Martin James Childs
−2003−

C000001055

(Twelve Pounds)
Len

07/21

RELIGION AND THE ARTS

Series Editor: John Hinnells, *University of Derby*
The arts have always been one of the primary means of communicating religious traditions; indeed, visual or performing arts may complement, predate or supplant many scriptural sources. This series explores how the visible has been used to express the invisible, and is designed to provide an understanding of the world's religions through the various art forms associated with religious practice and experience.

Already published
Art and Religion in Africa by Rosalind I. J. Hackett
Arts in the Religions of the Pacific by Albert C. Moore

Ganesa, Orissa, thirteenth century.

Hinduism and the Religious Arts

Heather Elgood

CASSELL
London and New York

Cassell
Wellington House, 125 Strand, London WC2R 0BB
370 Lexington Avenue, New York, NY 10017-6550

First published 1999

British Library Cataloguing-in-Publication Data

A catalogue record for this book is available from the British Library.

ISBN   0-304-33820-6

Library of Congress Cataloging-in-Publication Data

Elgood, Heather, 1950–
    Hinduism and the religious arts / Heather Elgood.
        p. cm.–(Religion and the arts)
    Includes bibliographical references and index.
    ISBN 0-304-33820-6 (hardcover)
    1. Art, Hindu–India. 2. Art, Indic–India. 3. Hindu symbolism.
    4. Art patronage–India. 5. Art and religion–India. I. Title.
    II. Series: Religion and the arts series.

    N7301.E38   1998
    294.5'37–dc21   98–24595
                                                              CIP

Designed and typeset by Ben Cracknell Studios
Printed and bound in Great Britain by Redwood Books Ltd,
Trowbridge, Wiltshire

Contents

List of Illustrations

■ Acknowledgements

This book is conceived as part of a series inspired by Professor John Hinnells (formerly at the School of Oriental and African Studies, University of London and now at the University of Derby) and originally under the aegis of Pinter Publishers. I am grateful to Professor Hinnells personally for his support and encouragement and more generally for initiating a project which is so close to my own interest in an area where art, religion and anthropology meet. In the research for this text I have drawn on the ideas of many scholars from these disciplines and have attempted to form these into a seamless whole. For this research I am grateful to SOAS whose library resource was a vital component.

Amongst those who helped me to write this book I would like to give special mention to Dr John Marr, not only for suggesting that I should work on this series but for being a constant source of encouragement, support and inspiration over many years. I am also profoundly grateful to him for a critical reading of the text prior to publication. For a valued contribution, welcome criticism and support in the reading of the chapters at an early stage I would also like to thank Dr Stephen Huyler. In the final editing I would like to thank Veronica Brinton for her patience and time, and Alix Lawrence for her help and encouragement. My own original contribution to my writing has been inspired over many years by working alongside and by listening to many of my friends who have given me encouragement and advice. Of these I would like to mention, in particular, Dr Anna Dallapiccola, Robert Skelton, Dr George Michell, Dr Stephen Huyler, Dr Vivek Nanda, Dr Michael Willis, Dr Angela Hobart, Richard Blurton, Dr Giles Tillotsin, Dr Linda Leach, Alastair Shearer, Rosemary Crill, Dr Don Stadtner, Dr Adam Hardy, John Burton Page, Vena Gheerawo, Stella Marsden, Dr Julia Leslie, Professor Piatigorsky and Dr Rashmi Poddar. I would also like to thank my many students from the Asian Arts Programme, who are responsible for inspiring some of my ideas and who have read selected chapters of the manuscript. I would also like to thank staff and students of the Bharat Vidya Bhavan for so often providing me with insight into the practical demonstration of the visual arts, and the Director Nanda Kumar, and Dr Shastri. I would also like to thank Janet Joyce as Director of Cassell's Academic Division who showed understanding, patience and gave much needed encouragement and enthusiasm. With regard to the illustrations I would like to thank Pat Barylski, Madhuvanti Ghose, Naman Ahuja,

Robert Skelton, John Marr and Stephen Huyler who were kind enough to lend me some of their slides. I would also like to thank Debbie Swallow at the Victoria and Albert Museum and Michael Willis at the British Museum for their kindness in allowing me to use some of the photographs in the collection. Finally, I would like to thank my husband who took many of the pictures of shrines and temples that I selected during a field trip to India in 1997. I would also like to thank Chris Glanville for his line drawings.

This book is dedicated to my husband and family. My husband showed unfailing patience and encouragement in helping with the editing of this book; without him it would never have been completed, and my children who put up with my work on this book for several years.

Map of the Indian subcontinent, showing the places mentioned in the text. Drawing by
Christopher Glanville RWA.

CHAPTER 1 Introduction

In prehistoric times in the Indian sub-continent, man's sense of wonder and enquiry into the mysteries of existence appeared to be satisfied by communal song, masked dance and ritual spirit possession, which met a deeply felt need to communicate with the supernatural. In time these wild occasions of release became ritualized, and this proved comforting since in continuity there appeared to be certainty in an uncertain world. It became necessary to convey abstract concepts about the gods in a form that changed words into images that were recognizable to the whole community. These images became known and acknowledged across wide areas. Religious art was created, not as art for art's sake but rather to meet the burgeoning spiritual needs of the community. It was believed that these images provided protection from the fickle, invisible spirit world.

The desire to propitiate, protect and secure wish fulfilment from the gods was the simple but essential element leading to the formation of Hindu ritual practice. In Vedic times (from 1500–300 BC) a sophisticated ritual sacrifice developed under the direction of a priestly class known as the Brahmans, who believed that human or animal sacrifice imitated the initial dismembering of the Purusa (primordial man), resulting in creation. Sacrificial offering was believed to bridge the void between their world and that of the gods, who were identified with the forces of nature. Their purpose was to ensure the continuance of the cosmic order of all things great and small. This objective continued a concern with the regulation of rainfall and the seasons, and a preoccupation with the natural elements of fire and water, which had been crucial to the Indus valley agricultural society of 2500 BC. In its attempt to understand, control and even transform nature, the ancient world of religious or magical powers, of which the rite of sacrifice is a part, resembles the modern world of scientific technology.

Definitions, Hinduism, Hindu Beliefs and Concepts

Religion, in the context of this book, may be defined as a particular system in which myths, rituals, sentiments and institutions are interconnected for the purpose of more effectively reaching out to a divine authority that is believed to regulate and control society, the environment and the individuals within it. The communication of Hindu religious beliefs and concepts was from an early stage facilitated by the development of ever more sophisticated iconographic symbols which incorporated proto-historic cult images and visually defined the earlier Vedic oral tradition. Symbolic diagrams, folk images, dance or mime linked to belief in sympathetic magic were also involved. One might suggest that art in proto-historic times was a magic device which was so strongly rooted in folk custom that it became necessary to absorb it into mainstream Hinduism.[1] For the purpose of this book magic may be defined as the attempt to achieve deliberate ends by the unorthodox use of orthodox religious practices. This depends on a belief in the supernatural and the paranormal operation of unmeasurable and invisible laws beyond the normal principles of science. A continuing use of magic from as early as 1000 BC can be seen in the unorthodox use of mantras or prayers, probably by shamans (referred to in the Vedic sacred text, the *Rigveda*, as 'munis'), to achieve powerful and specific objectives. It is also seen in the rich collection of spells and magical rites[2] found in the *Atharva Veda*, the last book of the four ancient religious texts known as the Vedas. Some women's folk rituals continued the use of these spells in practices which are still current and are known as Vrat. Mystery is also inherent in the Hindu belief in the invisible but living divine presence within icons.

The actual word 'Hinduism' stands for the civilization of the inhabitants of Hindustan, which literally means the land surrounding the Indus river (referred to by ancient Persians as Hindhu). Hinduism as a term was not common until 1830, when it was used by English writers to refer to the civilization in the Indian subcontinent, which has gradually evolved from Vedic Brahmanism over the last 2000 years. Brahmanism was the religion of the ancient Indo-European people, known as the Aryans, who were perhaps originally from the steppe country of Southern Russia and Central Asia, over the last 2000 years.

Hinduism should be understood more as a social system, or fabric of diverse religious customs than a religion, which has been codified and transmitted by a single inspired individual. Its beliefs are found to have no clear beginning, founder or central authority. It has been eclectic, retaining ancient practices and absorbing others. Today it is perceived predominantly as a faith of prescriptional devotion. Essentially, religious truth is believed to be a matter of personal spiritual vision but is also believed to be beyond philosophy or imagination. This has led to a characteristic religious tolerance and eclecticism.

Unlike the Western linear and chronological patterns of ethical thought, with their preoccupation with division and categorization and absolutes, the Hindu philosophical mind, expressed in verse, image, music and drama, is cyclical, synthetic, subtle and inclusive. Despite this flexibility, certain key concepts and a tendency to hierarchize characterize Hindu belief.

First, there is Atman-Brahman, the doctrine which links the self and the whole or universe. Atman means self or soul and Brahman ultimate reality. Brahman gives rise to the universe and to all beings which emanate from this ultimate reality. Brahman being all things is the self or soul (Atman) of all living beings. The personal search for Atman-Brahman, the one that is all, has been a focus of religious enquiry in India's spiritual life for 3000 years.

Second, the concept of a divine trinity comprising Vishnu the preserver, Siva the destroyer and Brahma a personification of the impersonal Brahman, is a physical depiction of more abstract and elemental forces. This trinity also serves to describe in philosophical terms the synthesis of unity in diversity. This concept is largely forgotten, however, in individual devotion towards one or other of the gods. Devotees generally choose Siva, Vishnu or the goddess as the focus of their worship and requests.

Third, there is recognition of the Vedas, the corpus of hymns and prayers transmitted orally and later written in the form of sacred literature.

Fourth, ahimsa, or respect for life, is linked to ideas of the unity of life symbolized by Brahman, which shows itself in the avoidance of meat eating and the veneration of the cow and other sacred animals.

Finally, there is a continued preoccupation among Hindus with the related concepts of dharma and karma. Dharma stands for a concept of right living which should correspond to caste laws and expectations, while karma, literally action, is the accumulation of past deeds that determine rebirth or reincarnation. The fundamental objective of every thinking Hindu is moksha, 'liberation' from samsara, the cycle of rebirth.

According to Biardeau, the Hindus have 'constructed a universe of logical coherence, which is almost too perfect, both in mythology and philosophically and a system of logic, which is breathtaking in its subtlety.'[3]

Despite Western criticism of Hinduism as glorifying in contradictions such as 'being and non-being', the sophistication of the philosophy lies in an understanding that the absolute is a reality that cannot be confined in normal structures of thought.

Aims of this Book

These essential elements of Hinduism are well known and scarcely need repeating. However, religious art has given boundless variation to this fundamental core while dramatically influencing ritual development. It is difficult in the twentieth century to conceive the fearful dramatic impact of the first encounter of a devotee with the image of his god. It is to give art a more central role in the study and understanding of Hinduism that this book has been written. Pre-Vedic and Hindu religious art was and remains functional. Its role was to act as a threshold between the worlds of gods and man; as a vehicle for defining, transmitting and preserving ideas. Hindu art will be seen to have an essential relationship with ritual practice.

Hindu art includes the performing arts such as theatre, songs, masked dance and a variety of sacred dances, but this book will be mainly concerned with the monumental arts, which include sculpture, painting, architecture and religious folk art. It attempts to look at the origin of Hindu images and to analyse the extent to which these images are representations of or actually become vessels for the numinous presence of the divine. The book also analyses the function of images, their use by the devotee and the representation and character of the actual deities in the Hindu pantheon and the manner in which this deepens our understanding of Hinduism. The didactic role of monumental temple art and folk art is also considered as well as an analysis of the multivalent symbols of Hinduism together with the role of patrons and artists and the principles that governed both royal and folk patronage. The book also takes account of the fact that recent scholarship no longer makes clear-cut divisions between traditional and modern, folk or royal patronage or the oral or written traditions. Such theatrical and dance performances as the Yaksgana dance or the dance of the Kuravanci are examples of this interweaving of folk and classical traditions. This can also be observed in the pan-Indian traditions of Bhakti worship which has common features at the simplest shrine or in the most complex temple setting. This testifies to the universality of the essential structures of the Brahmanic complex now referred to as Hinduism.

The study of the arts of Hinduism cannot ignore the art produced for Buddhist and Jainist patrons, though Western scholars perceive distinctions of greater significance than do the Asian devotees. There are many shared visual elements in the otherwise distinct religious sects of Buddhism, Jainism and Hinduism. These similarities were perpetuated by a hereditary group of craftsmen who used a limited range of image and symbol in their work for patrons of varying sectarian beliefs.

The Historical Development of Hinduism

The earliest traceable civilized culture in the Indian subcontinent dates from around 2000–2500 BC, from a community settled on the banks of the river Indus, commonly known as the Indus valley or the Harappan civilization. The archaeological finds of the Indus valley reveal a conservative culture with advanced building technology, a complex drainage and water system and an advanced system of writing. Artefacts such as seals and a few sculptures have also been unearthed. These objects have been subject to varied interpretation, such as an association with bull worship, tree worship,

goddess or fertility cults, and the reverence of a horned bull-masked deity. The Vedic text, the *Rg Veda*, refers to the Indus valley people as 'phallus worshippers' (Shishnadevas and Muradevas, literally meaning worshippers of the phallus and the fetish). It has been suggested that from this period terracotta figurines, seals and sculptures provide the earliest glimpse of what became Hindu iconography 2100–2500 years later. It has also been suggested that the most significant structure in this urban culture was a large water tank which may prefigure the water tanks or the ghats (bathing steps on riverbanks) associated with Hindu temples.

In around 1500 BC, a group of nomadic tribesmen, known as Aryans, arrived in the Indus region and eclipsed the Harappan civilization. Their success has been attributed to a variety of causes, most commonly to military success, due to their use of the horse and chariot. Despite the fact that the Aryans were non-literate they had a highly structured society based on a fourfold class division, of priests, warriors, merchants and artisans, which became the caste system (referred to as 'varna'). The priestly class had pre-eminence and sole responsibility for religious ceremonies, which revolved around ritual sacrifice. This religion grew out of an earlier worship of elemental deities, a part of the ancient pre-Zoroastrian Indo-European culture. The Vedic deities were of a recognizable Euro-Asian elemental type such as Indra (god of the storms), Surya (god of the sun) and Varuna (god of the rain and the waters). They shared features with deities of other Indo-European peoples such as the Persians, Greeks and Romans. The priests were responsible for preserving in an oral form the sacred ceremonial prayers or hymns known as the Vedas. These are thought to date from around 1200 BC and were subsequently written down. The first of these sacred texts was known as the *Rg Veda*. This was the earliest literary source for what developed out of Brahmanism and became known as Hinduism from AD 100–300. The hymns of the first of the Vedas contain none of the sweetness of expression in addressing the deity nor the emphasis on fertility which are features of later Hinduism. The *Sama Veda*, the third Veda is made up of transposed sections of the *Rg Veda*, while the *Yajur Veda* is concerned with correct sacrificial practice. The last of these Vedas, the *Atharva Veda*, which was composed around 900 BC, is more magical in tone and already displays pre-Aryan elements. It comprises a collection of magical spells and incantations and refers to holy men (vratyas) in the community who were patronized by the masses alongside orthodox priests. At around the time of the composition of the *Atharva Veda* several priestly schools began to record and preserve their expositions or commentaries on the Vedas. These are known as the *Brahmanas*, compiled about 900 BC, each attached to one of the Vedas. These were followed by the *Aranyakas* or the 'forest books'.

The Aryans gradually spread across Northern India, and were said to have begun by around 700–600 BC to settle in kingdoms and republics in the Ganges plain. From 700–500 BC there was a period of material progress, and a rapid increase of far-reaching international contacts through trade. This trading relationship gave rise to contact with Achaemenian Persia. Trade also brought new ideas and led to an imitation of the central Achaemenian preoccupation with a complex system of kingship. The centre of the region was

known as Magadha (a region now covered by areas of modern Bihar). Coincidentally, a period of intense religious speculation and enquiry developed in the more settled urban centres. Paradoxically, this period of urban growth gave rise to a retreat to the forests in search of truth. This retirement from society and the search for truth was later recorded and compiled in religious texts known as the *Upanishads* around 700 BC. This latter movement gathered momentum and attracted more followers who engaged in ascetic practices. It has been suggested that the four stages of man were developed in later Hinduism as an attempt to check the early rejection of family responsibilities by young men and to continue this to the end of their lives. Reference to an earlier practice of asceticism is seen in the *Rg Veda* in the presence of munis or shamans. By the fifth century BC the vratya (a wandering holy man) was commonly found in the region of Magadha. These vratyas (literally vow takers) were approachable, travelled from village to village and provided for the people's everyday needs with a profusion of magic spells and ancient folk customs. These unorthodox holy men were said to have been revered, to have supplied spells and performed acts of power and blessing.

In the *Upanishads* one finds repeated reference to reincarnation. This became a key concept in the development of Hinduism. Reincarnation was defined as the rebirth of men and women in the form of other human beings, animals, snakes or insects. The *Upanishads* also refer to the concept karma (actions), a related judgement, the measure of which determined rebirth.

It is in this atmosphere of religious enquiry that one must understand the

Figure 1.1 Cauri bearer, commonly known as the Didarganj yakshi, third–second century BC. Madhuvanti Ghose.

and spiritual freedom. This resulted in their following the contemporary teachings of Buddha and Mahavira. Buddhism and Jainism discouraged sacrifice and taught the doctrine of freedom from suffering and worldly existence by ascetic and meditative practices.

From about 600 BC written texts (*Sutras*) appear, which codify instructions for lesser sacrifices and domestic rituals. Each level of society had its own related dharma or norms of conduct. The philosophical texts are regarded as smrti (remembered commentaries) or sruti (revealed truth). Unorthodox Buddhist and Jain sects themselves began to make written records. These records describe the religious life of the orthodox Brahmanic majority which was said to feature the worship of Brahma and Indra with a widespread belief in the doctrine of rebirth. They also described the popularity of village cults, where there was continued practice of the worship of yaksha and yakshi (tree spirits), naga (snake spirits) and sacred chaitya (groves), while retaining the Indo-European ancestor cult. Apart from terracotta figurines, there was apparently little religious imagery.

The expansion of centralized authority in the period before Christ culminated in the establishment of the first great empire of India known as the Mauryan dynasty. The most famous of the rulers was Asoka, who ruled from 265–238 BC. Asoka, himself a professed Buddhist, established this teaching as a national faith through edicts, the construction of stupas and the building of columns. Asoka's patronage of Buddhism, declaration of non-violence (ahimsa) and vegetarianism did much to undermine the previous power and control of the Brahman priests. The Brahmanic religion also began to undergo a change,

appearance of Siddhartha Gautama, commonly known as the Buddha (the enlightened one), from the Sakya clan, and Nattaputta Vardhamana, called Mahavira (Great Hero), both born into the Ksatriya varna. Class discrimination, which prevented the lower classes from participating in the Brahmanic ritual, encouraged these individuals to search for alternative social developing a shift in focus from the worship of Vedic gods to that of Vishnu and Siva. Inscriptions reveal the worship of the god Vasudeva who was apparently worshipped in West India and later became identified with the god Vishnu. From this period date the earliest Hindu stone images, appearing not in the form of any gods but of monumental statues of the male and female tree spirits, yaksha and yakshi (Figure 1.1). These images were probably erected in sacred enclosures, while simple snake shrines also coexisted with the yaksha images. The Gudimallam linga (Figure 2.6a) attributed to the second to first century BC testifies to the practice of image worship at sacred shrines. Rare examples of the image of Siva in the form of the phallus are found on coins of this period.

Following the decline of the Mauryas, Buddhism continued to flourish under the first-century BC Sunga rulers of central India and the AD first- to third-century Kusana rulers of Gandhara and Mathura, but there was a Brahmanic revival. The older orthodox form changed its focus from actual to symbolic sacrifice and developed theistic tendencies centred around the gods Vishnu and Siva. The great Hindu epic, the *Mahabharata* popular from AD 300, in which appears the *Bhagavad Gita* (Song of the Lord) underlines this shift in the description of the pivotal role of Vishnu's incarnation as the god Krishna and his direct dialogue with the charioteer Arjuna. The text also attempts to restrain the influence of the ascetics by stressing that obedience to dharma, selfless action, was more effective than sacrifice or mortification of the flesh. The period from the second century BC to the rise of the Gupta empire in the fourth century AD was one of great change, with the conquest of most of the area of Pakistan

and parts of western India by a succession of invaders. Art and architecture began to reveal the effect of this new influence, particularly through contact with Greek culture and the Roman Empire. The cult of Vishnu, and that of Rudra who developed into the god Siva, and the worship of the Goddess, were the three most important cults.

Many of the principal Hindu deities appear for the first time in the art of the Kusana rulers of Northern India from 100 BC to AD 300. Shrines, temples and religious icons became common. A growing pantheon of deities including Lakshmi developed from the first to third centuries AD while Siva's son Ganesa, the elephant-headed god, did not become apparent until around AD 500. Surya, the sun-god, had many temples constructed in his honour from the sixth to twelfth centuries AD, following which he experienced a rapid decline in popularity. The earliest written prescriptive text, the *Dharma Sastra*, is contemporaneous with the *Epics*. This text illustrates doctrinal points with little or only brief narrative. In the period from the fourth to eighth centuries AD stories, later called the *Puranas*, were compiled to educate, entertain and glorify the gods. The *Puranas* literally 'ancient texts', are compendia of myth, ritual, philosophy, history and dharma.[4] The great narrative *Epics* and *Puranas* tell longer stories. These were usually acted or recited in villages, sometimes with accompanying story boards. The Hindus regard the *Epics* as great poems and textbooks. According to O'Flaherty, while we think of them as being about the war of the Bharatas and the battle between Rama and Ravana, the Hindus believe they are about dharma.

The Gupta period was one of great prosperity and calm, Buddhist pilgrims reporting on the high degree of prosperity and moral standing of the lords of India. The kings, encouraged to acquire merit by religious donation, began to patronize the Brahman caste again. The relationship between the religious texts and family law became more defined and rigid. Marriage was solemnized by lengthy sacred rites, in which the Brahmans held the key role. In the Gupta period the rise of patronage brought an increase in the development of free-standing temple architecture. From the seventh century AD the temple became increasingly significant in the functioning and forms of the religious and secular order. A proliferation of temple building occurred in Madhya Pradesh, Gujarat and Rajasthan under Hindu and Jain patronage. The great temples became the repositories of immense wealth through taxes, donations and fees. The running, administration and worship of the temples became the responsibility of the hereditary priests and temple servants. *Sastras*, or prescriptive textbooks, listing the rules governing the creation of many art-forms, were compiled at this time. The design of the temple, as this book will later explain, was strictly codified by *Silpasastras* (craft textbooks), where every measurement and decoration was meaningful and efficacious. Elaborate Indian sculpture was also incorporated into the temple which served to express the numerous aspects and manifestations of the spirit world.

From the seventh century AD there was a rise of a much earlier esoteric tradition which dealt with the purification of the body and attempts at self-mastery. This involved certain mental and physical processes in the transformation of energies and ultimately the devotee himself. This group of practices is known as 'Tantric'. Tantric devotees (or tantrikas) worship the goddess, and use meditative devices such as ritual diagrams (yantras) and prayers (mantras). Despite the fact that some of their actions oppose caste rules and some customs shock and create fear in more orthodox society, Tantric philosophy has from the medieval period had an impact on the use of images and on wider aspects of Hindu philosophy. Tantrism had a prevailing influence on courtly society during the Chandella period in Central India in the tenth century. Tantrism, associated with the worship of the goddess Sakti, also increased in popularity at this time.[5] There was also a predominance of the cult followings of Vishnu, Siva and the goddess, coexistent with some local cult deities.

From the eighth century, following the decline of the Gupta empire, there was a period of fragmentation. The arrival of the Muslims in North India in the twelfth century discouraged the continued patronage of temple architecture. Despite Muslim hostility Hindu society continued to thrive, integrally linked with the priestly requirements of domestic ritual and personal sacraments. In South India temples continued to be built, and retained their religious and political prominence. The southern temples reached their apogee in the great Rajarajesvara temple of Tanjore (Tanjavur). In South India the orthodox cults had been aristocratic in character, with a strong patronage of kings and chiefs who in turn acquired prestige by their patronage of Brahmans and by adopting Aryan ways. There continued to be worship of the local deity Murukan, who became identified with Skanda, as was his mother the fierce war goddess Korravai with Durga. Mayon, a South Indian rural cult deity described in contemporary literature as having a black colour, was absorbed into the Hindu pantheon, subsumed into the legend of the god Krishna, also portrayed as dark blue or black in colour.

This brief account of the historical development of Hinduism from as early as 2500 BC demonstrates the extent to which many extraneous sources are responsible for the ever-changing character of the eclectic form of current devotional Hinduism. The Vedic texts themselves refer to the fact that even contemporary Aryan society engaged in a practice which, as early as 1200 BC, revealed a variety of different sources. These sources derive not only from the Aryans, who share a common ancestry with Indo-European tribes, but also Iranians and indigenous Indian elements. Examples of these were practices such as the ancient Indo-European custom of the circum-ambulation of fire which became absorbed into Hindu wedding ceremonies, the crema-tion and ancestor cults, and the earlier Indo-European male sky gods. The Indo-Iranian elements are to be seen chiefly in the initiatory ceremony upanayana, the tying of a sacred cord performed on boys when they have reached a certain age, and the Vedic god Varuna. Varuna shares many common features with the Zoroastrian Ahura Mazda, while the narcotic drink Soma corresponds to the Zoroastrian drink haoma.

The indigenous elements of the Indian subcontinent itself, perhaps deriving from the earlier Indus valley civilization, may be seen in, first, the emphasis on fertility and by association water, and second, a concern with cleanliness which may well be the source of the concepts of ritual purity and taboo. Other features were the worship of the snake, trees, the mother goddess and the phallus. Another element was the tribal preoccupation with ancestor worship, and

fear of spirits seen in spirit possession rituals and the propitiation of ghosts (bhutas). Further tribal characteristics may be seen in the concepts of transmigration, the absorption of animal worship, localized cult deities and the later ecstatic devotional character of modern Hinduism. The tribal and village peoples of India coexisted with the more sophisticated culture of the Indus valley and themselves worshipped sacred animals, trees and terracotta figurines.

Vedic texts refer to earlier cult practices. Artefacts from the Indus valley testify to the use of common symbols and images, such as the snake, the tree, the earth goddess and an object believed to be a phallus. These reappear as Buddhist decoration from the second century BC and devotional Hindu sculpture and village art from the third century AD. It has been suggested that a synthesis took place between pre-Vedic fertility rituals and Vedic sacrifice. The earlier cult offerings to tree and snake shrines became absorbed into the ritual reverence which previously took the form of sacrificial offerings and a more abstract and descriptive hymnal evocation of the gods. Several passages of the *Ṛg Veda* give poetic description of the gods, and how these acquired visual form is described in Chapter 2. These were at this early stage to be propitiated but not revered, unlike the medieval rise in devotional spirit of the evolution of Hindu practice.

Textual Limitations to the Understanding of Hinduism

Historically, the study of Hinduism by Western scholars has been largely based on translations from Sanskrit of the sacred texts of the Indo-Aryans, the society and religious group from which much of Hindu social conventions was said to be derived. These texts, written in Sanskrit, are known as the Vedas, or the later commentaries the *Puranas*. Nineteenth-century scholarship in the study of Hinduism was largely based on these scriptures and the theological writings of the most famous Hindu philosophers such as Sankara (*c.* 788–820), Ramanuja (eleventh century) or Vallabha (1479–1531). Any translation has the potential for misinterpretation. The earliest Vedic text, the *Rg Veda*, had the character of a lengthy recipe book full of ritual prescriptions comparable to the Christian hymnals, with little religious theory or principles of doctrine. In the twentieth century, religious scholars widened their selection of literature to include folklore, mythology, poetry and philosophical writings, and ethnographic studies have also provided valuable interpretations of Hinduism by exploring its interrelationship with art or myth. Clearly there is a role for the study of both written texts and art and a need for their interaction to enable a comprehensive understanding of Hinduism on both the Brahmanic and the popular level.

There are a number of reasons why Vedic literature provides an inadequate picture of Hinduism, the first being that in Vedic society the oral tradition, *sruti* or revealed truth, believed to be derived from the gods, held pre-eminence over *smrti*, the remembered literature.[6] Written texts were not compiled until Brahmanism became threatened by the growth of Buddhism in the fifth century BC.

The second reason for this argument is the fact that these texts, like the oral tradition, were preserved for an initiated minority. The masses were non-literate and, with the exception of the Brahman castes or wealthy Kshatriyas, would have failed to have any direct contact with this literature. The Hindu majority would have touched on its content only by hearing the Sanskrit prayers during the priestly ceremonies; or in the mythical tales performed by village story-tellers carrying visual accompaniments such as painted story boards.

Fuller so clearly observed:

> Themes central in the scriptures are not always central in ordinary people's beliefs and practices, and textual scholars' conclusions do not necessarily provide good guides to the workings of popular religion. For the anthropologist of popular Hinduism, ethnography – not scripture – is both the major source of evidence and the touchstone of interpretation.[7]

The third justification for this approach is that the artisans, whose role it was to provide religious images to a wider audience, were themselves prevented on the grounds of illiteracy and caste exclusion from direct access to the texts, though they received priestly supervision. These craftsmen were subject as much to a pre-Vedic cult or folk background as to Brahmanical prescriptions. Evidence from Indian sculpture from as early as the second century BC reveals the inclusion of pre-Vedic cult images. Popular local cults attracted considerable followings which may have included artisans from conservative hereditary groups such as craft associations, which preserved techniques and a common visual vocabulary. Many Hindu devotees, while partaking of Brahman ceremonials for life's major initiations of birth, death and marriage, continued a complex pre-Vedic practice involving ritualized reverence and focused offerings. Dana, or gifts for wish fulfilment, continued in ancient form and involved offerings to deities in the form of stones, animals, snakes, water and trees, and by association contributed to the development of symbols and images.

The origin of Hindu reverence for such natural forms from pre-Vedic local cults and their place in Hindu ritual is clearly revealed by the study of sacred images, while analysis of Hindu ritual reveals the coexistence of Vedic and pre-Vedic cult practice. The fourth reason why Vedic literature is an inadequate source for the understanding of Hinduism is the extent to which Hindu ritual plays an essential part in defining a Hindu. Art, in the form of images, is an integral part of this ritual and therefore of particular significance. According to Wendy O'Flaherty: 'Hinduism as a whole has been well characterised as orthoprax rather than orthodox. Hindus define themselves by what they do rather than by what they think.'[8]

A Hindu's characteristic lack of dogma contributes to the argument that a Hindu may be defined more by what he practises than by what he preaches and his religious practice is inextricably intermingled with so-called art.

Fifth, the fixed nature of the ancient source books limits their contribution to an understanding of evolving Hinduism. In practice, the perception of contemporary artists, corresponding more closely to the changing requirements of society, provides a more faithful record of popular religion than the textual equivalent. There are many examples of this but it can be particularly seen in the development of devotional bhakti imagery.

Finally, devotional Hinduism reveals physical and psychological practice which is scarcely addressed in the written texts but which is directly related to art. The ordinary Hindu has a practical approach to his faith which is characterized by obedience to social pressures and certain traditional rituals relating to his caste, family and profession. The factors that determine these rituals are believed to relate to his individual dharma, the results of his actions (or karma). In practice the daily religious life of the average Hindu requires assistance from the mediation of priests and images, the former believed to possess authority, the latter potency.

Hindu art remains an integral part of ritual custom in the daily lives of devotees. Domestic details of family life mirror the grander dimension of the individual's relationship with the divine. This is most simply expressed in the customary Hindu greeting 'namaskara' which is also a gesture of respect: 'The gesture symbolizes in a condensed form the principle of hierarchical inequality that is so fundamental in Hindu religion and society. Thus a human worshipper, like a lower deity, gestures in respect to a superior deity.'[9]

This can be observed in the relationship between the priest and the icon he tends, similar in Indian society to the love and care of a mother for her child, the ideal wife for her husband and the widespread respect for the elderly. There is an inherent reverence, a worship which manifests in an almost maternal, practical devotion to the deity. This behaviour is as much a part of Hinduism as the profound but intangible philosophy expressed in sacred literature and mythology.

Hindu religious practice involves not only an emotional and/or intellectual response but also contains a sensory dimension. It involves touch in the rubbing of oil or powder on the idol; smell in the offering of incense; hearing and chanting in the participation of prayer, and sight and being seen through darsan and the offering of the sacred flame in the darkness of the interior shrine. Sexual sensuality in both denial and sexual fulfilment are also given a philosophical place within Hinduism. This sensory impact is an essential part in understanding ritual practice and it is expressed through relationships with art images. The monk Ramacandragani, in his poem known as the *Hundred Verses on King Kumarapala's Temple* which was dedicated to the king on his conversion from Saivism to Jainism, expressed this as follows.

> There in that temple, people experience a strange desire to renounce further pleasures of the senses; their ears were filled with the singing; their eyes were intent upon the marvellous dancing, and all they could smell was the fragrant water that was being used to bathe the main image. So satiated, they no longer yearned for any other objects of the senses.[10]

Experience through bodily sensation is a part of Hindu religious understanding, the body being itself a temple and, like the temple, a repository of the divine. The architectural elements of the temple are based on and named after the human body, and it is the human body that is the ground for religious experience and transformation.

In short, the religious arts of Hinduism have played an essential role as an integral part of ritual over the centuries. They provide a neglected but distinct devotional text of their own. Examination of Hinduism through the images that it uses to reveal itself gives us fresh insights into the ritual practices of devotees and details of behaviour and a deeper understanding of the nature of Hinduism.

Notes

1 This is, however, to view with hindsight the development of two levels of ritual as though they were separate and to assume Hinduism to be mainstream and orthodox, which it eventually proved to be. As a means of communicating with divine forces, the evident satisfaction given to a large part of the population by magic practices, some of which continue to be used to this day, suggests that it is wrong to marginalize magic in this fashion.

2 See Crooke 1894; Goudriaan 1978; Stutley 1980.

3 Biardeau 1981, p. 77.

4 According to O'Flaherty (1975, p. 17; 1988, p. 5) the approximate dates for the texts are as follows: *Rg Veda*: 1200 BC; *Atharva Veda*: 900 BC; *Brahmanas*: 900–700 BC; *Upanishads*: 700 BC; *Mahabharata*: 300 BC–AD 300; *Ramayana*: 200 BC–AD 200.

The *Puranas* are just as difficult to date, but she gives them this rough chronology: *Agni*: AD 850; *Bhagavata*: AD 950; *Bhavishya*: AD 500–1200; *Brahma*: AD 900–1350, *Brahmanda*: 350–950; *Brahmavaivarta*: 750–1550; *Brhaddharma*: 1250; *Brhannaradiya*: 750–900; *Devi*: 550–650; *Devibhagavata*: 850–1350; *Garuda*: 900; *Harivamsa*: 450; *Kalika*: 1350; *Kalki*: 1500–1700; *Kurma*: 550–850; *Linga*: 600–1000; *Mahabhagavata*: 1100; *Markandeya*: 250; *Matsya*: 250–500; *Narasimha*: 400–500; *Padma*: 750; *Sambha*: 500–800; *Saura*: 950–1150; *Siva*: 750–1350; *Skanda*: 700–1150; *Vamana*: 450–900; *Varaha*: 750; *Vayu*: 350; *Vishnu*: 450.

5 The chief centre was modern Bengal, Bihar and Assam.

6 O'Flaherty 1988, p. 1.

7 Fuller 1992, p. 6.

8 O'Flaherty 1988, p. xi.

9 Fuller 1992, p. 4.

10 See Granoff, in Mason 1993, p. 90.

CHAPTER 2 Sacred Imagery

In this chapter we will examine the meaning and significance of the Hindu sacred image, its origin, how it was made and its various forms. We must however be aware that this focus solely on Hindu imagery, ignoring other Indian religions, is a Western and inappropriate approach. The distinction between Hindu, Jain and Buddhist art is largely one of iconography and this division holds little meaning for non-Western devotees. Indians are not concerned with exclusive gods or primarily with the aesthetics of sacred images, nor do the majority of practising Hindus contemplate philosophical questions. Their devotion centres on a close relationship with a god or goddess chosen from a range of distinctive deities whose characters and visual characteristics are well known and comprise in effect an extended family. To this day the Hindu concept of a single supreme deity (the transcendental Bhagvan or Isvara) is too remote and impersonal and is not represented visually. The difficulties of expressing such a complex concept visually are obvious. From the early Vedic texts compiled from about 1200 BC, it seems that the deity was not represented by the Vedic priests in sculptural form.[1] Divine power was instead expressed in colourful and detailed mental images obtained by revelation or perhaps induced by the effects of soma, an intoxicant drunk during Vedic ceremonies. Some considerable time later this early oral tradition was written down in the ancient Vedic text, the *Bhagavad Gita*, which was compiled between 300 BC and AD 300.

For I am the sacrifice and the offering, the sacred gift and the sacred plant. I am the holy words, the holy food, the holy fire, and the offering that is made in the fire. I am the Father of this universe, and even the Source of the Father. I am the Mother of this universe, and the Creator of all. I am the highest to be known, the Path of purification, the holy OM, the Three Vedas. I am the Way, and the Master who watches in silence; thy friend and thy shelter and thy abode of peace. I am the beginning and the middle and the end of all things: their seed of Eternity, their Treasure supreme.... I am life immortal and death; I am what is and I am what is not.[2]

It is not known for certain when the intellectual struggle was determined to relate the nature of God, which is formless and infinite, to a finite, tangible form, which can be comprehended by the layman. The search for an appropriate means of reflecting the unfathomable, unknowable nature of the divine presumably continued in Hinduism, for centuries. In some instances in later Hinduism, the deity can

13

be described by what the deity is not.[3] A word that is used in the *Bhagavad Gita* and the *Upanishads*, whose meaning at that time is uncertain but which is subsequently known to indicate shape and form, is murti. The word 'murti' came to mean not only a likeness of the deity but the deity itself in concrete form. By this means, the worshipper was able to make eye contact on a personal level with the divine. This presence may on one level be perceived as formless, from which issues a hierarchical complex of powerful deities.[4]

Religious ritual in Hinduism revolves around the devotion and ultimate identification of the worshipper with God. Hindu art is created to assist this process and combines imagery and allegorical symbolism to represent the deity, to make visible the invisible. This finds expression in a large range of styles, all of which may in Western terms properly be considered as art. Simple geometry such as the square and circle, inorganic, organic forms and the human figure have been used as symbols of the divine.

Why the need for the image, the need for God and what is dedicated to Him – in other words, the sacred? A sense of mystery and belief in the existence of a spirit world and fear of the unknown have always driven man's search for a means of participating in the cosmic order. With order comes certainty and preservation. Irregularity in the seasons, for example, can mean starvation or death in an agricultural society. The world of religious or magical powers is an expression of the age-old human desire to understand and coerce a generally symbiotic relationship with nature.[5] The desire to propitiate and protect are crucial factors in the formation of Indian religious practice. As the separate roles of the gods in the cosmic order became recognized by man, they also acquired the iconographic emblems of their powers which on a mundane level served to instruct and identify. Brahmanic Hindu worshippers, villagers and tribal communities to this day continue to worship images and to maintain the ritual of votive offerings for wish fulfilment. Fertility images and a concrete locus for offerings almost certainly existed throughout the Vedic period on a village or tribal level in a manner entirely different from the sacrificial ceremonies of the Vedic priests.

Hindus believe gods and spirits are peripatetic and have a potential for varied manifestations. Chief deities appear in a wide variety of forms, expressing their multiple roles and moods. These forms can be iconic, that is, with a resemblance to human form; or aniconic, in other words, in an abstract symbolic form such as a pile of stones or a linga. Organic and inorganic matter is perceived as a potential residence for a deity or spirit, particularly the sacred images produced for veneration in a temple or domestic shrine. The image is generally required to be beautiful to encourage the deity to enter it, and the material from which it was made must be unblemished. Divine energy is believed to be infused by ritual, and the final task of the ceremony is to open the eyes of the image by means of a specific chanted mantra (spoken or sung religious formula) and the completion by the artist of this part of his work.[6] To be ritually effective and sacred an image must be given the correct preparation and invocation, after which it is perceived not only as an icon or symbol but is also believed to hold a numinous presence. The image is also said to emanate a particle of the divine whole, the divine perceived not in man's image as a separate entity but as a formless, indescribable omnipresent whole. The image allows the worshipper to catch a reflection of the deity whose effulgence transcends what the physical eye can see. This divine effulgence is beheld in man's inner vision.[7] An image is a murti not because it resembles the deity it represents but because it conforms to prescribed measurements and symbolic conventions. It is subsequently consecrated and offered devotion by the initiated artist (sthapati), priest (acharya) and devotee (bhakta). The requirements for the materials, measurements, proportion, decoration and symbolism of the murti are provided in technical manuals known as *Silpasastras*. Explanation of the metaphysical significance of each stage of manufacture and the prescription of specific mantras to sanctify the process and evoke and invoke the power of the deity in the image are found in the liturgical handbooks (the *Agamas* and *Tantras*). The process is modelled on the instructions for building fire altars found in the Brahmanas.[8]

Hindu images seek to express essential truths concerning divine forces. An iconography developed which was based on a code of symbols that assumed an interrelationship of forms and ideas. In a world where the phenomenal is believed to be illusory and the senses subjective, words and images are held to be an approximation of truth. They make visible the invisible, the essential transcendent and immanent unity of God. They are analogous of and act as reference to the existence of forces which can only be understood directly at a certain level of consciousness. They reinforce that which can be dimly sensed through myths and parables. The rituals associated with images in a Jain context have been suggested by Humphrey and Laidlaw to be like objects, describing worship (puja) as a pattern of action:

> The patterns rituals take, beyond our purposes, beliefs, or intentions, propose their own time, and to step into this, to enact it ourselves, is perhaps to defy our transience and death.[9]

> The visual equivalent of vocalized mantras, such images – I think to an extent all Hindu images – act as mechanisms (yantras) to support and sustain the effort of man to transcend.[10]

These sacred images (murtis, icons or sculptures) are meditative supports and are used in conjunction with other devices such as yantras[11] (abstract maps of energies likened to geometrical diagrams) and mantras[12] (verbal formulae or incantations). These visual references give form to the formless and make visible the invisible.

The devices referred to above act like a language of pun and allegory echoing in the multiple facets, reflections of the essential transcendent unity of form. The images cannot be taken separately from sound, since the vibrations of sound give them vitality.

Staal points out that the ritual function of mantras does not lie in their language or even their metrical structure but in their sounds, with their themes and variations, repetitions and inversions, all of which are executed in accordance with fixed rules.[13] Staal's interpretation is that this essential musicality shows mantras to be a form of ritual expression which preceded language. He describes them as units of sound, patterns or sections, which allow the devotees to be relatively fluid in the time taken and the number of mantras recited. Even in the Minakshi temple at Madurai the ritual model leaves out one part and concentrates on the central section: 'Although the "full" worship in the Minakshi temple comprises only four rituals, which leaves out at least eight of the sixteen textual upacars, it is common practice merely to offer food and wave the lamps.'[14]

It is also suggested that:

> The identity of ritual acts depends on a priori prescription, and not on intentional understanding, the elements can be arranged in purely formal structures which have no relation to the intentions and purposes for which the ritual as a whole is undertaken.[15]

Despite this however, an understanding of the meaning of the mantra may enhance its efficacy.

The Origin of Hindu Imagery

Hindu images have a very distinct appearance. The deities possess human or animal characteristics but represent superhuman beings. They are portrayed sometimes with many upper limbs, sometimes with more than one head. They express mood and movement in their posture and gesture; they hold emblems and can be placed in dynamic relation to other figures or symbolic animals. They inhabit realms beyond our normal existence. This mythical world and the gods who inhabit it express the Hindu belief that 'the universe is boundlessly various, that everything occurs simultaneously and that all possibilities are not mutually exclusive'.[16]

The origin of the formulae and components of religious imagery in Hinduism is shrouded in mystery. Were the forms of deities profound visions of real beings or did they arise from deep meditation, from an interior silence and formlessness, becoming clothed in imagination and translated into form? Or was it the result of intoxication induced by the ceremonial drink soma? The early text the *Vishnudharmottara Purana*[17] refers to the origin of sculpture. It says that in the Satya, Treta and Dvapara ages (Yugas) people could see the gods with their eyes, but in the Kali Yuga they lost that power. To help them in the worship and meditation of the Supreme Being who is formless, images were made as intermediaries.

> Out of these generations of seers (rishis) has grown the communal understanding of all life, its balance: through them is glimpsed, beyond the self-perpetuating fabric (prakriti), beyond the semblance of reality (maya), the one Being through Whom all live (purusha), Who is sacred (brahman), and to Whose myriad appearances and manifestations is returned His share in the ritual of the sacrifice. For the balance (rita) is always to be renewed, restored, confirmed.[18]

Despite the lack of evidence of sculptures or icons, the Vedic poets portrayed their deities in colourful imagery expressed in verse and hymns sung at ritual ceremonies. Intensified vision through heightened consciousness or the effects of soma may have contributed to the Hindu gods being portrayed with multiple heads and arms (multi-headed images have been discovered even among the remains of the Indus valley culture). Agni is described in the Vedas as having seven red tongues, seven faces and gleaming hair, while Indra is characterized as carrying a thunderbolt. Certain colours subsequently acquired individual symbolic meaning. According to the Vedic priests, all phenomena in the world were interrelated, with no fundamental distinction between powers and processes, symbols and the symbolized and so forth. Reality was perceived as a network of affinities or connections (nidana) which can be detected, evoked and activated by man.[19] The key to the hidden reality was the realm of sound or vibrations.

The focus of Vedic ritual was not the image of the gods but the re-enactment of creation in the rite of sacrifice. According to Baumer, another possible origin of the anthropomorphic image was the golden figure of the purusa, which was built into the Vedic fire altar. She relates this to the Stupa containing relics of the Buddha and to the simple stylized shape of the purusa drawn even today on earthern pots which comes close to the shape of a swastika.[20] The emphasis moved from the worship of the deities themselves (part of the ancient pre-Zoroastrian Indo-European culture) to a concentration on the sacrificial rite itself. The ritual prescriptions were laid down in the Brahmanas. Here the offering was the symbol of the 'purusha', the god itself. This action, together with the sacrificial fire and the soma, ascended with the smoke to the gods and thus maintained the right cosmic order.

The ritual elements contained in the sacrifices were the soma, the offering itself, sacred sound (mantras), the fire and the sacrificial altar, and the yupa, otherwise known as the sacrificial post.[21] The Vedic sacrifice later provided Hinduism with a kind of standard of worth by which non-Vedic religious practices may be gauged. New and relatively simple Hindu practices are said to contain the power of the most complex Vedic sacrifices. The shrouding of new Hindu practices in sacrificial clothing is not to present the new as the old. One might describe sacrifice to have functioned throughout Indian history as a marker for traditionalism and as a means for acceptable innovation.

According to Bhattacharya,[22] anthropomorphic descriptions of gods are not found in the early Vedas, and the iconographic texts originated after image worship had become customary in the later Vedic period.[23] In the Upanishadic era images were referred to which could be summoned by meditation. This was an interior (subtle/suksma) worship as opposed to an exterior worship of a material image (gross/sthula). In the *Epics*, image worship is mentioned and accepted, but it is given only marginal and fleeting notice, while the major interest is centred on fire sacrifice.

Supporting the idea of the mind as the source of creation are texts which instruct the Hindu craftsmen in the need for visualization and devotion as prerequisites for artistic production.[24] There is a direct link between the images of the mind described in the Upanishadic period and later Hindu guidelines for sculptors, as the following text from the *Vishnu Purana* demonstrates.

I will describe to you the perceptible form of Hari (Vishnu), which no mental retention will manifest, except in a mind that is fit to become the receptacle of the idea. The meditating Vishnu, as having a pleased and lovely countenance with eyes like the leaf of the lotus, smooth cheeks, and a broad and brilliant forehead; ears of equal size, the lobes of which are decorated with splendid pendants; a painted neck; and a broad chest, on which shines the Srivasta mark; a belly falling in graceful folds, with a deepseated navel; eight long arms, or else four; and firm and well knit thighs and legs, with well-formed feet and toes. Let him, with unremitting attention, Hari, as clad in a yellow robe, wearing a (rich diadem on his head), and brilliant armlets and bracelets (on his arms) and bearing (in his hands) the bow, the shell, the mace, the sword, the discus, the rosary, the lotus, and the arrow.[25]

A Hindu craftsman was obliged to go through a process of prayer and self-purification before he created a religious image. The image was expected to become potent and to suggest imminent movement. Its potency and dynamic emanations or forcefield were maintained by the cumulative effect of the chanting of mantras.

> Thus the stone or bronze image of a deity in a temple or shrine is believed to almost pulsate with life, containing the combined presence of the deity who invests it and the accumulated force-field of years of devotion. Conversely an object that is abused and desecrated, or that is in close proximity to expressions of hostility, vengeance, is likely to absorb negative energy, or to be polluted by its treatment or surround-ings. The purpose of many Hindu ritual acts is to rid objects or places of their negativity, to remove the contagion of evil spirits.[26]

According to current research, the Jain faith held images as an important part of the transmission and focus of their teaching. This may have had an impact on the acceptance of a concrete form of image making from the third century BC.[27]

Aniconic Symbols

Hindu aniconic and iconic symbols seek to represent forces and energies – aspects of a single supreme undifferentiated Isvara which is unmanifest and in real terms unrepresentable.

The swastika and the ringstone are two early aniconic sun symbols in use in the Indus valley culture. The image resembling a phallus found at Mohenjo Daro dating

from 2500 BC is perhaps a further variation of the use of aniconic imagery (Figure 2.1). The vulva, circle or ringstone, the aniconic form of the mother goddess, may also represent continuity from a matriarchal fertility cult of the pre-Vedic period.[28] The Vedi (Vedic altar), perceived as the symbol of the goddess, may also be seen as a possible early aniconic symbol.

Remnants of pre-Vedic cults, in their worship of aniconic natural symbols such as stones, earthen mounds termite mounds (Figure 6.3, p. 195), pillars, trees, snakes and rivers are still seen in present day tribal and village India. These sacred natural forms were held to be signs of the deities' presence before the existence of Hindu icons, and are revered to the present day.

Tribal religion in India

> is characterized by aniconical symbols as the seats of deities, by irregular worship and the carrying out of blood sacrifices, by tribal priests as being in charge, and by priests and worshippers being possessed in front of the deities. Hindu religion, by contrast, is marked by the existence of anthropomorphic murtis as the seats of the deities, by the conduct of regular puja-services under the control of Brahman priests, and by the deities' vegetarianism.[29]

The most sophisticated form of aniconic imagery is the yantra or geometric diagram, expressed as a formula, which attempts to describe and contain the dynamic force of the cosmos (Figure 2.2). Yantras often act as substitutes for the image of the deity. They are also used as ground plans for the conceptual foundation of the Hindu temple. Yantras are also placed in the foundation of temple sanctums and were used as compositional diagrams in the execution of sculptural images adorning temple walls.

Many elements in Hindu worship echo the pre-iconic past:

> The hallowed pit or cave, the breast stone or well, the bloodlike splash of vermilion, the circle-glyph or fullness, the female triangle of fertility, they signal with startling vividness and immediacy and are as natural to the Indian landscape as the land itself.[30]

Iconic Hindu Deities

According to Coomaraswamy, the Hindu Isvara is not a jealous god, because all gods are aspects of him imagined by his worshippers. In the words of the god Krishna, an incarnation of Vishnu:

> When any devotee seeks to worship any aspect with faith, it is none other than Myself that grants his prayers. Howsoever men approach me, so do I welcome them, for the path men take from every side is mine.[31]

Below Isvara in the hierarchy of the Hindu pantheon are the most well-known Hindu deities, Vishnu, Siva and Brahma, who form a triumvirate, together with the goddess Devi, who is worshipped in many forms, in some of which she is the consort of Vishnu, Siva or Brahma. A detailed account of the gods themselves will not concern us here, except to note that some of these deities are derived from gods referred to in the sacred book of the Aryans – the Vedas. The Hindu gods Agni, Indra (god of the storm), Rudra, god of destruction, the god Dyaus cognate with Zeus (god of heaven) and Varuna, the wind god, come from the Vedic pantheon. The earliest ancient Vedic text the *Rg Veda* itself, refers derisively to the pre-Vedic Indus peoples as *Sishnadevas* and *Muradevas*, literally meaning the worshippers of the phallus and of the fetish, implying the

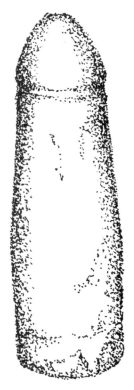

Figure 2.1 A stone linga, Indus Valley. Harappan period, *c.* 2300–1750 BC. The whereabouts of the original is unknown. Drawing by Christopher Glanville RWA.

previous existence of idol worshippers. The earliest unambiguous reference to the worship of images is found in the writings of Panini in the fifth century BC. This text refers to the worship of the images of the yaksha and yakshi, male and female tree spirits, associated with the ancient cult of tree worship and nagas (snake deities) and not Vedic deities. Offerings to monumental yaksha and yakshini images and to sacred trees for wish fulfilment are still a vital part of some village rituals. It is interesting to note that some elements associated with tree worship, such as flags, the offerings of flowers, incense and fruit have become part of later Hindu ritual.[32] The popularity and mention of images in the Jain tradition

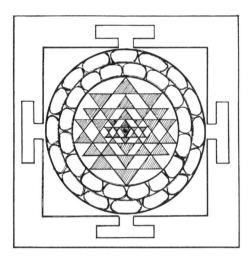

Figure 2.2 Yantra. Drawing by Christopher Glanville RWA.

which has largely been ignored may be a further factor in our understanding of this development.

The earliest sculptural evidence for specifically Hindu gods dates from the first century BC.[33] Several factors are believed to have contributed to the form of these deities. Besides the inspiration of Vedic gods was the existence of pre-Vedic gods, such as a possible proto-Siva deity (bull-masked), revealed in the cross-legged figure on an Indus valley seal (Figure 2.3);[34] or tribal sacred animals such as the boar or the lion subsequently seen as the avatars of Vishnu, Varaha and Narasimha.

Of supreme importance in the religious history of India is the worship of the mother goddess, together with the associated ideas of the desire for children. The female in her encapsulation of the mysterious power of reproduction and fertility was both feared and revered. The mother goddess and fertility ritual has been an element of continuity in Hindu worship on a monumental and village level to the present day.[35] A belief in spirits, ghosts and tree

spirits and their propitiation coexisted with the worship of the powerful trinity of gods and their consorts. Other lesser deities existed such as local ancient folk heroes and regional beings, some of which were animal or inorganic in form, and exist on a level between the primary Hindu gods and man. These were all subsumed in Hinduism into a pantheon of deities and spirits. There is no sharp division between the gods and man, as is found, for example, in the Judaeo-Christian tradition.

History of the Development of Images

As mentioned above, archaeological excavations in the areas of Mohenjo Daro and Harappa revealed numerous crudely made terracotta images of animals and female figures. Also found were a few skilfully carved and lifelike stone sculptures of humans, and steatite seals (Figure 2.3) attributed to the Indus valley civilization of 2500 BC. However, the subsequent Indo-Aryan culture from 2000–300 BC has so far failed to provide any significant material evidence of any fine-carved stone image making. Despite the absence of surviving artefacts from the period following the Indus valley culture it is difficult to imagine that this form of craftsmanship completely disappeared. Initially, as has already been mentioned, the Aryan deities referred to in the sacrificial hymns were not given sculptural form and were only described verbally. In the later Upanishadic tradition the personalized deity was to be summoned through meditation. The probability that image worship continued in the Vedic period in the lower levels of society is widely accepted.[36] Archaeological evidence suggests continuity in the making and use of crude terracotta animal and human

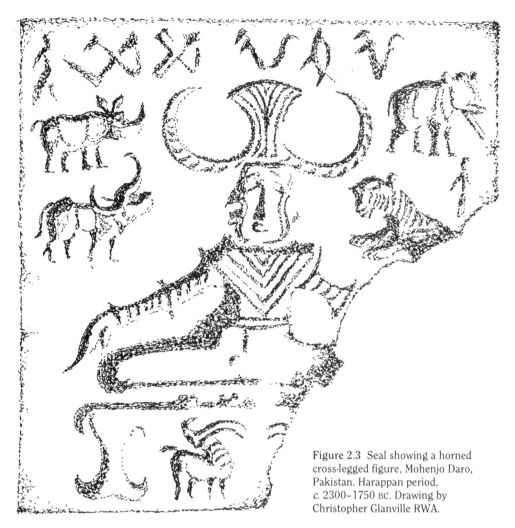

Figure 2.3 Seal showing a horned
cross-legged figure, Mohenjo Daro,
Pakistan. Harappan period,
c. 2300–1750 BC. Drawing by
Christopher Glanville RWA.

images. The practice of such votive offerings still persists in village and tribal India today.[37]

Stone monuments and edicts produced under the patronage of the great emperor Asoka survive from the Mauryan period which dates from the third century BC, but most other materials proved less durable and have perished. Asoka supplanted the 'revealed' Vedic sacrifice with a form of Buddhist ceremonial. This practice became the central cult of his empire and involved gift giving to Buddhist monks alongside a stupa cult, where signs of the Buddha were honoured. Magnificent buildings produced by the neighbouring Achaemenid empire inspired a new style of Indian architecture in stone to meet Asoka's requirements for monumental stupas and stone pillars. The first century AD Sanchi stupa has an inscription which refers to the work of ivory carvers, and further evidence of this work is provided in the early Sastric texts but nothing has survived. These textual prescriptions actually favoured images in impermanent materials such as clay and

Figure 2.4 Male figure (possibly a yaksha) from Parkham, Uttar Pradesh. Sunga, second–first century BC. Mathura Museum, Mathura.

wood rather than stone, and state that these images will bring the worshippers long life, fortune, strength and victory.[38]

The role of wooden architecture and its influence on the design of early Buddhist rock-cut and Hindu free-standing architecture is well known. The ancient text known as the *Vishnudharmottara Purana* devotes a whole chapter to the details of procuring wood for temple building and image making. This text also suggests that stone was used less frequently than wood. It is possible that wood as a material for sculpted images was selected for spiritual reasons as much as for ease of working and availability. Certainly the relative ease of carving a detailed figure affected the development of the free-standing image.[39] Perhaps the yaksha image, when carved in wood, was thought to be a suitable home for the vital pulse of the tree spirit, being of the same material substance. The *Brhatsamhita* gives the words of a mantra to be uttered by a craftsman about to cut down a tree in order to make an image:

> Oh though tree, salutation to thee, though art selected for (being fashioned into) the icon of the deity; please accept this offering according to rules. May all the spirits which reside in this tree transfer their habitation elsewhere after accepting the offerings made according to rules; may they pardon me today (for disturbing them) salutation to them.[40]

From this exhortation it is evident that society believed yakshas to be capable of transmigration and this may have contributed to the Hindu belief in the peripatetic nature of spirits generally;[41] it may also have contributed to the idea that a sculpture as well as a person may be possessed by the deity. It cannot be proved that pre-Vedic tree worship influenced the development of Buddhist, Jain and Hindu icons or images, though a very early Jain text refers to a statue of the yaksha Moggarapani in a shrine outside the city of Rajagraha.[42] The transfer of beliefs from one era to another and from one philosophy to another can be seen in the continuous use of sacred sites by successive religious groups. These sites acquired sanctity by identification with a former sacred presence, an idea which is part of the spiritual mythology of India.[43]

The earliest examples of free-standing anthropomorphic figures are of yakshas and yakshinis from the third to second century BC (Figure 1.1). Whether the early yaksha and yakshini sculpture attributable to Maurya and Sunga patronage had ritual or royal significance is uncertain. However, it is interesting to note that an early sculpture of a yaksha found near the ancient city of Vidisha (Figure 2.4) was still being actively worshipped as 'Jakheiya' by the local community at the time of its discovery earlier this century. Coomaraswamy refers to aspects of the tree worship cult and offerings to trees which in many ways are similar to the kind of offerings made to Hindu gods or village deities today. The full frontal and monumental form of the earliest free-standing yaksha images echo the solidity and verticality of the pillar. These monumental yaksha images influenced the form of the early images of the Buddha and Jain icons.[44]

Associated with the idea of tree worship is another vertical form, the sacred pillar. There is an acceptance in many cultures of the association of a sacred pillar with the world axis. The tree and the pillar are symbols which may have links in pre-Vedic and Vedic iconography. Even today the Gonds worship their tribal deity, Aki Pen, in the form of a wooden pillar.[45] The importance of the tree can also be seen by its continued worship in villages (Figure 2.5) and in the courtyards of several temples in India, one example being the Tiruvannamalai temple in Tamil Nadu. Vedic texts describe the pillar as the instrument

which separated heaven and earth during the creation of the universe. According to Irwin, the earliest record of this belief occurs in the *Rg Veda*,[46] where a tree was the sacrificial post (yupa or stambha) which represented the axis of the universe.

Indra himself is said to be the stambha which holds apart the worlds. The gods live at the top of the pillar, while man and the ancestors abide at the lower regions. Communication takes place along this post or tree, for the sacrificial offering is tied to a pillar and thereby delivered upward to the gods, while the yupa acts as a fecundator bringing the celestial waters to the earth.[47]

According to Irwin, evidence of a pre-Mauryan date for the earliest known stone pillars is given by their varied methods of construction. Furthermore, he suggests that wooden pillars may well have been common earlier.[48] Asokan pillars proclaimed written edicts and used images of the lion and the bull to assert their royal authority. Even today in South India in many temples, a flag on a tall pole is placed in the centre before the principal shrine. The devotees must first offer worship to this post or flag. The meaning of this flag is unclear nowadays and has become merely a ritual observance. It is possible however that this is an ancient remnant of the pillar and tree concept which is still incorporated into Hindu ritual practice. It is also true that even the simplest wayside shrine is declared sacred by the presence of the flag. The flag may also suggest the element of wind.

As already mentioned, the earliest known images of Hindu deities date from the first century BC and were found with free-standing Jain and Buddhist images in the region of Mathura. Whether these were inspired by Graeco-Roman examples or in emulation of free-standing monumental

Figure 2.5 Sacred tree hung with cradles. Tamil Nadu. Stephen Huyler.

yaksha sculptures remains controversial.[49] The ritual practice relating to this early monumental stone sculpture is unknown, but it probably echoed earlier folk traditions of the worship of the tree spirits and snake deities. A distinction must be made in the Sunga period (first century BC) between free-standing images and the decorative and illustrative relief carvings which adorned the railings and great toranas of the Buddhist stupas of pre-Hindu India. These reliefs not only tell a story but may also have attempted portrayals of actual places and events.

A precursor of the Hindu goddess Lakshmi dating from the Sunga period of the second century BC can be seen in a female image found on the Buddhist stupa at Bharhut. This image is in the character-istic form associated with Lakshmi – a female, supported by a lotus, flanked by and lustrated by two elephants. An early image referring to a Vaishnavite deity is seen on a large first-century BC stone pillar. This pillar bears an inscription which states that this 'standard' was set up in honour of the deity Vasudeva, by a man from Taxila named Heliodorus, the ambassador of a Graeco-Bactrian king to King Bhagabhadra in 120–100 BC. This pillar bearing one of the most popular names for Vishnu was probably surmounted by the bird Garuda, the vehicle of Vishnu.

One of the most important examples of early Saivism in South Asia is the linga presently enshrined in a temple of a later period in the village of Gudimallam. The figure of Siva carved on the linga resembles that of a yaksha and is in an early Sunga style suggestive of first-century BC origin. The figure of Siva has only two arms and holds a ram, or possibly an antelope, and a water pot. An axe rests on his shoulder, and he stands on a dwarf. Some of these attributes become standard elements of his later iconography (Figure 2.6). Also in South India, evidence of shrines from the Ishvaku period suggest the early covering of images.

Despite these references to Hindu images, the surviving sculpture produced during the Sunga and Satavahana periods from the first century BC to the first century AD is predominantly Buddhist or Jain, and Hindu sculpture is rare. The decoration of these Buddhist monuments reveals many examples of pre-Buddhist, non-Vedic iconography. The frequent appearance of inscribed yaksha and yakshini,[50] naga and nagini images, the solar symbols and the lustrated female on a lotus demonstrate the coexistence of these cults with Vedic Brahmanism.

The region of Mathura, from the first century AD under Kusana patronage, is responsible for many of the earliest examples of Hindu sculpture. The apparent increase in the making of stone images is generally attributed to familiarity with Greek sculpture, a result of increased trade with the Graeco-Bactrian community in North-west India. Some of the earliest Hindu images known to us are seen in the image of Kartikeya found in Kankali Tila and an image of Surya at Mathura.[51] The

Figure 2.6 Linga from Gudimallam, Andhra Pradesh. *c.* First century BC. Madhuvanti Ghose.

Lakshmi image of the first century BC on the stupa at Bharhut and the reliefs of Indra and Surya at Bhaja on the western ghats south of Bombay do not appear to have been worshipped. An architectural fragment of a Sivalinga from Mathura is also evidence of linga worship. The strength of this sect is demonstrated by the appearance of Siva on Kusana coins and the existence of the Gudimallam linga shrine which proves that the linga was used as a cult icon at this time.

From the fourth century AD, Vidisha and nearby Udaygiri in Central India were important sites developed under the patronage of the Kusana dynasty. The earliest intact body of Hindu art in India is seen in Udaygiri, in twenty rock-cut chambers. These caves contain carvings which are vital for the study of the creation of Hindu iconography. An inscription securely dates the cave complex to AD 401 and mentions the patron Candragupta II. The sculptures in these caves demonstrate that by the early fifth century much of the Hindu iconographic formula was well established. This multilayered language of form was mirrored in the love of verbal pun and allegory found in contemporary Sanskrit literature.[52] A pantheon of deities was now represented with clearly formed iconography. Gods such as the elephant god Vishnu, the goddesses Durga in the form of Mahisamardini and the river goddesses appear in the caves of Udaygiri. Other representatives of the Hindu pantheon may also be seen on the fifth-century Durga temple at Aihole near Badami and the fifth-century Vishnu temple at Deogarh. Sculpture was now involved not only in the making of the central cult icon but also in a highly complex arrangement of stone carving on the temple, predominantly around the outside with a smaller amount inside.[53]

One of the most important images at Udaygiri is that of the boar incarnation of Vishnu known as Varaha, which appears in cave 5. He is depicted as half-man, half-boar, with his left foot on a submissive naga.

Isolated sculptures from the Gupta period at a number of other sites reveal that many of the Hindu deities known today were already widespread by the fifth century. The sophisticated symbolism present in this early corpus of Hindu art suggests a lengthy formative period, while the complete absence of any examples from this earlier phase suggests the use of perishable materials.[54] With the growth in popularity of Hinduism, temples dedicated to various Hindu deities were constructed throughout North and Central India. The image was not only protected by ritual and architecture but served with the temple to protect the surrounding community. This dual function of manifestation and protection underlined the important relationship between temples and images.[55]

Surviving wall panels from these Gupta temples show a growing complexity in iconography including such images as the man-lion (Narasimha), the dwarf incarnation (Vamana), Vishnu lying on Sesa (snake), Vishnu as Nara and Narayana and the sculpture of Gajendramoksa. Some temples used specific complex imagery in an attempt to convey a message to the devotees. A common theme was Anantasayana representing the beginning, Nara and Narayana denoting the means through which moksa can be achieved, with Gajendramoksa being the final result. Parallel to stone sculpting in the Gupta period there existed a well-developed terracotta tradition. The sculptures from such sites as Ahicchattra demonstrate the high standard of craftsmanship, while the brick temple of Bhitargaon is one of the best preserved of its type. On stylistic grounds the first half of the fifth century has been suggested as the date of this building.

The sophistication and allegorical nature of the surviving Hindu sculpture leads one to conclude, despite the lack of material evidence of a formative phase, that Hindu sculpture from the first century BC to the fifth century AD represents not the formation of Hindu iconography but the crystallization of a long period of development. Over the next few centuries the trend was towards an increased elaboration in the depiction of Hindu relief sculpture. Examples of this may be seen in the panels decorating the cave temple of Elephanta assigned to the patronage of the Kalachuri dynasty in the mid-sixth century.[56] Sculpture from the first century BC generally comprises single figures or shallow narrative friezes. Gradually in the sixth century, free-standing figurative sculpture began to appear on the outside of the temples and became an increasingly important component of the architectural design. The naturalistic portraits of the human figure, accurate in details of dress and physiognomy, became less important over the next two centuries, to be replaced from about the eighth century by figures intended to enhance and promote a unified architectural design rather than realism.

> The loss of anatomical credibility, exaggeration of movement, simplification of the body, hardening of carving, bold elaboration of details and reduction and multiplication of single images that occurred between the sixth and fourteenth centuries can thus be seen for what they were – not a deterioration in quality but a change in intention.[57]

The relief sculpture resembles Buddhist wall painting at Ajanta in that it portrays figures which, like the actors in Sanskrit drama, appear in a series of apparently unconnected vignettes. These were seen by an audience able to absorb simultaneously many elements of the whole sequential story. These wall panels and the ever-increasing complexity of plot foreshadow the exuberant carvings on temple walls in subsequent centuries when sculpture played an even greater role in carrying out the programme of the temple than it did in the Gupta and immediately post-Gupta monuments. The cult icon retained identifiable attributes seen in the earliest period of Hindu sculpture. Emblems and vehicles had become firmly established as part of the code of effective identification and aesthetics, reinforcing the essential spiritual message of Hinduism in a manner that was readily understood by the people.

The Purpose of Images

For the Hindu the image is an instrument of purpose, significant only in its role as a vessel fit to contain the deity with little consideration as to its intrinsic value. Images are discarded once they have served their spiritual purpose. The purpose of the image, as has been already described, is to represent some fundamental aspect of the universe which is not perceptible to our senses, and to act as a metaphor to enable the religious devotee to more easily recognize that truth. Essentially the image is intended to reveal divinity to man and to help manifest divinity in man, in other words, to represent and participate in this process. The image is also intended to assist the concentration of the worshipper by providing a focus for his devotions. According to the Indian art historian Meister:

> Images that designate divinity, clothe the absolute, specify a path for meditation, give form to devotion, even specify a sociology for kingship or society; they contain divinity called down by human ritual, embody the potency of patronage, the beauty of their craftsman's inner vision, the subtle body that is real form. This is their function and their history.[58]

If these images have received the appropriate ritual invocation they are believed to hold a numinous presence and to radiate some particles of divine energy. In the innermost shrine many icons are blackened with smoke and, when seen by devotees, so heavily draped in cloth that details of their form are not as important as the splendour of their adornment. Many writers have observed that the services and offerings constituting worship are expressions of homage or respect for the honoured guest, seen as represented by the image as the deity. While this is one aspect of the ritual, some of the elements – for example, the lamps – are rarely used for an honoured guest. The final objective of worship in Hinduism is to overcome the differences between gods and men which lie at the root of the problem of their dialogue and to encourage a progressive identification of the worshipper and god. The ultimate aim for them either before the personal shrine at home or in the temple is to become one by the devotee identifying both inwardly and outwardly with the deity. The potential for the interchangeability of nara and narayana – man and god – is fundamental to Hindu theology. The strongest expression of this idea may be the ritual's use of a flame, with its strong smell and brilliance which acts directly on the senses, and yet expresses the insubstantial yet transforming spiritual power of the deity.[59] The rapid extinguishing of the flame also symbolizes the transience of imperfect man's communication with the deities and his need to repeat it continually.

In other words, while it seeks to produce (or restore) an identity of god and man, worship simultaneously emphasises their differences, because the identity cannot be sustained. Moreover as only gods know how ritual should properly be performed, worship must always remain the inadequate work of humans.[60]

The study by Humphrey and Laidlaw of the variety of individual aims in the ritual practice of Jain puja, however, revealed a wide variety of individual motives, some of which reflect a habitual approach to its practice as a dutiful part of the customary round of their everyday life.[61] Throughout this study one must acknowledge the discrepancy between the theological or philosophical claims of Hinduism and the

varied multilayered concepts and aims held by individual Hindus. Despite these differences improvisation takes place within a carefully prescribed form.

Ritualized acts in liturgical traditions are socially prescribed and present themselves to individual actors as 'given' and external to themselves. Because ritualized acts are stipulated in this way, a new situation arises: instead of, as is normally the case in everyday life, a person's act being given meaning by his or her intentions, with ritual action the act itself appears as already formed, almost like an object, something from which the actor might 'receive'. In this transformed situation the intentions and thoughts of the actor make no difference to the identity of the act performed.[62]

Darsana (literally viewing), an act of positive visual and mental engagement with the god or the seeing of or being in the presence of an image; and funding, or the making of a religious image, are believed to lead to the acquisition of spiritual merit, both for the donor and, by association, the craftsman. The craftsmen making these images were concerned with more than mere aesthetic achievement.

He [the craftsman] also makes them [the image] act effectively by means of their aesthetic presence whose magic literally secures for the donor a place in heaven while on earth, and whose virtue acts for the well-being of those who are in the orbit of power or connected with the patron.[63]

The artist's work becomes 'concretely real, subtly effective and transcendentally existent', as indicated in the sacred text the *Vishnusamhita*.[64] The physical presence of the work of art was felt to have beneficial influence, primarily on the patron but also on all who saw or worshipped it. Statues were said to weep, to shake and to address the spectator, as did the royal portrait statues in the drama *Pratimanataka*.[65] The effect of the image on the worshipper involves a charged atmosphere of expectation, smoke from the incense and flames, and a darkened mystery of the inner shrine. Hindu preoccupation with the universal rather than the individual, and therefore with form rather than strict portraiture, contributed to the need for general attributes in the depiction of the figures rather than specifics. The Hindu artist became adept at conveying bhava (mood) with a subtle portrayal of feelings, without it degenerating into sentimentality.

Associated with the image is the devotion itself, which is an aspect of ritual practice that is difficult to quantify or qualify. Devotional cults grew in popularity in Tamil Nadu from AD 300 and gave rise to the bhakti cults which soon permeated the whole of India. The exchange of devotion for God's grace is the fundamental purpose of temple worship.

The Making of Images

Among Hindus the act of sculpting or painting an image of the deity is sacred. Centuries of oral instructions regarding the making of images were later compiled in texts called the *Sastras*. In general, the *Sastras* were written by Brahmans to give guidelines for the correct performance of a range of activities from music, warfare and cooking to making love. The texts dealing specifically with sculpture are called the *Silpasastras* and those concerned with architecture the *Vastusastras*. The *Silpasastras* give precise instructions as to proportions, postures and the required number of arms and heads of the Hindu gods. The texts also suggest the most

suitable material for making these sacred images. Essentially, these texts attempted to guide the transformation of the ideal or numenal into the real or phenomenal world.

The *Sastras* specify that before beginning any new work the craftsman (silpin) should undergo ritual purification and conduct rites which include paying respect to the stone and paint he is to use and to his tools before beginning any task. Even today, craftsmen may still enter into a state of concentration or heightened consciousness by means of yoga or meditation before commencing a new project. The texts stress the need for the artist to be guided by inner vision and revelation, conceptualizing the appearance of the work during this mental state of openness and receptivity. The vision of the silpi yogins (sculptors) who follow this discipline represents a supreme form of concentration. Their art aims at the discovery and depiction of the true nature of reality. Sculptors do not see themselves as creators or innovators but as attempting to express an order that already exists (savam) of which they are a part and to represent it to the world.

Starting in the immediate and perceptible, ritual brings forth the vision of the ishta the desired object, and piece by piece the picture is completed until at last a moment comes when the vision is totally changed and subject and object, Siva and Sakti, become one. In the words of the famous Bengal boatman's song 'In search of thee I found myself'.[66]

In order that the form of an image may be brought fully and clearly before the mind, the imager should meditate; and his success will be proportionate to his meditation. No other way – not indeed seeing the object itself – will achieve his purpose.[67]

In the creation of free-standing icons and relief sculptures, correct proportions were imperative. Five different sets of proportions were devised for the male and female figure. The Indians, like the Greeks, held the view that beauty consisted not in the elements but in the harmonious proportion of the parts. Different regional schools of sculpture held different theories of proportion. The *Chitrasutra* states: 'For the rest of the princely figures, the measurements have to be provided by an intelligent understanding on the lines indicated and from one's own experience.'[68] Here, the artist is specifically told to study the differences in features, complexions, ornaments and dress from one region to another and where necessary to create proportions by his own genius.

An image should be seen from the front and should not be crooked;[69] it should be given a beautiful countenance, the cheeks well formed; the face should have a pleasant expression, the torso good arms, hands and a full chest. The limbs should be heavily decorated and the statue complete with its implements and vehicles (vahanas); it must possess bhava (literally mood) and action, and look lifelike.[70] The technical process of making the image brilliant was to rub it with oil, hair and diamonds and then to smear it with vermilion.[71] The majority of Sanskrit texts agree that sculpture and painting should be as beautiful and durable as possible and that this will be propitious both to the artist and owner. In order to encourage the gods to enter an image the manuals specify that it should be portrayed in a beautiful manner. They generally state that all figures in painting and in sculpture must be sundara (beautiful), sivam (auspicious), and also satya (real; that is, conforming to the form as known to the artist or to the devotee to whom God had revealed himself). Only then will the god enter the image and shower the worshipper with dharma, artha, kama and moksha. The essential features of sculpture and painting are also referred to in the six limbs (shadanga) of Chitra described by Yasodhara in his commentary on the *Kama Sutra* of Vatsyayana.

The proportional system referred to in the *Silpasastras* is both varied and complex. The *Vishnudharmatorra Purana* describes three basic units of measurement based on the human body: angulas, talas and mukhas. The angula is based on a measurement of the forefinger, the distance from the first to the second joint of the forefinger when bent, and the tala is made up of twelve angulas from which the calculation of the measurement of the human face or mukha is arrived at. The face is measured from the base of the chin to the hairline. There are nine mukhas in the overall height of a figure. Variations of this scale can be seen in the texts, depending on where they were written and their date. The proportions also vary depending on whether the statue is of a human being or a deity. Most religious sculptures in India were part of an architectural context, the sculptor varying his work to suit the location. To achieve the optimum effect, sculpture when viewed from below required deliberate distortion by the craftsman.

Pupils learn their craft by memorizing repetitive exercises from a teacher, first in isolation and then in combination.[72] A craftsman is expected to remember all the necessary calculations of proportions for the structure and composition of an image. There was a certain degree of artistic licence and interpretive freedom. According to the art historian Adalbert Gail, while the rules or guidelines reflect Brahmanic religious requirements there is a gap between theory and practice:

> One will not find a single case of full coincidence between textual injunction and the work of art in question. When I studied the tradition of varaha-murtis (boar incarnations of Vishnu) ten years ago I found not a single correspondence between image and shastric text.[73]

Another recent study of the rules governing proportion by the art historian Mosteller has also questioned the extent to which Hindu sculptors obeyed the formulae described in the *Sastras*. Mosteller suggests that the manuals on which Western scholarship has depended for its understanding about the proportions and methods of image making are unreliable. He suggests that these texts were not manuals in a Western sense, but are disjointed and fragmentary versions of a largely orally transmitted code of rules which do not accurately reflect the discipline. He therefore argues that the texts cannot be relied upon as a guide to the practical and theoretical foundation of Indian art.[74]

Mosteller analyses the images themselves and has interviewed contemporary Indian sculptors working in the traditional style. He suggests that in South India there was a correspondence between the width of the middle segment of the middle finger of the patron of the image and the image itself which bound the patron inextricably to the image. He argues that this confirmed the patron's acquisition of merit. Mosteller also suggests that the tala or palm of the hand, the next unit of measurement, was associated with the hand span of the patron. Mosteller also refers to a carving of the stone which is based on the removal of a line which has to be constantly redrawn. He

shows how this method results in the connection between the act of drawing and carving and the image being quite literally drawn into the third dimension.[75]

The formula used for early North Indian sculpture seems not to have been based on a measurement from a living body but was calculated, as it still is, by subdividing the surface of the raw material to be used for the image into a prescribed number of equal parts.[76] The key to memorizing style was, according to Mosteller, through an understanding of the essential pattern or form and this skill was transmitted within a hereditary group of artists who preserved its secrets.

Other details were referred to in the texts with a strict iconography. For example, the gods were given colours according to their status in the divine hierarchy (gunas);[77] the posture chosen for the statue was dependent on the intended mood or rasa.[78] The reason behind this rigidity lay in the concern for the ritual efficacy of an object. According to the *Vishnudharmatorra*:

> A rough image is said to cause death and an angry one destroys beauty. Even when (duly) invoked by the best of Brahmans, the gods never enter images short of (sastric) measurements and devoid of the marks (laksanas) (of divine form); (but) demons, ghosts and hob-goblins always enter into them, and so great care must be taken to avoid shortness of measurements.[79]

The restoration of old and dilapidated shrines and the replacement of broken, decaying and sometimes defiled images or other cult objects by new ones has long been regarded as a great act of religious merit in India. In some texts such actions are even described as more meritorious than the establishment of new shrines and the construction of new images.

31

Ritual Performance and Consecration of the Image

More important than the rules governing proportions of images is the correct procedure in their ritual preparation. The process of imbuing the statue with religious presence involved various rites of consecration to be performed by the reciting of prescribed Sanskrit mantras. This ancient practice is still meticulously observed today. Texts specify the correct performance of this consecration and worship of images. Yet a recent study by Fuller of priests in Madurai revealed that, despite Madurai being one of the most traditional Hindu temples and the priests being full-time ritual specialists, their regular rites are not closely guided by the texts. Fuller's informants agreed that the religious texts, the agamas, are the authoritative source on ritual performance, yet Fuller writes:

> Probably the most important sociological and historical fact about the Agamic literature ... is that it is nowadays largely unknown.... Neither the Agamas nor the ritual manuals actually contain the kind of explicit liturgical instruction that priests and others commonly suppose them to contain.[80]

On the education of the priests who perform the rituals, he says,

> The pupils mainly learn by memorising exactly the passages recited to them by their teachers. It is considered vital that these passages' words, pronunciation and scansion are all memorized absolutely accurately, and this cannot be done by reading books.[81]

Before an image is constructed, the Dhyana mantra is chanted which contains the iconographic descriptions and the definition of the power of the specific deity. When the deity is complete the eyes are opened (chaksunmilan). Consecration of the image often takes place in a specially consecrated booth outside the temple. There is an altar in the booth which is first sprinkled with sand and then covered with kusa grass. The image is purified with a variety of ritually pure substances, such as darbha grass, honey and ghee. When the image is bathed its head should face towards the East and an instrument similar to a trumpet should be sounded. Then, through a rite called nyasa (literally touching), various deities are established in different parts of the image: Brahma in the chest, Indra in the hand, Surya in the eyes, the directional guardians in the ears and so on. This is followed by the mantras of Pratishtha and those of the Adhivasana and Pranapratishtha which are responsible for the infusing of life in the image. Once this process has been completed the image should be laid down to sleep for the night and then roused at sunrise and worshipped with flowers, garments and sandal paste and the sounding of a conch shell. It should then be carefully taken inside the temple sanctum. A piece of gold should be placed in the base of the image before it is fixed. The installation of an image is particularly recommended in the bright fortnight during the period of the summer solstice.[82]

The function of mantras or prayers is crucial in the consecration of an image or a king. The chanting metaphorically anoints the king or image like the sprinkling of sacred water. It is said that the sound of the chant is the god Vayu. The verses addressed to different deities evoke their presence and activate them.

Rasa or the Experience of Feeling

It is considered important when creating an image to give it rasa; in other words, the taste or flavour received by the viewer. The Sanskrit word 'rasa' has a variety of meanings, its essence best conveyed as the sap or juice of organic life.[83] The differentiation of eight sentiments in the transmission of rasas was expressed partly by the use of distinct colours and partly by gesture, posture and hand positions.[84] A concern with the representation of hidden realities and the evocation and expression of the flow of rasa is behind the most successful Hindu sacred imagery. This rasa or the expression and communication of mood bhava and taste are fundamental to many forms of art. Its manifestation can be seen in many examples of religious painting, sculpture, drama, dance, music, poetry and literature. An example of this can be seen in the sacred dance performed by the Devidasis (female temple dancers) which still takes place in a few Hindu temples in India. Marglin in her study of these dancers points out that the highly stylized dance, with its large number of gestures (Figure 2.7), eye positions, rigid facial expressions and foot movements, distances the dancer from her own subjective states of mind. A total postural and gestural state accompanies an emotional-cum-mental state, aimed at arousing in the audience an erotic sensation which is, according to Humphrey and Laidlaw, transformed by the ritual to a spiritual-cosmic plane such that the spectators can participate in the 'divine play' of the gods. Humphrey and Laidlaw question whether the dance is more concerned with the representation of an idea or ritual action than with the actual communication of a message: 'What is

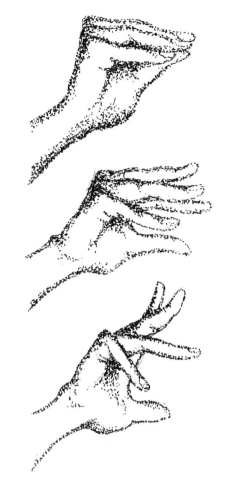

Figure 2.7 Hand gestures: the mukula mudra (closed lotus), padmakosha mudra and the alapadma mudra (open lotus). Drawing by Christopher Glanville RWA.

going on here is that the worshipper intends to represent an idea by means of a ritualized action, an action which could perfectly well represent other ideas.'[85]

Images in an Architectural Context

Within the decorative framework of the Hindu temple, sculptures assumed different emphases during the years AD 500–1000. Sculptures lost their individuality and

Figure 2.8 Nageswara temple, Tamil Nadu. Kumbhakonam, 886. Robert Elgood.

became valued less for their inherent vitality and realism than for their part in the cohesive dynamic of the structure of the whole as fragments from a divine cosmology.[86] Imagery began to fulfil a protective function as well as heightening the auspiciousness and beauty of the whole. According to Joanna Williams:

> Architecture became more complex and coherent as a religious experience, and sculpture was integrated into that larger purpose. This new role led to the patterning of detail, linking different parts of the temple's decor. It also led to the depiction of less credible human anatomy, the creation of less self-sufficient sculptural compositions and the organization of imagery in more inclusive iconographic programs.[87]

The characteristic small, free-standing temple shrine of the Gupta period was to a large extent replaced in the medieval period by the larger temple complex with an increasing ritual function. The most important and potent image in the temple was the icon enshrined in the sanctum known as the garbhagrha, or sanctum. This icon represents the locus of the deity from which the divine emanations are believed to proceed. All the other sculptures in the building relate to this image, being incarnations or variations of the same deity. The entrance to the garbhagrha with its protective door keepers became highly decorated. The door was perceived as the passage between the manifest and the unmanifest. The door sill (udumbara) with its attendant and auspicious figures was used to mark the liminal zone between the worshipper and the divine. The upper corners of the doorways bore the female yakshinis, although by the sixth century these were being increasingly replaced by images of the river goddess on the lower jambs of the door. The standard iconography from the Gupta period, such as an overall rythmical pattern of vegetation, aquatic and protective motifs, and celestial images on the lintel and above continued, but became more diverse and elaborate.[88]

The first free-standing temples possessed few external images, and sculptures appeared in only those that had exterior niches. Subsequently, secondary images began to appear on the corners (karnas) of shrines and then on the intermediary offsets (pratirathas). Throughout the eighth century eight guardians of the directions of space were placed protectively at each corner of the temple. These were originally elemental deities of the Vedic pantheon, who in later

Hinduism became subsidiary to such major gods as Vishnu and Siva. These elemental deities helped to support the structure and to protect it from external chaos.

They also helped the deity to communicate with and manifest itself in the world of man. They are the most important images on the wall and are placed on an axis with the centre of the shrine. The secondary images provide more intimate, individualized forms for personal worship.[89]

The figure on the back wall of a temple opposite the door is axially and spiritually the most closely related image to that of the inner sanctum. When the sanctum image is absent the identity of this image gives an indication of the temple's dedication. With the greater elaboration of figures on the external temple walls, a certain order in the arrangement of deities usually prevailed (Figure 2.8).[90]

By the ninth century images were left unframed. A mythical beast called Vyala frequently appeared on the vertical recesses of the temple walls (Figure 2.9).[91] Within an increasingly complex architectural form lesser beings were placed in the side offsets, vertical recesses which flanked the wider bhadra walls. In the ninth century female attendants became the usual occupants of these intermediary offsets, and mithuna (erotic couples), were sometimes placed in specific points of architectural weakness or juncture for protective purposes.[92] In Western India in the eleventh century sculptures of ascetics (munis) replaced the Vyalas in these recesses. These figures at times leer at the Apsaras, linking the indentations and projections of the temple building into a playful narrative.

Few images are placed above in the tower (sikhara) which is situated above the sanctum.

In its formal multiplicity ... the temple tower evokes the celestial realm of Mount Meru at the world's center and is crowned by the seed form capital of the cosmic pillar. Each temple thus both centers and reveals the world while offering the worshipper a path by which to transcend it.[93]

The North Indian temple is a cosmos translated into stone. On the temple surface is a hierarchy of images taken from plants and insects, animals and humans, celestial beings and divinities, representing the multifarious forms of the phenomenal world. Fire and flames are depicted on the walls by spiralling carved stone vines that encircle the temple to represent ritual.

The temple surface represents the atomic particles of creation; its base, superstructure, and upper altar the three levels of cosmic reality; and the multitude of deities enshrined by niches the particulate nature of divine manifestation.[94]

Ritual Worship

The three symbolic devices, mantras, yantras and murtis (icons or images), have a dynamic relation with one another. The chosen deity acts as the intermediary on the path to the worshipper's final objective. The image is a support for meditation. The mental discipline of the repetition of prayers (or mantras) and the focus on an image helps to prevent fragmentation of attention and distraction from the state of silent awareness. Initially the image is outside the worshipper's attention but gradually it fills the mind of the devotee. The ultimate aim is for the identification with and openness to the experience of silence, beyond sound and image, where the worshipper and worshipped are one and an experience is reached of a consciousness beyond the boundaries of time and space. The integration or unity of all things is frequently referred to as one of the fundamental characteristics of the highest state of mystical experience.

As the *Vishnusamhita*, a ritual Agama text, puts it:

> Without a form, how can God be meditated upon? If (He is) without any form, where will the mind fix itself? When there is nothing for the mind to attach itself to, it will slip away from meditation or will glide into a state of slumber. Therefore the wise will meditate on some form, remembering, however, that the form is a superimposition and not a reality.[95]

The *Jabala Upanishad* intimates that the image is only the support for the beginner: 'Yogins see Siva in the soul and not in images. Images are meant for the imagination of the ignorant.'[96]

This theological or philosophical category of the self and the ritual act should however be distinguished from the actual varied concepts that people hold or claim to hold. A study of Jain ritual by Humphrey and Laidlaw sees the act of intention and practice of ritual as independent and, by recording religious contemporary attitudes, suggests, as does Fuller in his study of Brahmans in Madurai, a gap between textual prescriptions, theory and actual thought, meaning and practice. Humphrey and Laidlaw, for example, in contradistinction to the ideals inferred in the above paragraph, see ritual acts as giving the devotees opportunities to allow the mind to wander by the repetition of the familiar.[97]

As is described below, in the temple, the image, like a revered monarch is woken, washed with water, milk or rice water, fed, dressed with cloths and garlands of flowers anointed with yellow sandalwood and red powder, and honoured with flames, incense and song according to the season. On an ordinary day there are traditionally four, or sometimes six ritual celebrations which take place at sunrise, noon, sunset and midnight. Once this ritual has been performed the curtain is pulled back (where it exists) to reveal the deity to the worshippers. Irrespective of the deity's needs, worship is carried out in order to please and for the hope on the part of the devotee for favour and protection. The image does not stand between the worshipper and the object of his devotions but acts as a vessel or form which facilitates the close relationship and provides the medium for the outpourings of reverence.

The cycle of service to the deity forms the programme for temple activity. The range of ordinary domestic tasks in the service of the divine make sacred the simple acts of duty and affection. There is usually no formal congregational worship, though the moments when the deity is revealed to the audience of worshippers is close to this. The religious attitude shown towards the image or icon is one of reverence and humility. The general term for this worship is puja. This includes the offering of flowers, water, receiving the darsan, or sight of the deity, and prasad (sanctified food offerings). Puja or worship involves gestures such as bowing, kneeling, prostration, touching the feet and placing the hands together in greeting, each of which is the individual choice of the devotee. Worship is performed not only in the home but also in the temple by special priests called pujaris. These priests offer upacaras to the deity. The number of these offerings in the temple varies, but they include food, water, fresh leaves, sandalwood perfume, incense, betel nuts and cloth.[98]

Other ritual actions such as waving a flywhisk[99] and the rite of circumambulation are considered as pleasing to the deity. Another important act is the honouring of the deity with light, during which the priest or householder slowly circles a five-wicked oil or camphor lamp before the deity, often to the accompaniment of the ringing of handbells and the singing of hymns.[100] This rite is called arati and is central to Hindu worship, and in some cases has become the general name for the daily rites replacing the term puja. In a temple there will be several aratis during the day, continuing into the evening.[101]

Associated with puja is the idea of bhakti (literally to share). According to Eck, bhakti is the love which is shared by God and the devotee.[102] Puja expresses not the deity's requirements but the most eloquent gestures of human devotion. Reverential humility expresses the feelings, while the incense, flowers, lights and food offerings delight the senses of the worshipper. The vision is not only sharpened by darsan but the heart and senses become tuned harmoniously in the final offering of the self.

Sometimes there are temples with several deities which are accorded worship. In one example, cited by Eck, the worship is called 'panchayatana puja' (the five-altar puja) in which five deities (Vishnu, Siva, Surya, Devi and Ganesa) are honoured in a single geometric diagram, with four images situated in four directions and one in the centre. This formula of the five shrines is the standard layout of the medieval North Indian temple. The worship of five deities simultaneously serves to remind the worshipper that the presence of God transcends any one single form.[103]

Worship is begun and concluded with certain rites. The rites of avahana (bidding)

Figure 2.9 Vyala. Drawing by Christopher Glanville RWA.

and visarjana (dismissal) are revealing. Siva may be summoned by the words 'O Lord, who protects the world, graciously be present in this linga until the end of the worship'.[104] When puja is over the deity may be dismissed with the words 'O excellent gods, O Supreme Siva, return now to your own abode so that you may come again for the benefit of the worshipper'.[105] These prayers acknowledge the Hindu belief in the transience of the deity's concentrated presence in any one form. Several images made for specific festivals underline this peripatetic nature of the deity. Durga is invited to depart and the image disposed of at the conclusion of a Durga festival. Even more temporary is the example of the Kanishka linga, where a worshipper offers his or her prayers with a moulded lump of clay along with perhaps a flower and some water, when Siva is given leave to go and the image destroyed.

Despite the philosophical interpretation of the aims of the individual in worship one should not ignore the very material qualities of this practice. The scholar Tachikawa, in his study of Homa in Vedic ritual, argues:

> Everything that is used during the ritual, be it offerings or utensils, must be transformed from a mundane state into a Vaidic state, and in fact approximately half of the ritual is devoted to effecting this transformation.[106]

Tachikawa suggests that the material qualities with which the priests conducting the ritual are concerned are not visible but involve the transformation of physical properties by an almost spiritual alchemy.

The Power of the Image

These ritual acts have in common a belief, even if only temporarily, of the potential for an image, however simple, to emanate and contain a powerful sacred presence in certain circumstances.

The relationship between the object and worshipper is one of continual recharging and renewal. The sacred object is believed to draw power from the energy of the reverence it receives.[107] It is popularly believed that the deeper the sense of reverence an object receives, the greater will be its spiritual power. For example, an icon or shrine's powerful reputation may be unrelated to its antiquity, physical appearance or authorship. In general, however, it is considered that the older a particular ritual object the more potent it is likely to be.

The power of the image is also demonstrated in the role of orthodox Hindu and tribal images in establishing the legitimacy of aspiring kings in 'little kingdoms'. Tribal goddesses and partially Hinduized goddesses possess a strong local rootedness, while the power of moveable goddesses was linked to their royal patrons. These moveable images thus provided greater mobility for the kings, and gave them a wider potential range of authority. It has been suggested that at certain periods in history, kings deliberately did not inscribe temples, which was believed would limit their power and area of influence.[108]

Conclusion

As we have seen, the origin of Hindu imagery is obscure. Images emerged from a pre-Vedic or coexistent tradition of terracotta votive offerings, an associated belief in burial grounds, spirit possession and the propitiation of spirits often associated with trees. This complex of ritual practice was combined with an oral immigrant mythology. Metaphor and verse described elemental gods and was incorporated into sacred formulae. The continuity of imagery over 3000 years is found less in stone than in terracotta. Wood may well have been a precedent not only for stone architecture but also for sculpture. Al-Biruni[109] refers to the image of the sun-god at Multan being made of wood and covered with red cordova leather; and also to the wooden idol of Sarada in Kashmir.

Throughout this chapter the sacred images should be seen in context. They can be inside a domestic household, in a forest shrine or at the edge of a village. The space where a Hindu image or icon is enshrined is not necessarily large or ritually complex. No congregational space is required, though space may be needed for certain rituals. Theoretically ritual worship or puja is an echo of the Vedic rite of sacrifice in its re-enactment of creation and contact with the divine and is faithful to precise ritual requirements. In modern Hinduism in the majority of cases, the sacrificial element is merely symbolic, echoed in the offering of a coconut or the presence of a sacred flame.[110] Worship is made up of offerings to the god, including incense, light and prayers with darsan the ritual's culmination.

It is said that in his making of the image the sculptor has not attempted to absorb or express something external to himself but to release something universal that he has experienced inwardly. His concern rests not only with form but with the forces that give rise to form. He is involved in a continuous process of discovery, not of himself but of the roots of the universe which he has been able to discover within himself. The characteristic product of the Hindu craftsmen may be seen in a sensual fluid form in sculpture and dance, the continuous narrative of fresco painting, the structure of Indian music and the cyclical structure of Sanskrit drama.

According to Lannoy:

One often sees the trunk of some huge tree locked in the embrace of a creeper, or one trunk coiled around another in a marriage as sensuous as the couplings (maithuna) of the Indian deities. The union of figure with matrix adorer with adored, subject with object, functions on the same analogy at all levels both abstract and plastic. Poet and dramatist also resorted to the image of the creeper for the same purposes as the sculptor.[111]

Religious icons or shrines are not the only objects to receive regular worship. Practical items of equipment are also shown reverence by their users with ritual ceremonial.

Perhaps in tantric ritual we are closest to a more conscious awareness of the aims expressed here for ultimate release with the assistance of imagery. Much of this theory depends for its realization on the subjective aims and experiences of the individual. The ultimate goal of release from the cycle of rebirth for each individual may be realized in one of several million lifetimes. This objective is profoundly connected with the aims of meditation in the search to ascend and transcend time and space.

Notes

1 For a clear account of these early texts and their approximate dates and chronology see O'Flaherty 1975, pp. 16–18.

2 Mascaro 1962, p. 81.

3 See Blurton 1992.

4 See Eck 1981.

5 Discriminating between magic and religion is difficult. In the Vedic period this may be discerned where important mantras were applied outside their original context for mundane objectives. In post-Vedic Hinduism there is a greater distinction between magic and religion, where magic is both socially approved and condemned. The *Atharvaveda* contains a rich collection of spells and magical rites (see Goudriaan 1978; Stutley 1980; Crooke 1894). Euro-centred cultures attempt through science and technology to control nature, while other non-European cultures such as North American, pre-Columbian and Hindu cultures suggest a symbiosis, rather than dominance.

6 Humphrey and Laidlaw (1994, p. 230) refer to the essential consecration of the Jain image with

the fixing on of the eyes: 'Without this ritual, people say, the statue is mere stone.'

7 The English word 'image' comes from the Latin word *imago*, meaning likeness. This concept of likeness is underlined by a custom in Bengal during the annual autumnal worship of the goddess Durga. A bowl of water is placed in front of the clay image of the goddess in such a manner that it reflects the goddess like a mirror. The goddess is worshipped by being bathed and the water used is then ritually poured on to the reflection, signifying that the reflection and the icon are equally divine. This use of a mirror image is also seen in Jain ritual – see Humphrey and Laidlaw 1994, p. 245 fn. 6. A quasi-narcissistic engagement may be seen in the worship of the idol of what is ideally perfect in oneself. This is heightened by the use of real pocket mirrors in ritual which may reflect the idol and oneself, by the building of some Jain temples in mirror-glass and the anointing of the self before a mirror at the beginning of puja. The idol is not a portrait of the Jina but an assemblage of qualities. Those who experience the identity with the Jina may undergo a cosmic resituating of the self, a feeling of being at the centre of the world as the Jina is represented in the temple. People would sometimes perform puja, dabbing sandalwood paste not on the idol itself but on a small pocket mirror. Words meaning an image may be found in the Vedas. The word 'pratima' is found in early Sanskrit texts such as the *Grihya Sutras* and the *Arthasastra*. All its synonyms – pratika, pratikriti, pratibimba, bimba – had the dual meaning of reflection, or a representative figure or symbol. Secular images which, according to Banerji (1941, p. 41), were not objects of worship were also mentioned in the Vedic texts. The sandstone statue of Kanishka at Mathura dating from the first century AD is an obvious example of this.

8 Vedic mantras are not only verses from the Vedic texts but also sections from the Vedas, used ritually.

9 Humphrey and Laidlaw 1994, p. 267.

10 Meister 1984, p. xix.

11 The deity can be given shape by the yantra, in which its presence during worship is laid out in a precise linear diagram within a polygon. It usually has around its centre several concentric primal shapes, such as triangles, hexagons, circles, octagons, and rings of lotus petals. The yantra's periphery is generally a square enclosure with four sacred doors opening towards the four cardinal points. The centrifugal yantras are conceived as a sacred dwelling in which the presiding deity and its retinue take up residence. The seat of the principal deity is in the centre while those of its emanations are arranged concentrically. They are known as avaranas (veils), so called because they conceal the luminous splendour of the deity in the centre. The yantra is a dynamic cosmic symbol and is always used in conjunction with mantras, or mystical sound units that correspond to the deity's subtle form. A yantra without its seed mantra is lifeless. See Khanna 1987, pp. 500–1.

12 All the objects we see and feel in this universe from abstract thought to matter are considered in Hinduism to be sounds of particular concentration. A mantra is primarily mental sound and regarded as fundamental in both the creation and dissolution of all form. It is believed to have the capacity to activate the divine forms invoked. A mantra exerts its power not so much through its meaning, but more deeply through its sound vibrations. Seers of ancient times who knew the secrets of the power of sound composed the mantras by joining together symbolic syllables in accordance with laws laid down in tantric texts. Mantras are believed to have corresponding colours and forms and Hinduism claims that each mantra relates to a particular power or deity (devata). Few initiates were given the knowledge of this science and great care was taken to guard its secrets. Modern physics in the study of harmonics continues to reveal the ever-present vibrations that are a component of matter, and the study of ultrasound is in its infancy. See Mookerjee 1968, pp. 57–8.

13 Staal 1984.

14 Fuller 1992, p. 68.

15 Humphrey and Laidlaw 1994, p. 104.

16 O'Flaherty 1975, p. 11.

17 Chapter 1 and Chapter 46, part III.

18 Vatsyayan 1982, p. 94.

19 For example, clear water not only purifies the body but also serves to wash off the impurity caused by untruth (Satapatha Brahmana). See Goudriaan 1987, p. 109.

20 See Baumer Vol. 2, 1988, p. 38.

21 According to Baumer (ibid., p. 38), some *Silpasastras* derive the anthropomorphic form from the yupa with which it shares its verticality and the round head. See also B. Baumer, 'Purusa and the origin of form', in Rupa

Pratirupa, Alice Boner, Commemoration Volume, New Delhi, 1982, pp. 27–34.

22 Bhattacharya 1947.

23 See Banerji 1941, p. 575. The Satarudriya section of the *Maitrayani Samhita*, while referring to the names of several gods and goddesses, also describes their iconographic features. Only with the emergence of sectarian Agamic and Puranic literature from the fourth century AD did the notion of murti and its use in puja become systematically formulated. For further reference see Bhattacharya, 1947, pp. 324–418. The *Mahanarayana Upanishad* (Vol. IV, pp. 1–18) elaborates the ethnography of some of these gods which were mostly folk gods absorbed into Vedic society. It has been suggested that the iconographic traits of the folk gods such as the yakshas arose before those of the higher cult gods and goddesses and may be traced to the pre-Buddhist period.

24 The earliest iconographic canons, according to Bhattacharya, 1947, pp. 326-7, are to be found in the Parisistas (appendix) of the *Grihyasutras* of which only one survives. Though the exact age of this Parisista is not known it may be placed in the latest part of the Sutra period and may be regarded as the earliest known iconographic text of India (1947, Table XI). Although a few texts relating to Hindu sculpture and painting may be placed in the third or fourth century AD their authors refer to the existence of innumerable earlier texts on which they had based their writings. The *Natyasastra* of Bharatamuni (*JBORS* (Journal, Bihar and Orissa Research Society) 1923, Part I, pp. 60–2) was composed between the third and sixth centuries AD. Bharata recommends wall paintings (Ch. 2, p. 83ff.) for stage scenery and shows his familiarity with colours and their variations of strength. The relations of various rasas with different colours are also described. Bhattacharya, (1947, p. 330) refers to sculptures known as pustas (dolls) mentioned in the *Silpasastras* and in the *Natyasastra*. These are placed at the back of the stage and are made of matting, cloth or skin. In front of this appeared multi-faced, grotesque or ugly beings. The *Natyasastra* also recommends that kings and princes should be bearded. The bearded image of Brahma of the third and fourth centuries AD in the Mathura Museum supports this reference. No early Silpa texts describe him as bearded but this detail may have originated from texts available to Bharata now lost to us. The *Natyasastra* may thus prove the existence of

technical literature on sculpture and painting before the third to sixth centuries AD.

25 Wilson 1870, Vol. 5, p. 234.

26 Huyler 1992, p. 6.

27 I am grateful to Madhu Ghose for her suggestion.

28 For discussion of this see ch. 3, p. 67.

29 See Schnepel 1995, p. 157; Eschmann *et al.* 1978, pp. 80-5.

30 See Mookerjee 1985.

31 See Coomaraswamy 1992, pp. 132, 133.

32 See Coomaraswamy 1971.

33 See Huntington 1985; Harle 1986.

34 For discussion of the proto-Siva image and its implications see Srinivasan (1984).

35 See Irwin (1973) for a discussion of the worship of the female in her manifestation as the queen, with particular reference to the queen termite and her many eggs in the termite mound. The termite mound was considered sacred in ancient India.

36 See Banerji 1941.

37 The *Sutras* refer to the existence of images. The *Jataka* stories refer to statues of Indra (Sakka) and the *Arthasastra* have clear references to images of gods. The *Grammar* of *Panini* also contains references to images.

38 See Banerji 1941 p. 222. Banerji refers to Chapter 58 of Varamihara's *Brhatsamhita* where details are given concerning the making of images.

39 See Michell 1992.

40 Banerji 1941, p. 223.

41 Coomaraswamy 1971.

42 The Jain text is the *Antagada Dasasp*, Chapter 6. Other references to wooden sculpture are to be seen in a wooden pillar bearing figure sculptures and motifs discovered at Arial near Dacca. See Banerji 1941.

43 Note the similarity between this and the concept of ley lines. The localization of the sacred was an idea common in Tamil Nadu.

44 See Huntington 1985.

45 See Haimendorf 1979.

46 See Irwin 1973, p.115. The *Rg Veda* reveals that the god Indra slew a demon, thus releasing the cosmic ocean and causing the separation of heaven and earth by pushing them asunder and propping the sky with a pillar.

47 Sutherland 1991, p. 25.

48 See Irwin 1973, pp. 115-18.

49 See Huntington 1985, pp. 151-2.

50 An interesting possible association can be seen in the carrying of the camar or flywhisk (a royal symbol and mark of respect). Humphrey and Laidlaw (1994, p. 228), refer to the waving of the flywhisk before the idol in Jain puja which can be accompanied by circular movements and a twirling dance which can lead to states of trance. The spirit possession associated with tree worship is well known.

51 The iconography of Surya is known in literature and occurs in pre-Kusana art. The moustache, garment, boots and representation of the fire altar carved in low relief betray the Iranian source.

52 See Desai 1992.

53 Ibid.

54 Other examples of deities represented from this period are Hari Hara (the union of Siva and Vishnu) and Krishna as bearer of Mount Govardhan (Krishna's name meaning 'the black one', has been suggested to be due to his tribal origin). His role of cowherd and links with the pastoral community also reinforce this relationship with a cow worshipping pre-Vedic society.

55 One such example is the Vishnu temple of Deogarh, dating back to the sixth century AD. The original five shrines of the temple are now empty but would probably have held five images.

56 See Huntington 1985, pp. 280-2, figures 13.5-8.

57 See Mason 1993, p. 122.

58 Meister 1984, p. xxiii.

59 See Fuller 1984, p. 15; Logan 1980, p. 24.

60 Fuller 1984, p. 15.

61 See Humphrey and Laidlaw, 1994, p. 169.

62 Ibid., p. 5.

63 See Kramrisch 1983, p. 56.

64 Kramrisch (1983) cites *Vishnusamhita* (c. twelfth century, 0 TSS 85 Trivandrum 1925, Chapter xiii).

65 Kramrisch 1983, p. 53. See also the Bhuta figure and other images in the Tamil epic *Cilappadikaram*.

66 See Mookerjee 1985, p. 21.

67 Coomaraswamy 1956b, p. 153.

68 Pal 1986, p. 47.

69 Bhattacharya 1947, p. 393.

70 Ibid., p. 394. See the regulations in the *Vishnudharmatorra* (Chapter 35) which are equally applicable to sculpture and paintings. The eyes of the figures, their expressions, limbs and hands have to be treated as in dance 'The Gods should be like youths of sixteen. Even when invoked by the best of Brahmans, gods never enters images short of enjoined measurements and devoid of marks.'

71 Ibid., p. 395.

72 See Dehejia 1988.

73 Gail 1989, p. 109.

74 Mosteller 1990, p. 389.

75 See also Bhattacharya 1947, p. 390.

76 Ibid., p. 393; Mosteller 1990, p. 393.

77 The gunas of the sculptures were the following: Sattva, Rajas and Tamas. These three gunas were possessed by men as well as gods. They vary in attributes and also in colours. The white colour is Sattvika, red indicates the Rajasa, and black is the Tamasika class. Images of gods in sculptural form or in paintings were thus to be coloured according to the guna possessed by each. South Indian texts lay down rules for colouring the images. North Indian texts on iconography also refer to the colour of the gods and their images.

78 Thirteen positions are mentioned in the *Vishnudharmatorra* that indicate the act in which the painted or sculpted figure is engaged; and also the bhava (mood) and rasa which are expressed on its face. According to the *Samarangana* (Chapter 82), 'By indicating the meaning (artha) with the hands and explaining or proving (pratipadayan) it by its looks, a figure appears to be alive (sajiva) for thus it exhibits all actions.' (Bhattacharya 1947, p. 408).

79 Kramrisch 1924, p. 25.

80 Fuller 1984, pp. 136, 139-40.

81 Ibid., p. 143. Fuller also points out that there are a whole range of ritual rules which all participants believe to be of the first importance and to be laid down in the agamas. For the most part they are not. This importance of oral rather than textual instruction is an important feature of all aspects of the historical continuity of Hindu precepts – it is a measure of the mechanics of the didactic elements and the quality of memory that it has survived at all and so faithfully.

82 Banerji 1941, pp. 373-5.

83 For many years rasa has been associated with the appreciation of the audience or

spectator – meaning liquid, juice or flavour. This meaning was originally ascribed to Bharata, author of the *Natyasastra*. However, according to the modern scholar S.S. Barlingay (pp. 11–24) Bharata was referring to a concept of rasa as solely describing some essential element of theatre. The idea that rasa meant spiritual joy or some kind of indescribable spiritual experience was not what Bharata intended and is represented by him using instead the word siddhi. Later commentaries such as Bhattanayaka and Abhinavagupta, according to Barlingay, have disguised Bharata's real theory by interpreting rasa solely from the perspective of aesthetic appreciation. However, the general use of the word rasa today is wider than Barlingay's interpretation.

84 The *Natyasastra* refers to eight rasas, and to 108 kinds of hand poses used in dancing. All these were not used in works of art however. The rasa is itself divided in the *Natyasastra* into sentiments or tastes: eight erotic (srngara), comic (hasya), pathetic (karuna) furious (raudra), heroic (vira), terrible (bhayanaka), odious (bibhatsa) and marvellous (adbhuta). Mahakala, for example, is associated with the odious sentiment, the colour blue, and is intended to evoke the sentiment of disgust, while Vishnu is associated with the erotic, and is bluish black, intending to evoke delight.

85 Humphrey and Laidlaw 1994, pp. 78.

86 Meister, in Mason 1993.

87 Williams 1982, p. 175.

88 Also discussed in Chapter 4.

89 Meister, in Mason 1993, p. 102.

90 For example, in the Siva temple the images are arranged clockwise, beginning with Ganesa on the south wall of the ardhamandapa and proceeding with Dakshinamurti on the south wall, Lingodbharamurti on the west of the vimana, Brahma on the north of the vimana and Durga on the north wall.

91 The Vyala image is found in this form in a number of temples and may have previously acted as a bracket on the sides of the bhadra's niche.

92 Desai 1985.

93 Meister, in Mason 1993, pp. 103–9.

94 Ibid.

95 Eck 1981, p. 45.

96 Ibid.

97 Humphrey and Laidlaw 1994, p. 181.

98 According to Coomaraswamy (1971), several of these were given as offerings (bali) by the tree worship cult.

99 The flywhisk has ancient royal associations seen in the depiction of the tree spirit and the yaksha.

100 Fuller (1992) convincingly argues that the camphor flame is the quintessential experience and key to Hindu ritual worship. He echoes Logan (1980, p. 123) in suggesting that the flame has symbolic properties, due to the fact that it burns with a strong light and fragrance. He suggests that the flame symbolizes both the deity's embodiment during puja, by appealing to the physical senses, as well as the transcendence of its embodied form, with the camphor leaving no sooty residue and providing an intense incandescent light and fragrance. Fuller also describes how the embodied deity is partly dissolved in the flame and how both deity and worshipper together may transcend through the reflection of each in the flame: 'the divine and human participants are most fully identified in their common vision of the flame and hence in their mutual vision of each other' (Fuller 1992, p. 73).

101 For further discussion on the temple ritual see Chapter 4.

102 Eck 1981, p. 48.

103 Ibid., p. 49, fn. 71.

104 Ibid., p. 49, fn. 72.

105 Ibid., p. 50, fn. 73.

106 M. Tachikawa in *Senri Ethnological Studies*, No. 36, ed. Y. Nagano and Y. Ikari (1993, p. 263).

107 See Mookerjee 1985, p. 18.

108 See Willis 1993.

109 Al-Biruni 1910, Part 1, p. 116.

110 Symbolic sacrifice has not always been the rule. Travellers in India in the sixteenth century, for example, report ritual suicides during temple services and human sacrifice is still reported in Assam today.

111 Lannoy 1975, p. 24.

CHAPTER 3 Hindu Deities

Hindu images serve to represent the deity and are believed to act as vessels containing the spiritual essence of the God defined. These images intentionally illustrate rich mythology and attempt to express hidden powers through visual allegory. Hindu worshippers seek release (moksha) from the circle of worldly existence attained through union with the Deity. This is achieved using a number of means (referred to in an earlier chapter) which bring about refinement of consciousness and inner transformation and thus makes possible the merging of the worshipper with that which is worshipped. The image in its many forms is therefore of crucial importance in the practice of Hinduism.

The earliest appearance of the gods with multiple limbs dates from the Kusan period of the first century AD. Many Hindu deities have fantastic forms with multiple heads and arms, sometimes with part animal bodies, in blue, black, white, green or vermilion colouring. These strange features serve to indicate the various functions and cosmic nature of the gods and to set them apart from man. They stretch the human imagination towards the divine by juxtaposing earthly realities in an unearthly way. Even to the dullest observer they illustrate the distinction between the human and the divine being. The collage of imagery

and telescoping of time sequence, in an oneiric sense, which can be found in Hindu paintings and sculpture reveals that the essential elements of time and space do not apply to these beings in a worldly sense. The worshipper is invited to approach reality through Maya, the dreaming phenomenal world.

Hindus believe in a supreme god who is formless, whose most popular manifestations are as Siva, Vishnu and the goddess, each of whom represents aspects of the supreme God.

Siva

The god Siva can have an iconic or aniconic form. Siva, like a complex personality, has multiple forms and a paradoxical character. He is a deity who often inhabits the extremes of human behaviour. Siva is sometimes perceived as supine, awakened through his union with Sakti which is both female energy and a goddess who personifies this active force.

Conversely he is also seen as the destroyer. His dance is sometimes destructive as seen in the destruction of Andhaka, but his more common manifestation as Nataraja depicts him performing the dance of bliss in a circle of flames, symbolizing creation and the perpetuation of the cosmos, while destroying ignorance in crushing the dwarf Apasmara. As an energy or force Siva is believed to have not only destructive and regenerative capabilities but also the capacity to transform man's inner consciousness. A paradoxical relationship of sexuality and asceticism in which the energy of sexuality is intensified by its denial, seen particularly in the retention of semen, is frequently associated with the character of Siva.[1] As an ascetic he is also perceived as mystic and teacher, the possessor of the secret doctrine and the achiever of enlightenment.

> In many myths Siva is merely erotic or merely ascetic, as a momentary view of one phase or another. But in the great myths, transcending the limits of mundane causality, he participates in cycles of cosmic dimensions which melt into a single image as they become ever more frequent, making an almost subliminal impression in their brief symbolic appearances, creating an infinitely complex mosaic.[2]

The visual origin of Siva is vague. Certain of his attributes suggest that he arose from the combining of several cult deities. The pre-Aryan fertility god and the fierce Rudra, a minor deity of the Vedas, may have contributed to his ultimate form. Artefacts believed to be stone-carved phallic symbols revealed by archaeology from the Indus valley culture of 2000 BC, for example, may be precursors to the characteristic features of the Saivite cult. No images exist from the period between the worship of the wild god Rudra whose description we know from the Vedic period and the first images of Siva in the first century BC. The paradoxical nature of Siva may well be due to the multitude of diverse religious cults which are believed to have spawned him, and which have become absorbed into the character of the deity.

Iconic Form of Siva

History

Siva's first appearance is in his aniconic form as the linga attributed to the second to first century BC from Gudimallam in South India, while the earliest examples of Siva's iconic form come from simple relief carvings from the Gandhara region of the first century AD. Features such as an erect phallus and a trident suggest the identification of the figure as Siva but in other respects it may be a subsidiary figure in an otherwise Buddhist composition. A number of Kusana coins of the second century AD which bear the figure captioned Okhsho also come from North-west India. The figure on the coins has multiple heads, an erect phallus and a bull mount, all common attributes of Siva's iconography. If this is not actually Siva it is a deity who may well have contributed to the overall iconographic character of Siva.

Attributes

In temple shrines Siva is most usually portrayed in the aniconic form of the linga (Figure 3.1) while his iconic form is more common in private worship, in processional images, in frieze sculpture on the outer walls of the temple and in its subsidiary shrines (Plate 1). Siva's iconic form is a complex combination of elegant proportions and allegorical forms and emblems. Siva is described and portrayed as beautiful, with a third eye in the centre of his forehead and a crescent moon on his brow. He is crowned with matted hair, within which is depicted a flowing river symbolizing the Ganges which is sometimes depicted as a goddess. This goddess is said to have landed on

Figure 3.1 Siva Lingodbhava, South India. Cola, 900. British Museum, mus. no. 1955, 10–18,1.

Siva's hair when she fell from heaven to earth. Siva is often shown smeared with ashes and adorned with shining armlets. A garland of rudraksha beads, snakes and sometimes skulls surrounds his neck. Siva often wears or sits on a tiger skin, and two of the hands of his four arms hold a trident and an axe. The other two hands are said to grant favours and remove fear. When he dances he dances on a demon called Apasmara.

Linga

The most common symbol of Siva is the phallus (lingam). According to Brahmanical literature, linga is the sign of the transcendental, unseen Siva and symbolizes Siva's capacity to produce life itself.[3] The Sanskrit word 'linga' literally means 'mark' or 'sign' and is the Hindu's most abstract expression of the creative energy of God. The linga as it is worshipped in India today is an aniconic image, sometimes referred to in the Saivite myths as a fiery column of light, rather than a phallic symbol. It can also be seen as symbolizing the axis mundi – the bridge between the earthly and heavenly energies. Siva in all his forms including the linga is regarded as expressing the whole universe as time and space being identified with life creation. The lingas in many of Siva's grandest temples are believed to have emerged naturally out of the ground, 'self-existent' and already full of divine power.[4]

Belief that Siva has a pre-Vedic origin is supported by his association with the linga. Archaeologists working on the Indus valley culture discovered several objects believed to represent the phallus at Mohenjo Daro and Harappa.[5] The *Rg Veda* also refers to people from the Indus valley as worshippers of the phallus (shishnevedevas). An ancient cult which has its roots in prehistory is said to have worshipped naturally occurring stones called Svayambhu lingas. These are still brought out of the river Narmada for worship and are set upright on stone or brass pedestals and honoured as the god Siva himself. The natural coloured markings on the stones are said to represent active female energy. Ammonites, found as pebbles in the Kala Gandali river in Nepal, are viewed in the same way.

From the second or first century BC, the linga was sculpted in stone, supported on octagonal and square sections embedded in the earth, at first in stone-railed open-air shrines beneath sacred trees. The earliest surviving carved linga is in South India at Gudimallam. Lacking any inscription, it has been dated between the second century BC and the first century AD. Gritli V. Mitterwallner places the Gudimallam linga after the sculpture of Bharhut and just pre-dating the sculptures of Bodhgaya, in the latter half of the first century AD.[6] The Gudimallam linga is naturalistic in form with the figure of Siva standing in front of the shaft of the linga (Figure 2.6). Siva is shown with full lips and thick curly hair, anticipating the matted locks associated with his iconography, and two arms carved in high relief. He stands astride the shoulders of a crouching dwarf-like figure – perhaps a yaksha or a gana. In his right hand Siva holds a small horned animal and in his left hand a battle axe and water pot. Several features of this sculpture are revealing about the early perception of Siva. The horned animal relates to the deer seen in the early proto-Siva seal from the Indus valley. This is an animal associated with sacrifice and death, the victim of the hunt. The axe reinforces this idea of sacrifice. Perhaps the most significant features of this

early portrait of Siva are the water pot in his hand and the crouching figure at his feet. These are clearly added by the sculptor as iconographic clues in order to identify the god and point to his powers. The yaksha was worshipped throughout India prior to the appearance of Siva as we know him in this form, and his inclusion here at Siva's feet is no doubt intended to mark the supremacy of Siva, shown absorbing the strength of the supporting figure. This figure was in later Hindu iconography reduced to the dwarf Apasmara, representative of man's ignorance, on which Siva dances in the Siva Nataraja sculpture. The root of this lies in the defeat by Siva of the worship of the earlier non-Vedic God.

The Gudimallam sculpture shows the yaksha with fish-shaped feet and conch-shaped ears. Both these features link the yaksha, and by association Siva, with water (as does the water pot in Siva's hand). The yakshas were seen as guardians of the vegetative source of life and therefore closely connected with water and in turn with prosperity and abundance. The association of Siva with symbols such as the yaksha, the tree and the lotus reinforces the idea that early lingas were not just phallic emblems but symbols of vegetation and thus prosperity and fecundity. Coins of the Kusana kings depict Siva pouring water on the ground from a vase. The early text the *Vishnu Purana* states that he who adores the linga continually enjoys great prosperity.

The linga at Gudimallam was placed within a rectangular enclosure, a common practice at tree shrines and other early sanctuaries. A few centuries later the linga was installed in the dark sanctums (garbhagriha) of rock-cut or free-standing temples dedicated to Siva. Buried in the

Figure 3.2 Trident in a secondary shrine, in a temple at Tiruvannamalai, Tamil Nadu. Robert Elgood.

there was a growing abstraction from 50 BC to the 11th century in the form of the linga. Usually the linga was carved as a simple shaped pillar, usually out of stone, but they can be hewn from any material.

The worship of the phallus is perceived as non-Vedic, but there is nothing non-Vedic in using the phallus as a metaphor. The linga, as has already been said, was a symbol in the early period for prosperity and fecundity as well as sexuality. These three conditions were directly linked by the need to produce offspring to support the parents in later life, a factor that still obtains in India today. Early phallic worship may relate to the ancient and persistent worship of the tree, subsequently symbolized as a vertical wooden post, both of which represented the axis mundi. Despite its phallic form the linga was sometimes placed in the open air and enclosed by a protective railing like a sacred tree (Figure 3.2). The trident pillar form is seen here as a symbol of Siva, placed in a secondary courtyard near a sacred tree in the temple of Tiruvannamalai. Certain locations in India were regarded as sacred sites and remained so across the centuries with only the object worshipped changing to reflect the evolving nature of belief. Later tantric reference to the transmutation of energy by the retention of seminal fluid suggests that the erect phallus may be an expression of restraint and transformation rather than sexuality and emission. Richard Blurton suggests that the 'linga rises up from the yoni rather than penetrates down into it as one would expect if the imagery was primarily sexual'.[8] That is certainly the visual impression. However, another interpretation is possible which is closer to the needs and intentions of the early worshippers. In the sexual act the phallus passes through the yoni to achieve

ground, the lowest part is cubic (like the sanctum) and supports a horizontal, circular base, shaped like the female vulva and known as the yoni. Rising from the centre of this is the linga. The channel formed by the yoni round the base of the linga served as a drain and carried away the liquid poured as a libation over the linga.[7]

Other forms of linga developed after the Gudimallam linga. Lingas were sometimes shown in later examples with just a face or sometimes with as many as five faces on the sides of the shaft of the phallus. It has been observed by Gritli V. Mitterwallner that conception. The symbolic womb chamber is the place where this occurs and where the prayers for fecundity are offered. The linga and yoni may represent the congress between Siva and Mother Earth for the benefit of all life.

Siva Nataraja

One of the most popular manifestations of Siva, Siva Nataraja, depicts Siva dancing in a ring of fire. A paradoxical range of mood from wild ecstasy to a controlled detached movement is expressed in this well-known image. Despite the violence of the dance his expression is detached, serene and uninvolved. Siva dances, surrounded by a fire which destroys ignorance while evoking creation with the sound of his double-sided drum. He crushes underfoot the dwarf demon Apasmara, the symbol of ignorance, while simultaneously showing mercy by raising his palm, a calming gesture, and pointing with his foot to indicate where the worshipper may take refuge. This image reminds the devotee of the circle of life and death and the reconciliation through Siva of these opposites. Several examples of this image were popular in South India during the early medieval period. The famous form of Siva Nataraj, known as Anandatandava, is worshipped pre-eminently at Chidambaram in Tamil Nadu (Figure 3.3). Siva as representative and centre of the universe is seen in this bronze sculpture of Nataraj. It expresses not just the movement of the dance but reveals the five elements: earth (kanchi), wind (kalahasti), fire (tiruvannamalai), water (tiruvanaikha) and space (akasha). The lotus is a symbol of water and of earth; the wind catches Siva's sash and hair; fire is expressed by the flaming disc, symbolic of the sun, which surrounds the dancing figure; and water is expressed by the river Ganges which flows through his matted hair. Space is seen in the areas in the sculpture between, defined by the intersection of the circle with the limbs and sometimes the sash of the dancing Siva. The earliest gods represented the primordial elements and in this sculpture of Siva these elements are brought together. The paradox of the interplay of the microcosmic and the macrocosmic scales of life, the profound and the banal are expressed by the image of Siva where, as O'Flaherty describes: 'he uses his magic eye to bring about the final conflagration of the universe and is then berated by his wife for using it to cheat at dice.'[9]

The subtlety of this interplay of the gods whereby they are capable of inspiring awe and then becoming insignificantly trivial is exemplified by such mythological tales. The incident when Indra, filled with pride, is made to see himself as one of a number of Indras likened to a swarm of ants is, according to O'Flaherty, another such example.

Dakshinamurti

Siva is the patron of ascetics. In the guise of a yogi Siva is seen as the wise and benevolent teacher Dakshinamurti (Figure 3.4). This Sanskrit term has two components: 'dakshina' meaning south, and 'murti' meaning image. Blurton suggests this may refer to Siva as a teacher facing south towards his disciples from his mountain home in the Himalayas. In comparison to the wild-eyed yogi or the dancing image, this is Siva as the young ascetic with long matted hair. Across his

Figure 3.3 Siva Nataraj, Tamil Nadu. Chola, 1100. British Museum, mus. no. 1987, 3–14.

forehead are sometimes displayed three stripes of ash which are the hallmark of the Saivite devotee. His hands are in the teaching position, and he is often portrayed sitting in front of a tree. The practice of preaching under a tree is an ancient tradition in India, both as a practical means of obtaining shade and as a means of relating the teacher to the spirit of the sacred tree. A well-known example of this can be seen in Buddha's enlightenment and his first sermon at Sarnath, both of which

Figure 3.4 Dakshinamurti Siva from Kailasanatha temple. Kanchipuram, early eighth century.
Robert Elgood.

took place under a tree. There may also be a link with the ancient custom of questioning a medium in ritual spirit possession beside the sacred tree who was believed to be possessed by the yaksha or spirit of the tree. In time this wisdom was transferred to the wish fulfilment tree, which itself answered questions.

Bhairava and Virabhadra

Other forms of Siva exist such as Bhairava and Virabhadra. Siva in the form of Bhairava can be recognized as an ascetic, with wild hair, a staff and an erect penis. A skull is fixed to his hand and he wears a garland of skulls. He is often accompanied by a dog. Bhairava is notorious for his beheading of a Brahman. As penance for this crime Bhairava was condemned to wander endlessly, with the fifth head of Brahma stuck to the palm of his hand. Despite his dangerous character Bhairava is still popular in North India and Nepal where he is known as Bhairon. The extreme Saivite sect, the Kapalikas, worship Bhairava. Their name is derived from the skull (kapala) which is their emblem.

Another manifestation of Siva which expresses the wild side of his personality is the form Virabhadra. Virabhadra was created in anger by Siva to avenge an insult from his father-in-law Daksha, the father of Siva's wife Sati. Daksha refused to invite his mendicant son-in-law to a sacrificial ceremony. Siva arrived at the occasion unannounced and beheaded Daksha. Siva repented this action and returned Daksha to life, but with a goat's head. Virabhadra is often seen with a goat-headed man standing diminutively at his feet. The worship of Siva as Virabhadra is popular in the south and in the Deccan.[10] He is also

worshipped in a variety of local forms. In Himachal Pradesh, for example, Virabhadra and his consort Sati are worshipped in the form of bronze masks which are carried in processions round the town. During these festivals men and women fall into trances and utter strange words believed to be induced by their being possessed by the gods.

Interpretations

The mythology and iconography of Siva still continue to develop in modern India. The understanding of Siva's personality and the interpretation of his attributes is controversial. Many of his characteristics, such as the matted hair and garments made of tiger skin are associated with ascetics. The scholar Danielou[11] suggests meanings for some of Siva's emblems: the crescent moon represents the power of procreation; the serpent, the cycle of years and dormant sexual energy; the matted hair, Siva's rejection of society; the tiger skin trophy, the power of nature; the drum (damaru) (made of the top part of two human skulls joined back to back, with a thong and a pellet), the power of sound; the trident (trisula), the three qualities of nature, creation, preservation and destruction; the skulls, the perpetual revolution of death and rebirth; the ashes, the burning of the universe with the power of a glance of his third eye. To this list one might add that Siva's nakedness expresses the rejection of the norms of society as does the act of rubbing ashes on the body. This also indicates sublimated sexuality and the abandonment of family life while fulfilling a practical function in giving protective warmth to the body. Siva's cosmic dance on the demon indicates both the destruction of ignorance and illusion and the destruction of the world and its rebirth.

Siva is sometimes described as lord of the animals. Various animals such as the bull, buffalo, snake and antelope are associated with him. The first three are symbolic of his sexual energy while the antelope, often a sacrificial victim, reinforces Siva's link with life and death, or renewal. For such parallel imagery it is interesting to recall the proto-Siva image from the Indus valley (Figure 2.3), a masked figure thought to represent a bull, below which sit two addorsed antelopes.

A degree of caution must be sounded in the acceptance of the above interpretations. Hindu art is composed of visual forms which are multivalent, rather in the manner that Sanskrit is a language where words have several meanings. An example of this multivalence can be seen in relation to the symbol of the moon and by Siva's association with it, his link with the natural world of cause and effect. The moon is suggested by Hindus to have power over procreation. The moon is also interpreted as the expression of the unconscious instinctive side of man's psyche. Siva manifests this in his state of withdrawal from the preoccupations of the phenomenal world. This is reinforced by Siva's circlet of snakes which are themselves creatures associated with hidden and dark places. The bull vehicle which expresses the power of sexual energy also relates to the power of the uncontrolled sexual forces of man. The combination and juxtaposition of gestures and emblems express Siva's varied nature with all its accompanying ambiguities. In order to interpret Hindu iconography it is helpful to use not only intellectual analysis but to experience the visual forms as a Hindu worshipper was expected to, in other words through the experience of bhava and rasa, through the senses and feelings.

What do the visual forms of Siva tell us about Hinduism? Siva's image portrays a being who is both beneficent as a revered teacher and powerful, violent, terrifying and destructive. The acceptance and reverence of such a personage expresses a faith which allows within itself non-conformable, provocative, disruptive and destructive elements. Siva echoes forces that run counter to the orthodox structure and obligations of society. It is the way of the outsider. Siva's origins lie in the destructive Vedic deity Rudra, and in a combination of pre-Vedic traditions of fertility, amalgamated with an esoteric mysticism revealed by forest sages. Hindu wisdom is suggested by the manner in which Siva's character reflects the power of nature which is both destructive and creative, the fury of floods and fire as well as their generative powers. This expression of Siva's powers is also expressed by O'Flaherty in her suggestion that:

> The control or transmutation of these forces may be seen on the cosmic level, where the continual interaction of the natural elements (primarily fire and water) animates the flow of vital forces within the universe.... On the symbolic level these are the moments when the forces of fire and water are simultaneously present but not mutually destructive; on the divine level, these are the undertakings in which creative and destructive divinities reinforce one another; on the human level, these are the episodes in which ascetic and sexual impulses combine within an individual, each impulse allowed to develop the full expression of its power without impeding the expression of the contrasting impulse.[12]

This interpretation of Siva admits to subtleties of energies at work in the pattern of the divine order, and the paradox and contradiction are seen as part of this fabric. The acceptance and need to propitiate Siva admits to the power of the uncontrolled and the fear of the unknown. This is a real terror and one which in our mechanized society with its virtual reality we try to suppress.

> The worship of Siva can be powerful, dangerous, beautiful, exciting, mystical, exultant and solitary. It satisfies one substantial sector of humanity. Another large group looks for security, certain knowledge and the strength of community. In India this second group turns towards the worship of Vishnu.[13]

Consorts of Siva

Scholars have suggested that the worship of the mother goddess pre-dates the worship of Vishnu and Siva. It has been suggested that any conflict ensuing from usurping the primacy of the goddess was resolved by her marriage to the male deities. An example of this can be observed in Madurai, where the cult of the goddess Minakshi is of greater antiquity than that of her spouse Siva, known as Sundaresvara. Each year a symbolic divine marriage of Minakshi and Sundaresvara is celebrated in the temple. This no doubt commemorates the incorporation of Siva into an earlier goddess cult. Many pilgrims also visit the temple of Khajuraho to celebrate the annual re-enactment of the marriage of Siva and Parvati.

Siva is often portrayed as passive and it is his consort or Sakti who is said to empower or activate him. Siva has several consorts who express his diverse nature. Parvati is one of Siva's wives but it is difficult to discriminate between Parvati, who has no major cult of her own, and the Great Goddess, who is known by the more generic name of Devi. Parvati is the most conservative, modest and benign of Siva's consorts. The goddess Annapurna is a popular form of Parvati, representative of plenty and abundance. Annapurna is recognized by the carrying of a ladle. Other benign forms of Parvati are Lalita, identifiable by the carrying of a mirror, and Gauri, whose name means the fair. Other consorts of Siva are the goddesses Ganga, Durga, Chamunda and Kali. These goddesses are energetic, vigorous and at times bloodthirsty. The goddess Chamunda was created by the goddess Durga. Chamunda's name derived from her victory over the male demons Chanda and Munda.

Siva's offspring

Siva has two sons, Skanda sometimes known as Karttikeya, and Ganesa. Legend recounts that Parvati did not give birth to Skanda, despite his being the result of Siva and Parvati's love-making. The intensity of the consummation of the union of Siva and Parvati was said to have been so great that it caused cosmic unrest and disturbance and gave rise to Siva's seed falling in the river Ganga. Despite the river's associations with Parvati, Ganga is also not considered to be the mother of Skanda. Ganga was said to have been unable to bear the heat of the divine seed and Skanda was apparently nurtured and born to the six Krittikas (the constellation known in the West as the Pleiades). This link with this constellation gives rise to Skanda's alternative name Karttikeya and his depiction with six heads. The earliest known depiction of Skanda dates from the second to third century AD and comes from North-west India. Skanda can be recognized by his carrying of a spear and sometimes a cockerel banner. His vehicle is a peacock.

Ganesa is one of the most popular deities; associated with Siva as the son of Parvati, he is immediately recognizable by his elephant head. Ganesa is evoked to remove obstacles at the beginning of each new venture and he is the guardian of entrances. Despite a complex mythology, Ganesa may demonstrate the absorption of an earlier cult of elephant worship. According to legend, Siva, on seeing a figure in Parvati's doorway, decapitated Ganesa, ignorant of the fact that he was Parvati's son. Repentant once he realized his mistake, Siva swore to replaced Ganesa's head with the first head he saw, which happened to be that of an elephant. Myth also describes Parvati making an image out of the dirt from her legs which brought Ganesa back to life. This may refer to the ancient idea of sympathetic magic where clay and flesh were seen as synonymous. Siva made Ganesa the leader of the dwarfs, or Ganas. Siva also made Ganesa the guardian of doorways as a tribute to his guarding his mother. As remover of obstacles he is known as 'the Lord of the Beginnings'. Some scholars link the corpulent Ganesa to Kubera Yaksha, king of the Yakshas. His attributes are an elephant goad, a noose and a bowl of sweetmeats. His vehicle is the mouse which perhaps signifies the proximity of mice to food offerings, or the paradox of the relative size of the mouse to the elephant.

Animals associated with Siva

Certain animals are associated with Siva who is depicted with a snake entwined around his neck. The linga is also sometimes carved with a protecting cobra. Association with Siva may well express the absorption of the earlier snake or Naga worship which was common throughout India. Fear and reverence of the snake and its powers was and still is a common feature throughout India's history. Snakes are often found in anthills and since anthills and nagas are both the object of veneration these places are natural shrines which are frequently visited by women who bring fertility offerings.[14]

The bull or nandi (Figure 3.14) is Siva's vehicle while the more docile cow is associated with Krishna one of the incarnations of Vishnu. It is the strength, virility and power of the bull which is expressed in the relationship between Siva and his vehicle. The frequent occurrence on seals of bulls or buffaloes or as terracotta figures suggests the importance of this animal in Indian culture from as early as 2500 BC. The existence of a possible buffalo mask on the proto-Siva image (Figure 2.3) may also suggest the existence of a bull or buffalo cult which has been absorbed into the cult of Siva. Traditionally the bull is always placed in the temple facing the enshrined icon of Siva or the Siva linga.

The antelope is also linked to Siva. As has been mentioned earlier, the antelope was frequently hunted or used as a sacrificial victim. It is therefore seen as a symbol of Siva's power over death and rebirth.

Vishnu

Vishnu, like Siva, has an iconic and aniconic form. Despite his varied manifestations he is consistently seen as the preserver of harmony and the maintainer of order and tradition. The name Vishnu is derived from the Sanskrit 'vish' literally meaning to 'work'. He is indeed regarded as the all-doing presence. Vishnu is the deity of moderation, prosperity, and obedience to the traditional values of society. He represents the good householder and the values of family and community. As Siva stands at the extremities, Vishnu supports the accepted social values of behaviour.

Devotees believe that Vishnu comes to earth in various forms to assist them at times of spiritual and political crisis. An example of this is the growth of the popularity of Vishnu during the expansion of Muslim power from the sixteenth to the seventeenth centuries. These partly animal avatars, or incarnations of Vishnu, can be interpreted as the absorption by Hinduism of earlier pre-Hindu cult deities. Vishnu as the saviour materializes in forms which are a blend of superstitions and cult images. It is generally accepted that there are ten avatars or incarnations of Vishnu; five are in animal and five in human form and some minor ones such as Mohini Vyasa and Hayagriva. Accounts of these incarnations were woven into expansive colourful legends. This mythology expressed social, political and religious ideals and values which contributed to an increased popularity of Vishnu. Some of the characteristics of Vishnu's personality may also have their source in the benevolent manifestations of the Buddhist Bodhisattvas.

Vishnu is perceived in the Krishna avatar as the god of love and emotion. Krishna's love for man was first expressed in the *Bhagavad Gita*, a section within the great epic the *Mahabharata*. 'Bhakta' or love is sometimes expressed by the Vaishnava devotee in 'bhajans', literally devotional songs. This 'bhakti' cult arose and developed in South India. This love is not wild ecstasy but is described as a steady,

selfless phenomenon. Despite the erotic element in the Krishna legend, in the majority of cults the love referred to is asexual.

The early history

Vishnu is mentioned in the *Rg Veda*, but was not an important deity in the Vedic period. By the time of the appearance of the *Mahabharata* and the *Puranas* he had acquired his supremacy. The deity referred to in the *Rg Veda*, the dwarf who strode across the cosmos, may well have been amalgamated with the Aryan god Varuna, the guardian of cosmic order. It is suggested that he absorbed some of the attributes of the Adityas, which were Vedic solar powers, of which Varuna was the chief deity. According to Gonda[15] this demonstrated the absorption of Vishnu, a God of rising power, who was in turn absorbed into the group of the Adityas. He later became loosely associated with the sun, demonstrated by his holding emblems which are solar symbols such as the discus (chakra), and by his vehicle the kite (garuda). Vishnu is not however the sole representative of the sun and is distinct from the solar deity Surya. In the later Vedic period Vishnu became associated with the human heroes Vasudeva-Krishna, Narayana and Krishna-Gopala. Vasudeva-Krishna was a Kshatriya warrior who fought at Kurukshetra and challenged the Brahmanic Vedic rituals. *Astadhyayi*, Panini's grammar of 400 BC, refers to Vasudeva-Krishna, who became the centre of a cult.[16] Evidence of the importance of this religious figure is seen by the column erected in honour of Vasudeva. The first dated monument linked with Vishnu is this second-century BC shaft of the Heliodorus column in Besnagar, where the inscription refers to the erection of a garuda column in honour of Vasudeva. His first appearance in the later characteristic form is on a coin from the Graeco-Bactrian king Agathocles (c. 180–165 BC) found at a site on the Oxus which was destroyed some time later in the second century BC. On one side Vishnu is shown with the chakra, conch shell and mace and on the reverse is Balarama with his plough and pestle. A later coin from the first century BC represents Vishnu as a four-armed figure grasping two poles, one surmounted by a discus, the other by what looks like a trident. On a Kusana seal-matrix from King Huvishka the god is more recognizable as a four-armed figure with a wheel and a mace.

The earliest surviving statues of Vishnu are found in Kusana sculpture from Gandhara and Mathura of the first century AD, where there was a simultaneous production of Buddhist, Jain and Hindu images. The extent to which Graeco-Roman sculpture inspired the style or character of these early figures of Vishnu is still a matter of conjecture. Vishnu first appears in regal form with a royal head-dress (kiritamukuta) which was to become a regular feature of the god. His physical appearance was that of a normal human being, a form which continues up to modern times, while a parallel form subsequently developed into a multi-armed and multi-headed supreme deity known as Visvarupa. One temple in Nagarjunakonda of AD 278 shows Vishnu in his eight-armed form. The depiction of Vishnu in the avatar of the boar Varaha and Krishna began to appear for the first time as early as the first century AD. Examples of the early forms of Vishnu (such as Varaha from Udaygiri and the Mathura image of Krishna now in the museum of Bharat Kala Bhavan) show a statuesque being with

greater power and strength of character than appears in later carvings. Among the earliest sculptures representing Narasimha is the fourth-century AD relief panel from Kondamotu in south-eastern Deccan.

Attributes

Vishnu (as distinct from his avatars) is generally represented as a tall, handsome youth with dark blue skin and the attire of an ancient king (Figure 3.5). He is carved or painted with long earrings, large decorative armlets, a high royal crown, four arms, and on his chest the distinctive curl and the jewel Kaustubha. His four arms hold characteristic emblems such as the conch, discus, lotus and mace (Figure 3.6). Occasionally one attribute is absent, and instead one of Vishnu's hands grants a boon or favour. His vehicle (vahana) is the bird known as the garuda which is sometimes described as an eagle, falcon, or more accurately a Brahmany kite. Garuda has wings and a birdlike human head with a curved beak. Due to his flight across the heavens, the kite and by association, garuda, can be seen as a solar symbol and as in the wild, as the kite is the enemy of serpents. The discus and the dwarf Avatar are also associated with solar imagery.

Aniconic forms of Vishnu

The simplest aniconic forms of Vishnu are saligramas. These are round black stones which sometimes contain fossilized ammonites and are found in the gorge of the Kali-Gandaki river in Nepal. Naturally occurring concentric rings on some of the saligramas resemble the spiral and discus, Vishnu's emblems. These circular forms are

Figure 3.5 Vishnu,
Kanauj, Central India.
Late tenth century.
British Museum,
mus. no. 1872, 7–1, 41.

all seen as solar symbols which reinforce Vishnu's association with the sun. Pilgrims decorate themselves with stamps bearing the discus and the conch shell or wear block-printed clothes in the same pattern. The body stamps may also display other symbols connected with Vishnu, such as representations of his feet or written epithets.

Creation

Creation is visualized as Vishnu asleep, lying on the snake Sesha. Vishnu is here perceived as the source of the universe. Legend recounts Vishnu's awakening and the emergence of the flowering lotus from Vishnu's navel. The earth emerges from the petals of this lotus. Vishnu in his incarnation as guide and saviour first appears in the world in a form which is linked with creation myths.

Avatars

The worship of Vishnu in the form of one or other of his avatars is popular with his devotees. Particular favourites are the later incarnations of Rama and Krishna. The early legends are now reduced to stories with a few episodes, while those of Rama and Krishna are expressed in a complex web of mythology.

The fish and turtle

Of the ten avataras attributed to Vishnu the first four are partly animal in form. The fish (matsya) and the turtle (kurma) are no longer important deities. The fish, reputed to have saved the world from the great flood and the Vedas, and the turtle, revealing the divine nectar by churning the ocean,

created links with Varuna, the Aryan god of the waters.[17] The probability that these incarnations were the means by which local cults were absorbed into mainstream Hinduism is shown by the fact that the tribal group the Gonds still worship the tortoise as their cult totem.

The boar

In his third appearance on earth, Vishnu adopted the guise of a boar to kill a demon who had cast the world into the depths of the ocean. Vishnu succeeded in killing this demon and raising the earth (personified as the goddess Bhu) on his tusks. In this story Vishnu released the imprisoned earth from the bottom of the ocean and restored her to her rightful place, thus reinforcing and maintaining the status quo.

The worship of Vishnu in this form was particularly popular in the Gupta period (fourth to sixth centuries AD). Several remarkable depictions of Varaha survive from the sites of Udaygiri and Eran, dated to the fifth century AD, and also at the seventh- to eighth-century site of Mamallapuram, south of Madras. Varaha was also adopted as the royal emblem by the Chola and Vijayanagara dynasties of South India. Today Vishnu in the form of the boar attracts fewer devotees than do other incarnations.

Narasimha

The fourth Avatar Narasimha is depicted as half-man, half-lion (Plate 2). This form of Vishnu is mentioned in the *Mahabharata*. Vishnu takes the form of Narasimha to overcome a foe who was insuperable by day or night, man or beast. Vishnu's foe was a proud royal devotee of Siva called Hiranyakasipu, who received a boon as

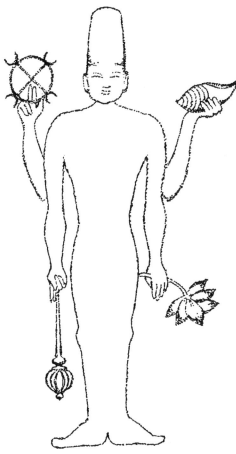

Figure 3.6 Vishnu holding his key attributes. Drawing by Christopher Glanville RWA.

to blood sacrifices is revealed by the lion ripping open the stomach of the king in an expression of a ritual blood-letting, behaviour which would be unacceptable to the orthodox Vaishnavite devotees. Evidence of this is given by Blurton, who refers to a long tradition of the worship of a lion deity in the Deccan and Orissa. He refers to one of the earliest known depictions of Narasimha, which is found in an area of south-eastern Deccan in a fourth-century relief panel from Kondamotu. In local and tribal cults, the lion deity required sacrificial offerings. Even today in the temple town of Ahobilam in southern Andhra Pradesh, blood offerings of goats and rams are made to Narasimha at specified times of the week.[18]

The dwarf incarnation

Vishnu's fifth incarnation on earth was in the form of a dwarf, who holds a water pot in one hand and a parasol in the other. Legend recounts that a powerful king, Mahabali, who threatened world order, granted a wish to the dwarf. The dwarf requested ownership of whatever land he could cover with three strides. On securing the king's agreement the dwarf rapidly became an enormous giant and with three strides encompassed the earth and the nether regions. Vishnu granted the king control of the underworld. This granting of a consolation prize is an example of the Hindu tradition of reconciliation and reverence by the victor for the vanquished enemy. Despite the king's acquisition of power through the performing of ritual penance, Vishnu's action serves to remind one of his supremacy and the underpinning of all human and divine activity by the laws of karma.

the result of ritual penances to Siva. Hiranyakasipu could neither be defeated on the ground nor in the air, nor in his palace nor outside it. Narasimha appeared at sunset as half-man, half-lion, held the king Hiranyakasipu on his lap and sealed himself in the palace doorway, thus evading Siva's boon to the king; he thus succeeded in slaying and humbling the king. An inherent conflict between Saivite and Vaishnavite sects is revealed in the reference to Vishnu's victory over the king, who had acquired power through penances to Siva. Narasimha's tribal source and the reference

Rama with an axe

The next avatar with a human form is Rama with the axe. Although bearing the same name as the seventh avatar, there is no clear connection between the incarnations. When the warrior caste or Kshatriyas attempted to overthrow caste hierarchy and to rule without Brahmanic sanction Rama restored the previous order. He thus defends the divinely sanctioned structure of society. His worship occurs in Kerala, and also in Indonesia.

Rama

The second heroic figure of Rama is the main protagonist of the *Ramayana*. According to Sanskrit legend the acts of Rama were told by the sage Valmiki. The stories of Rama, one of the most popular incarnations of the god Vishnu, are often acted out in community theatre and puppet shows and are well known to audiences. Rama may represent an actual historical personage who participated in the Indo-Aryan advance through India south of the Ganges plain in the late centuries BC, while Ravana, his antagonist in the *Ramayana*, may represent the indigenous population. Rama is even today viewed as the ideal king and husband. According to mythology Rama was the king of Ayodhya and established a golden age of justice, helped and revered by the monkey god Hanuman. The story of Rama revolves around his consort Sita. In one version of the story she returns to rule with Rama; in another she once more goes into exile. Her exile resulted from suspicion concerning her integrity and honour which was thought to have been compromised by the unsolicited advances of Ravana. Rama's suspicion of a rela-

tionship between Ravana and Sita is an interesting expression of the tensions between tribal, licentious, indigenous India and the orthodox Indo-Aryan society. The relationship of Rama and Hanuman may also be another instance of a former sacred animal becoming adopted and absorbed into Hindu mythology.

Balarama

The brothers Krishna and Balarama were incarnations of Vishnu and are therefore sometimes regarded as joint incarnations. According to the *Vishnu Purana*, Vishnu took two of his hairs, one black and one white, and implanted them in Devaki's womb. Shortly before they were born the resulting infants were transferred to Rohini's womb in order to prevent them from being murdered at birth by the tyrant king Kamsa. Krishna was born with a dark complexion and Balarama was white. Balarama shared many exploits with Krishna but is not regarded as very saintly. His attributes are the club (gada) and the plough.

Krishna

Krishna is the most popular of all Vishnu's avatars. He has a blue skin colour and is often depicted playing a flute. Krishna is a god associated with romantic love. Krishna's concern and love for humanity is first expressed in a famous text the *Bhagavad Gita*, literally meaning 'Song of the Lord'. In this text Krishna is consulted by the hero Arjuna, who hesitates before launching a great battle against members of his own tribe. The most romantic and selfless expression of Krishna's devotees is seen in the performance of devotional

Figure 3.7 A modern painting of the baby Krishna.
Pat Barylski.

songs, music, dance, lyrical poetry and paintings. Celebration, joy and play are associated with the worship of Krishna. His mythology is retained, with wide regional variations. The earliest stories of the life of Krishna are found in the *Bhagavata Purana*, and later in the *Gita Govinda* which was written by the twelfth-century Bengali poet Jayadeva. A prolific number of sculptures and paintings, in particular illustrated manuscripts from the sixteenth century, testify to the popularity of Krishna and Rama. These images suggest different strands of the rich personality of Krishna, while story scrolls from Bengal and Maharashtran Paithan paintings retell the narrative of Rama.

Krishna legends refer to the child Krishna playing tricks and stealing butter, with an early life associated with Vrindaban on the river Jumna (Figure 3.7). The adult Krishna is seen as a cowherd renowned for his erotic play with the milkmaids. The most romantic and surprising of the Krishna stories is the one concerning his relationship with Radha, a married woman. This has been one of the frequently illustrated sequences of the Krishna legend, a particular favourite of the royal patrons and courtly ladies. It has been suggested that this tolerance and the acceptance of codes of behaviour outside the norms of Hindu society may suggest the absorption of a more liberated tribal pastoral deity. The playing of bamboo flutes by the Bhil tribesmen of Rajasthan, Gujarat and Madhya Pradesh are evidence of the tribal origin of the dark-skinned pipe-playing Krishna. This emphasis on the erotic may also derive from fertility or tantric rites or may be seen as a symbolic analogy for the pining of the soul for the divine. The expression of freedom seen in the relations between Krishna and the milkmaids may well reflect the ease of contact between men and women which is found even today in tribal groups. A study of the Bhils[19] reveals this greater sexual licence and a sense of female emancipation and gaiety. There is promiscuity among young men and girls, which is discreetly practised out of sight in the jungles.[20] Extra-marital relations are also common in Bhil society and may lie at the root of Krishna's affair with Radha.

Further evidence for Krishna's tribal origins is expressed in the almost abstract image of Krishna from Orissa in the Jagannath temple in Puri. This sacred object was originally worshipped by the jungle tribes in the interior of Orissa. One of the distinctions between tribal and orthodox Hindu worship was that the former worship the divine in the form of a heap of stones or a wooden post and the latter a representational icon. The seizing of a tribal deity by a powerful monarch is common practice and one that transfers authority to the king, who has earned the right of power over the tribal region by his courage and possession of the icon. The occasional renewal of the image associated with tribal practice, a practice carried out at the Jagannath temple, is perhaps another reference to this tribal heritage. Another Vaishnava temple, which periodically renews its images associated with the worship of Krishna, is the temple in Rajasthan dedicated to Sri Nathji. Elaborate rituals have developed around the worship of the icon Sri Nathji, and different paintings or hangings portraying the god are produced at various festivals. It is interesting to note that this image was regarded as a Naga deity, which was formerly worshipped by the shepherds of Mount Govardhan near Vrindaban, who made offerings of milk to it in the open air.

One of the earliest examples of the depiction of Krishna is from the sixth century in Benaras.[21] This shows him as a powerful youth wearing a tiger claw necklace, lifting up the mountain to protect his devotees. Another scene which is often illustrated and associated with Krishna is the overcoming of the snake deity. Krishna is described as defeating and dancing on the snake demon, who in turn worships him. The vitality of the new faith over the old is suggested in this victory over Indra and the snake demon Kaliya. Plate 3 shows Krishna being fed milk by one of the cowherdesses.

In devotion to Krishna, man expresses his most romantic and colourful feelings through music, dance and celebration. Ideas of play or 'lila' are connected to this devotion to Krishna.

Buddha

Buddha, the great prophet and teacher, became absorbed into the pantheon of Hinduism as an Avatar of Vishnu. Buddha as an Avatar has no substantial cult. Bodh Gaya itself was a Saivite rather than a Vaishnavite place of worship. Between the tenth and twelfth centuries the interaction between the two religions became very close, with similar practices and doctrines such as the tantras. Both the Buddha and Vishnu are seen as divine saviour figures.

Kalki

The last of the avatars of Vishnu and the one that is yet to come is called Kalki. He is depicted as a human figure with a horse's head or as an actual horse. The texts say that his appearance in the world will come at the time of dissolution or at the end of the present time cycle. The choice of the horse for this future saviour of the world may well express India's attitude to the horse as an animal that was not indigenous and was identified with the powerful Aryan invaders whose arrival astride these fearsome animals must have seemed like the end of the world. The horse was a feared and valued animal. In South India offerings of terracotta horses are made to propitiate the spirit Aiyanar and for protection against any other ghosts or spirits believed to inhabit the forest.

Vishnu's consort

The usual name of Vishnu's wife is Lakshmi (Figure 3.8). She represents prosperity and bounty. She is worshipped so as to ensure blessings and affluence to her devotees. Lakshmi is often depicted seated in the lap of Vishnu and in this form the couple are known as Lakshmi-Narayan. As the goddess of good luck she has a long history reaching back to the late centuries BC. She is first seen sitting on a lotus flower and is lustrated with water from two elephants. The lotus is associated with Lakshmi and Vishnu. The lotus and the water are associated with prosperity and life. Lakshmi's other name is Sri. The other consort of Vishnu is Bhu. Bhu was the earth goddess who was rescued from the depths of the ocean by the Varaha incarnation of Vishnu.

Interpretation of Vishnu

What does the worship of Vishnu tell us about Hinduism? It tells of a society at pains to maintain the continuity of its traditions. It expresses a belief in 'bhakti', literally a shared relationship with God on a personal level and an expectation of love and fair dealings. Vishnu as a deity is seen as the deliverer. Vishnu is known as the source and preserver of the world and for this reason is often shown as the king, or

Chakravartin. As such, he becomes an analogue of the earthly king who is 'wedded' to his territory in the manner in which Vishnu is wedded to his second consort, the earth, or Bhudevi. Kings today, such as the king of Nepal and the former Maharajas of Travancore, are regarded as Vishnu's representation on earth.

As in the case of Siva, the interpretation of Vishnu's attributes cannot be precise. Understanding has to be associated with vision or enlightenment, which comes as much from unconscious perception as from a conscious reading of symbols. The characteristic elements and emblems of Vishnu have been analysed in the following way. The four arms may represent the four stages of human life, the four hands the dominion over the four directions of space and thus Vishnu's absolute power. The conch may represent the creative spiral, or its sound 'om' held to be the origin of existence. The discus, the weapon which cuts off demons' heads, may symbolize the power of the mind which destroys ignorance. The lotus may represent the universe, the rising of beauty of form from the formless, or literally the swampy depths of the pond. The lotus may also symbolize the egg of nescience, or the seed of endless millions within the universe. The mace is said to symbolize the power of knowledge and of time, which destroys all who oppose it. The jewel on his chest is supposed to represent consciousness, which manifests itself in the sun, moon, fire and speech. The lock of hair on the chest represents the source of the natural world.[22]

The first two avatars, the fish and the tortoise, are strongly linked to water symbolism. Mythology recounts the tale of the fish who saved the world from the great flood and the tortoise who churned up the

Figure 3.8 A modern painting of the goddess Lakshmi. Robert Elgood.

ocean and revealed the divine nectar. The boar and the half-man half-lion incarnations represent the absorption of local cult deities into the orthodox pantheon of Hinduism. Boar worship had been recorded in Malwa and the half-lion beast has a long tradition of worship in the Deccan and Orissa. The four next avatars, the dwarf, Rama in two incarnations and Krishna, are more frequently represented in epic narrative. Rama and his wife Sita described in the *Ramayana* still today represent the perfect ideal marriage. Krishna on the other hand expresses the joyful celebration of divine love and play. The acceptance of Krishna's love for Radha, a married woman, is revealing. Perhaps this unorthodox relationship is on one level symbolic of human passion for the divine but on another releases emotions which are of necessity restrained in marriage rules and obligations. Marriage decisions are usually governed by an overriding sense of duty and obligation, not love or passion. A common thread in all the manifestations and forms of Vishnu is the link with local heroes and animals sanctified in tribal and local myth. As has been already suggested, the absorption of the Krishna legend into Vaishnava mythology may represent the acceptance of a more lax and yet joyful message from tribal society into the more rigid orthodox code. The worship of Vishnu as Krishna conveys in particular a sense of play, joy and lightness of spirit.

The final two avatars Buddha and Kalki demonstrate Hindu absorption of later religious movements. The consorts of Vishnu – Lakshmi, Sri and Bhu – echo the prosperity and fruitfulness expressed in the form of Vishnu. The relationship between Vishnu and Lakshmi is the more normal orthodox relationship.

Brahma

Brahma as a deity is not actively worshipped. Brahma never presents himself as a great yogin. The only temples dedicated to Brahma are at Ajmer, and near Kumbhakonam in Tamil Nadu. Brahma is the source or seed of all that is; he is the place wherein the union of Siva or Vishnu may occur. He is the point of balance between the poles of concentration and dispersion.

Brahma is represented with four heads, originally five (the fifth was burned by the fire of Siva's third eye). His colour is red or pink and in his four arms he holds either the four Vedas or a sceptre, ladle, string of beads, bowl or water jug. His vehicle is a swan or goose, the symbol of knowledge. His consort is Sarasvati, the goddess of knowledge or speech.

The Goddess

A sixth-century Hindu text recounts the deeds of the Goddess and suggests a single powerful female deity. The Goddess 'Mahadevi' may be regarded as personifying the thousands of local Devis as well as the pan-Indian goddesses of orthodox Hindu tradition. The assimilation of the Goddess into the Hindu pantheon may be represented by two distinct phases: the first when the Indo-Aryan Gods were given consorts and the second under the influence of tantric movements in the medieval period, when the female goddess emerged with supreme independent power. Despite the fact that the goddess retains many names and distinct personas,[23] the subsuming of all female deities into one great goddess has however continued to the present day.[24] In the medieval period the Goddess, and the female energy which she represents, became known as Sakti. Today she is commonly called Mata or Ma in North India and Amman in the south.

History of the Earth Goddess

The Earth or Mother Goddess pre-dates the Hindu period. Worship of the Goddess is directly concerned with fertility, procreation and abundant harvest that is valid even today, with a large percentage of India's population still depending on agriculture for its livelihood and survival. Archaeology has revealed continuous production of terracotta female images with pronounced breasts, hips and stylized features throughout the history of India. The earliest female images, presumably of a goddess, come from sites in West India such as Mehrgarh and Sheri Khan Tarakai during the sixth and fifth millennium BC. Although we have no evidence of their ritual function, the exaggerated generative organs strongly suggest associations with fertility and the Mother Goddess. Terracotta images discovered in Mohenjo-Daro and Harappa from the second and first millennium BC show less exaggerated female forms.

What was the actual purpose of these terracottas? The answer may be found by examining the form and purpose of similar more recent clay images. Even today, votive offerings are left in rural and tribal shrines. These tokens, usually but not exclusively made of clay, symbolically represent the ancient sacrificial victim, or perhaps can be seen as offerings that become real in the spirit world. These were sometimes offered in thanks for the fulfilment of requests. Another purpose of clay votive figures was the ancient belief in healing through sympathetic magic, seen in the offering to

the Goddess of damaged or sick parts of the body made of clay. Women desiring pregnancy or the safe delivery of a child have for many generations moulded and placed clay images of mother and child before the Goddess. These practices depend on a belief in magic and a miraculous interdependence of earth and flesh.

History of female tree spirits and river goddesses

Despite the continuing devotion to the Earth Goddess in pre- Vedic and post-Vedic rural India, it is apparent that in the orthodox Brahmanic texts the pantheon is dominated by powerful male gods. The goddesses, Ushas (the dawn), sometimes likened to a cow and associated with light and Prithvi (the earth), are briefly referred to, but there is no mention of bloodthirsty female deities or tree spirits. Despite this lack of literary reference, lifelike female images representing tree spirits (yakshinis) decorate Buddhist stone monuments from as early as the second to first century AD. At Bharhut, a second-century stone carving shows yakshinis' in supplication to the Buddha; and at Amaravati, the second- to third-century site, a male yaksha is depicted appearing from a stone altar under a tree to greet and worship the infant Buddha. The nubile yakshinis and other sensual female deities are shown entwined with lotuses and branches of trees. The inclusion of these spirits in early Buddhist art marks the new faith's absorption of earlier beliefs and the use of sculptors practised in an earlier artistic tradition. It is unknown what values early Buddhism attributed to these ancient deities and spirits, but they arrived in time to have an auspicious function, ensuring the spiritual potency of sacred sites. This no doubt derived from the ancient practice associated with tree worship, where the breaking of the branch of a tree by a beautiful young virgin was believed to bring about the arousal of the tree spirit and the tree's fruitfulness.[25]

The earliest post-Harappan free-standing stone sculpture is believed by some to be a sculpture referred to as the 'Didarganj Yakshi or Chauri-bearer'. Similar female images with increasingly sensual overtones are frequently to be found on Buddhist monuments from AD 200–400. From the fourth century AD however the yakshi was often supplanted by the river goddess. The river goddess and the tree spirit both suggest water symbolism in their association with the flowing water and rising sap. They appear to be initially interchangeable, until the river goddess surpassed the yakshi image in popularity. Garlands were thrown on to the surface of rivers to honour the goddess, in the same way that devotees had respectfully adorned sacred trees with garlands.

Present day village deities

The worship of the earth goddess and tree spirits continues in village and tribal India to the present day. Throughout village India in rural areas, shrines to a variety of goddesses are common. The village mother deity of the Gonds, for example, is represented by a sanctuary where round stones and a number of small clay animals are presented to the goddess as votive offerings. The extent to which they are separate or part of the cult of some greater female deity is impossible to determine. Sometimes the names are the same, but the goddesses possess different characteristics. These goddesses may be tribal in origin and

can be guardian deities known as gramadevata. The gramadevata is a generic term for the deity or goddess identified with the village and towards whom the villagers have a special affection. The goddess can both terrify and protect with gentle benevolence. Many goddesses of this type are associated with agriculture, plentiful rain and good harvests. These goddesses embody fertility and are without male consorts. According to Kinsley, the mythological origin of the village goddess of South India expresses injustices done to women by men.[26] It explains their ambivalence and their independence from the male consort, and the required sacrifice of a male animal to be offered to the goddess. In order to protect the village's interests she needed a fierce countenance. Examples of regional goddesses are Mariyamman in South India and Manasa in North India. When they receive blood offerings it is often a male animal whose life blood is offered and they are often worshipped by men. Many village deities require offerings of blood or alcohol, the former in the guise of chickens, goats or occasionally buffaloes. Symbolic associations can be made between the natural cycle of seasons and the menstrual cycle of the goddess. Blood, alcohol and fertility are all hallmarks of the goddess.

The seats (pithas) of these village goddesses are frequently found in the open, sometimes in fields (Figure 3.9). A shrine with buildings dedicated to the goddess is less usual. Instead of an image there is often merely a pile of stones marked by a flag or pole. Some shrines are maintained and honoured by a priest while others are tended by a temple keeper, who is paid no renumeration and acccorded no special status. All tribal groups have a priest or a

Figure 3.9 Village shrine in Tamil Nadu. Robert Elgood.

group of sacred specialists generally limited to two or three in number. Its membership is confined to the priest's family or those of his assistants. Different tribes call them different names. For example, the Hos of Bihar call them Pahan, the Gonds of Madhya Pradesh call them Baiga Kanikkars and the Uralies of Kerala call them Plathies. The Kuvi Kandhas of Orissa have female priests assisted by a number of female assistants to propitiate the deities. The duty of these priests is to propitiate the village deities and to ward off disease and misfortune. The Bhils call their priest Badava, who may combine in himself the roles of a medium, diviner, worshipper and healer. The ceremony is essentially that of sacrifice. The offerings range from eggs to buffaloes. New

cereals like maize, paddy and country liquors are offered to the god. Ritual worship commences with offerings, followed by a noisy summoning of the goddess and the belief in her arrival. Spirit possession is a frequent occurrence in village worship[27] and a common characteristic is the medium's loss of bodily control. The village goddess or devi, like the tree spirits, is believed to be a quixotic bearer of both bounty and catastrophe so that spirits need to be propitiated to avert any evil consequence of their presence. At the end of the worship the tribal people enjoy a feast where drinking and dancing takes place. Many villagers believe that the outbreak of some diseases such as smallpox represents the anger of the goddess. Other goddesses inhabit cremation grounds, and are placated with blood or flesh offerings. The goddess Chinnamasta is frequently depicted drinking her own blood while striding over a copulating couple. Many aspects of the ceremonies and practices of the tribal groups of North and South India show common features even today which may reveal a faithfulness to ancient ritual practices. A practice which may represent a continuation of the ancient ceremony of tree worship is seen in the spring annual festival of the tribal group the Oraons. This festival is held in a sacred grove where blossoms of the sal tree form an essential element and the ceremony is known as Sarhul. Features such as blood sacrifices, shamans and simple natural shrines of trees or stones represent some of these aspects, underlying which is an apparent belief in a deity or spirit form. This impersonal force is given the title Bonga by the Indian Ho tribe. Other tribes conceive of a similar presence or force, which forms a substratum of primitive religion. Any stone marked with vermilion and unidentifiable as any particular deity will be explained by the Birhors as some sort of bheru which acts as boga or mana power. The tribes also consider the sun, moon and earth as supreme powers, while ancestor worship plays a decisive role in tribal life in general, and in religious life in particular. The mystery of the goddess cannot be understood rationally. The unpredictabilty of the goddess enables people to come to terms with fate and to attempt to manage the uncontrollable. The view of reality where tragedy and success are ever present is more real than the single view of life where bad times are repressed. The goddess reminds us that life must contain her and thus prepare us for the truth of the fragility and uncertainty of our hold on it. This in some ways helps us to digest the tragedy of our daily lives.

Aniconic form of the devi

Whereas Siva's symbol is the phallus, called in Sanskrit the linga, or standing pillar, the goddess is sometimes depicted in the form of a stylized representation of the female genitals, which in Sanskrit is known as the yoni. The two organs often appear together, with the linga seeming to pass through the yoni and to rise above it. The yoni without the associated linga is worshipped as Kamakhya in Kamgirim near Gauhati in Assam. This is the place where, according to tradition, the yoni of Sati was thrown by a distraught Siva. Another place containing this solitary symbol of the goddess is the temple site of Alampur.

A more abstract image of the goddess is depicted in the symbolic form of the yantra or geometric diagram. This is primarily associated with the goddess although not exclusively so. Different names are given to the yantras in the worship of different goddesses. The geometric form is based on a combination of triangles and circles. It is suggested that the triangle represents the approximate shape of the vulva. Sometimes the triangles are superimposed to form a star, which stands for the union of the male and female principles. This form is placed within a circular diagram, representing the lotus flower in all its subtle varieties of meaning. Sometimes the lotus flowers are raised in the form of a small mountain culminating in the star, in the centre of which is said to be the absolute point of the godhead reached from the union of the active female and the passive male energies. The history and use of yantras is linked to other sacred diagrams used as aids to meditation.

As well as the wilder forms of the pre-Vedic goddess, the female deity became absorbed into the orthodox pantheon of Hindu gods and goddesses, in which the wives of the gods reflect subtle aspects of the nature of their husbands. One of the most revered of the Hindu goddesses is Siva's wife Parvati. Siva's consorts express benevolence in the form of Parvati and power and possible destruction in the persons of Durga and Kali.

Parvati

As already mentioned, unlike Lakshmi, Parvati has barely any independent history of her own. Her nature is defined by her relationship with her divine husband. Parvati has already been identified as a reincarnation of the goddess Sati. Not until the *Puranas* or the plays of Kalidasa of the fifth and sixth centuries do we find the central myths of Sati and Parvati told in detail. Legend describes Parvati as the child of the sacred mountains, the Himalayas. Mythology relates Parvati's determination to win Siva. She was said to have been undeterred by Siva's worldly detachment and preoccupation with asceticism and to have become an ascetic herself to earn his respect and attention. She is often depicted on Siva's lap, demure and beautiful, and looking at him tenderly. The sons of Siva and Parvati are known as Skanda (Karttikeya) and the elephant-headed Ganesa.

The theme of the Parvati cycle of myths is to represent the tension between the householder and the ascetic. Parvati, representing the householder, tries to lure Siva from his ascetic preoccupations. Another important element of Parvati's character is a role model for the perfect devotee or disciple.

Durga

Durga's primary purpose is to combat demons who threaten the stability of the cosmos. Durga is depicted as a queen armed for battle. Her most common manifestation is as Mahisa Mardini, slayer of the buffalo demon. At a certain point in history she became associated with Siva as his wife.

Perhaps one of the most popular cults is that of the goddess Durga who is described in the *Devi Mahatmya* as a powerful goddess created from the combined anger of several gods. Durga is armed with the principal weapons of the major gods, the javelin of Agni, the trident of Siva and the discus of Vishnu (Plate 4). She rides a lion and confronts a buffalo which has been possessed by a demon. The buffalo (perhaps symbolic of indigenous nonconformist cults) is said to threaten the stability of the gods themselves. Durga's victory over the buffalo demon is frequently depicted and shows Durga placing a foot on the decapitated buffalo while spearing the demon who possessed and now emerges from the dying animal. The example of the buffalo warns devotees of the danger of possession by the spirit world, and is a reference to the ancient tradition of buffalo worship which continues to be practised in tribal communities such as the Bhils.

The cult of Durga is ancient. Yet no goddesses are cast in the role of demon slayers in Vedic literature. Although the name Durga is mentioned in Vedic literature, no figure resembling a warlike goddess appears in the early texts. An indigenous non-Aryan origin for Durga is reinforced by her association with areas such as the Vindhya mountains, and tribal peoples such as the Sabaras, who drink liquor and eat meat.[28] In many respects Durga stands for qualities diametrically opposed to the general ideal for the Hindu woman. Unlike the normal female she does not provide her consort with her power or sakti but takes power from the male gods in order to succeed in battle. In doing this the gods surrender their potency to her.

Aside from possible links with proto-Durga Sunga terracotta figurines, earliest known examples of the image are from the first century AD in the vicinity of Mathura. From the fourth century AD, images of Durga slaying the buffalo become common. Durga's image is also found in the rock-cut temples at Ellora which date from the seventh and eighth centuries AD, and in the south on rock-cut temples, where there is more than one depiction of her at Mahabalipuram. Throughout North and South India it is a common theme sculpted on Hindu temples.

Today, Durga is still a popular form of the goddess. Durga-puja in the autumn is an important festival, known as Dasara. The festival takes place over nine days and is often called the Navaratra festival. In many parts of India this was an occasion in which the rulers would celebrate military might and royal power and petition for military success in the coming year. Worship of weapons was a part of the festival in many cases.

In Bengal she is given a particular place of importance and the story of Parvati's return to her family after the bleak sojourn with Siva in the mountain is re-enacted annually. At the festival of Durga-puja she is shown surrounded by four deities, Karttikeya, Ganesa, Sarasvati and Lakshmi. She is also associated with plants and receives blood offerings at the festival, perhaps suggesting the renourishment of her powers of fertility. The legend is echoed

by the return of married daughters to their maternal home for one day to be looked after and cosseted. Special icons of the goddess vanquishing the demon are made for the festival in clay by a specific subcaste of artisans. These images are often large and are housed in temporary shrines. At the end of the festival the images are immersed in the river, returning to the elements from whence they came.

A fundamental difference between South and North India is seen in the perception of the relationship between Durga and the buffalo demon. In the south the implied sexual tension between Durga and the buffalo demon is heightened. Durga is seen to be dangerous and violent and world safety is secured by taming the sexuality of the goddess by marriage. In the north on the other hand, Durga-puja stresses the aspect of the gentle young wife and daughter.

Annapurna

While Durga is the fierce goddess of the battlefield, Annapurna represents the goddess of plenty. She is calm, fruitful and fertile. Her symbols are the overflowing pot of rice and the brimming vessel of milk. In aniconic form she is worshipped as a full pot. In Central India she is depicted seated with a ladle across her lap. Unlike most goddesses, Annapurna carries no weapons. Her most famous shrine is in Benaras, the city sacred to Siva. In Bengal during March and April there is a tradition of producing clay images of the goddess ladling out food to Siva, who is shown as a begging mendicant. At the harvest festival of Annakuta, the 'mountain of food', which takes place in the autumn, Annapurna's Benaras temple becomes the focus of elaborate activity. This festival is usually associated with Krishna but in Benaras it is Annapurna whose temple is filled with food by her devotees, to be given away to the needy as prasad, food sanctified by contact or association with the deity.

Kali

Kali is the most terrifying manifestation of the Goddess, sometimes indistinguishable from the goddess Chamunda (Chamunda is usually depicted as an older, more withered hag). Although she is portrayed as a wild, violent and sometimes hideous being, she is often the object of intense devotion. She is also depicted as black or dark, usually naked with long, dishevelled hair, severed arms as a girdle, and severed heads as a necklace. She is seen with a lolling tongue bitten by long teeth and with clawlike hands. Although she is sometimes regarded as an independent deity she can be associated with Siva.

The name Kali (literally 'the black (female) one') may suggest the deity's tribal or southern origin. References to the indigenous population as dark-skinned appear in the ancient text the *Rg Veda*, notably in hymns to Indra as 'subduer of the dark (dasa) colour'.[29] The earliest references to Kali in the Hindu tradition date to the early medieval period around AD 600 and locate Kali on the battlefield or on the edge of Hindu society. She is mentioned in the *Agni* and *Garuda Purana*, and in the *Bhagavata Purana* as the patron deity of a band of thieves. Her most famous appearances in battle contexts are found in the *Devi-mahatmya*.

Kali's association with the cremation ground which is always on the outskirts of any settlement reinforces her status as a terrifying outsider. Kali, like Siva, inhabits the regions on the edge of society, a place historically occupied by the untouchables and tribal people. Kali is seen with sagging breasts, a necklace of skulls, a skirt made of severed arms and a large red lolling tongue, sometimes dripping with the blood of sacrificial victims (Figure 3.10). Some devotees describe Kali's act of biting her large protruding tongue as an expression of the control of the senses. The skulls around Kali's neck stand for the cycle of life and death. Whereas Parvati receives devotion and symbolic offerings as the bounteous and fecund goddess, Kali, like Durga, requires mollifying sacrificial offerings in human or animal form.

Kali is particularly popular in Bengal, although she is worshipped and known throughout India. She is also worshipped by many who see her as their mother. It is remarkable that despite her gruesome appearance Kali holds such a key position in Hindu religious devotion. She is of central importance in tantrism. Kali dominates tantric iconography, texts and rituals, especially in left-handed tantra. The approach of the devotee to Kali differs from the approach of the tantric sadhaka. The former becomes a child returning to the fierce mother for protection, while the latter approaches her in a heroic and fearless way. In both approaches the devotees or the tantric heroes accept or confront the truth of life and death and through their accept-ance or confrontation become liberated.

One of the most famous temples dedic-ated to Kali is located on the steps (ghats) of the river Hooghly in Calcutta, an area known as Kalighat. This temple has been the major source for painted icons of the goddess Kali. Kumartully, also in Calcutta, is the centre for the production of the clay images already referred to in connection with Durga-puja, where in the same

Figure 3.10 A modern painting of Kali. Pat Barylski.

workshops similar life-sized images of Kali are produced.

Kali is the predominant goddess in tantric painting, which emphasizes the active female, passive male roles by depicting Kali striding over or dancing upon either a supine Siva, or Siva in sexual union with the goddess Parvati, with the latter taking the dominant role. Kali is portrayed with a necklace of skulls suggesting her devouring nature. For the Western mind accustomed to the portrayal of the Virgin Mary as gentle, modest and nurturing, the concept of a terrifying death-dealing goddess who at the same time attracts intense devotion is difficult to grasp. Philosophically, the sacrificial offerings required by Kali express the paradox that life requires death for sustenance and that without this replenishment there can be no renewal. The result of this belief was the formerly widespread practice of self-sacrifice to Kali on the assumption that human beings have the potential to be transformed by allowing themselves to be devoured by the goddess, and thereby achieve ultimate absorption into the state of formless bliss.

The goddess is sometimes depicted as the old hag Chamunda, expressing Indian societies' ancient fear of post-menopausal old women. (The demonizing of old women has historically been widespread in many societies.) From a female point of view the associated fear of ending the useful fertile years when sons might be produced on a regular basis and the physical rejection that might ensue was in itself terrifying, as was the state of widowhood. Chamunda also reflects an ancient belief in the empowerment of old women in a ritual, magical sense associated with witchcraft. The change in hormone levels and the subsequent madness of menopause may be associated with this power and loss of ordinary control. The power in the domestic sphere and respect for the paternal grandmother may also be associated with the respect for old women, despite their loss of status due to infertility. Chamunda embodies the contradictions between these positions representing fear, rejection and respect. In Chamunda there is also an element of deliberate self-emaciation and ageing in order to repel mortal suitors as distinct from Lord Siva.

Essentially, Kali is remarkable in her association with blood and death, both held as pollutants by the purity-conscious Hindu society.

> Kali puts the order of dharma in perspective, perhaps puts it in its place, by reminding Hindus that certain aspects of reality are untamable, unpurifiable, unpredictable, and always a threat to society's feeble attempts to order what is essentially disorderly: life itself.[30]

Lakshmi

As has been already mentioned, Lakshmi is the consort of the god Vishnu. She is one of the most approachable and benign forms of the goddess, and has her own cult independent of her role as Vishnu's wife. Lakshmi embodies auspiciousness, prosperity and abundance. Lakshmi in the form of Sri does occur in the earliest Vedic literature.[31] Associated with Lakshmi, Sri is one of the first to be mentioned in the ancient Sanskrit texts. The term is used to suggest beauty, lustre and glory, and is used in later Vedic literature to refer to ruling power. Kinsley refers to it as a kind of disembodied power that is acquired by kings in various ways, one of which is ritual lustration. Sri also refers to riches and abundance and is associated with fertility or the potency of the earth. An example of this in modern Hinduism is given by the women worshipping Sri in the form of cow dung. Sri-Lakshmi is depicted visually in an image as early as the second century BC at the stupa of Bharhut, which may be interpreted as Lakshmi. This shows her seated cross-legged on a lotus being lustrated by two elephants. Both the lotus and the elephant are associated with Lakshmi. The lotus refers to life and growth, while the elephants are associated with clouds in ancient Indian traditions and royal authority. This lustration of Sri echoes the ancient royal consecration where the head of the Indian monarch was anointed with water. A similar image of Lakshmi with four arms sitting on a lotus appears on certain Gupta coins. As Vishnu's consort, she is defined by the perfection and beauty of the lotus and associated with the creation myth. Her frequent depiction with elephants suggests her royal status as consort to the regal form of Vishnu.

Some traditions associate Sri-Lakshmi with the god Kubera, the lord of the Yakshas. Sri's relationship with Kubera is especially revealing, as both are associated with wealth and prosperity. Lakshmi is extremely popular throughout India and is worshipped each year in a variety of festivals, the most important being the festival of Divali held in late autumn. Even temples not dedicated to Vishnu will contain an image of Lakshmi. Her image is often carved on the door lintels of Vaishnava temples and by her presence at the entrance she guarantees the auspiciousness of the shrine. Associated with prosperity, Lakshmi is particularly popular with the business community of India; she is worshipped at New Year when new ledgers and accounts

are opened. Special pujas are conducted and reverence is paid to articles such as pens, ink and paper. This aspect of her character is celebrated at the festival of Divali in the autumn, when lamps are lit in all the houses so that by her presence misfortune will be dispelled.

As Sri-Lakshmi is regarded as the consort of Vishnu she is also considered to be the model Hindu wife, loyal and submissive to her husband.

Sarasvati

The consort of Brahma is the goddess Sarasvati, sometimes depicted together with the same vahana, the swan or goose. Reference to her appears in the *Vedas* and she is honoured by Hindus and Jains. She is one of the few goddesses from the Vedas who remains significant in modern Hinduism. In the early *Vedas* she is clearly associated with the river, praised for her cleansing and fertilizing power. One could say that Sarasvati was a prototype of the important later river Goddesses the Ganga and the Jumna. While Sarasvati was once worshipped as an actual river which has now largely dried up, she also represents a mighty yet far from ordinary river, an ever-flowing grace from the heavens which purifies and fertilizes the earth. Vedic sacrifices on its banks were made. According to Blurton, the deification of this river was a precedent for the later worship of the Ganges.

Today, Sarasvati's old association with the river is seen only by her depiction as seated on a lotus. She is described as white like snow, and this transcendent nature is suggested by her vehicle the swan. Later Vedic literature such as the *Brahmanas* associate Sarasvati with the spoken word and she becomes known as the goddess of speech. In time she came to represent poetry, music and all intellectual pursuits and is depicted holding a musical instrument (vina). Sarasvati's connection with literature and knowledge is the reason for her popularity in Jain temples. The Jains are renowned for their ritual recitation of texts and their interest and investment in manuscripts and literature. Special puja to Sarasvati is conducted in the spring when images of the goddess are established in schools and universities; this is not the goddess of the domestic world but one who involves the worship of books, pens and musical instruments.

Sita

In the *Vedas* Sita meant 'furrow' and was the name of a goddess associated with ploughed fields in Vedic literature. She was however not a very significant deity prior to the Ramayana of Valmiki. As Rama's wife in the Ramayana, by her self-effacing nature and her steadfast loyalty, Sita is seen as the ideal Hindu wife.

Matrkas

A group of goddesses is known as the 'matrikas' or simply the mothers. Early references to this group of goddesses date to around the first century AD, rarely mentioning their number and stating only that they are innumerable.[32] The earliest clear descriptions appear in the *Mahabharata*. In the medieval period they become known as the seven matrkas. They take on names and characteristics which associate them with important male gods in the Hindu pantheon. The matrikas were initially described as dangerous, fearsome

Figure 3.11 Terracotta female figurine, Indus Valley. 2600–1500 BC. National Museum, Delhi.

and threatening to new-born children. Finally they appeal to Karttikeya to adopt them as his mothers; he agrees on condition that they protect rather than harm children. Behind this concept of child-threatening goddesses is possibly the belief that women who die childless or in childbirth linger as jealous spirits ready to steal or harm other children, and need to be propitiated to forestall danger to offspring. In the *Mahabharata* it is clear that the matrikas were associated with non-Aryan traditions. They may well have represented the many village goddesses who needed appeasement. From the fourth century AD the number of mothers became standardized to seven, and are patterned on male deities of the Hindu pantheon, yet rather than be regarded as saktis of the male deities they are seen as extensions of the Devi, and as fierce, effective warriors who protect the world and combat demons.

Interpretation of the goddess

A hierarchy of female deities, tree and river goddesses, bhutas (ghosts), heavenly courtesans and spirits existed in female form in the Indian imagination. Over centuries a composite goddess evolved which was a compilation of various elements such as the non-Vedic village goddesses or grama-devatas and the earth goddess. This composite goddess was absorbed into the Hindu pantheon by marriage with the chief Hindu male deities which gave her a place in the religious hierarchy, though she also retained an independent status. In some cases the goddess is seen as a source of vital powers. The Nayak rulers of Madurai received their sceptres, symbols of temporal authority, from the hands of Minakshi, at the temple of Madurai in South India. Other lesser female spirits existed such as tree and river spirits, apsaras, heavenly courtesans and Devadasis.

Reference to two female roles exists in Sanskrit literature: the fecund Mother goddess and that of the vesya (courtesan). Ancient pre-Vedic terracottas and the earliest known free-standing female images (Figure 3.11) depict the Mother or Earth Goddess. The vesyas, like their prototype the apsaras, are associated with fertility and rainfall. Unmarried and therefore incapable of widowhood, the vesyas are auspicious

(nityasumangali). Their role was to stimulate and bring about the forces of auspiciousness and fertility without involvement through emotional attachment or their own pregnancy.

> The wife and the vesya have split between them the roles of fertility and eroticism; but we are then left with the paradox that a symbol of barren eroticism (the courtesan) is needed to bring about the longed for state of non-erotic fertility in the home .... The king lives a life of eroticism marked by a certain prescribed recklessness, and by excess; he is himself seductive, energized, and open to the emotional labyrinth of love; he symbolizes and focuses the fertile and auspicious forces necessary for the kingdom's growth.[33]

The development of more sensual and erotic female images is first seen on Buddhist monuments and later proliferate on the outer walls of Hindu temples. A growing sensuality is shown in the stone carvings of these secondary images from as early as the first century AD. These sensual courtesans also serve to tempt and test the detachment of the king and devotees.[34]

The development of the Hindu cult of the goddess, more usually referred to as sakti worship,[35] was contemporary with that of Siva. The change in the nature of sakti was based on the elaboration of texts known collectively as tantras. These texts describe a terrifying, bloodthirsty and energetic goddess who was the centre of all power (sakti). Adepts believe that the power of the goddess could only be experienced through invoking her by a combination of ritual actions and the recitation of texts. The actions required by these rites were often unorthodox in terms of Hindu religious practice and included ritual sexual intercourse, sometimes group sexual intercourse on cremation grounds, and the ritual eating of meat and consumption of intoxicating liquors.

Despite the numerous names and manifestations of the goddess, her identities share many common features. One of these is the idea of the goddess as the creative energy or power (sakti) of the male god who is her consort. According to Fuller, one of the factors which accounts for the fact that single goddesses are more violent than married goddesses is revealed by the concept of ritual temperature. Great heat is attributed to the unmarried goddess, her power equated with heightened sexual energy and a capacity for angry violence. The concept of intense heat embodied by the goddess is clearly associated with the goddess of smallpox, a disease causing raised temperature or feverishness. This heat is also symbolized by the red forehead marks which are prominent on these goddesses.[36] The cult of the terrifying and powerful goddess is associated with the male idea of the potency and sexual appetite of the unfettered and uncontrolled female[37] and that only when ritually shackled to a male can female sexuality be safely channelled and restrained. Tantrics believe that men and women contain both male and female energy and that the union of these two forces by ritual means brings enlightenment and liberation. Female energy (sakti) is visualized as Kundalini, a curled serpent residing at the base of the spine which, when aroused, rises up the spinal column. In contrast, male energy, which takes its power from the sun, resides above the cranium and is believed under certain conditions to pass through the foramen of the skull. Tantric followers desire liberation which they believe will be achieved through the union of female energy with the descending male energy. The historical origins of tantrism are unknown but are presumed to date from a period preceding the Vedic period in India. The tantric tradition that power passes through the female suggests it dates from the time when India was a matriarchal society. Furthermore, the secret nature of the sect and its initiates has resulted in no written records from its early period. From the earliest period of the formation of Hindu art for spiritual purposes the influence of the female principle has been a dominant force. The concept of sakti is regarded by historians as a later development, primarily because there is no academically historically acceptable evidence for it, but it undoubtedly reflects the undocumented cults of an earlier period. The best evidence of the early themes that came to be called tantrism can be seen in the preoccupations of early Hindu art.

In conclusion, certain core features of the goddess must be stressed: first, the existence of a generic form of goddess which manifests in benign and terrifying forms: second, a belief in a goddess who is propitiated with sacrificial offerings, and third, a belief in the transmigration of spirits, manifest in spirit possession, where in a trance state man's conscious mind is suspended to allow the entry and presence of the goddess. The generic goddess is part of a female spirit hierarchy including tree and river spirits, vesyas and celestial maidens and the earth mother. The vesyas reflect women's sexuality which in Indian society is considered to be stimulating and powerful, desirable and uncontrolled, tempting and terrifying. By contrast, the fecund earth mother goddess reflects nonsexual, fertile and controlled womanhood which relates to the theme expressed in

Chapter 1 of early religion being an attempt to control nature for the benefit of society as a whole. The active, creative role of the goddess and the matriarchal tradition is also reflected in the predominance of women in religious rituals in Indian village life. The continuing importance of the goddess in India demonstrates India's acknowledgement of woman's potential power and her significant conservative role in the continuity of the social order.

Elemental and Lesser Gods

Several of the Vedic gods have continued to receive devotion during the Hindu period. Some of the more important deities of the *Vedas* such as Agni (fire), Indra (warrior god), Vayu (god of the wind), Varuna (guardian of cosmic order and chief of the six celestial deities known as the adityas) and Surya (god of the sun) persist in Hinduism and form a background to later complex legends and mythology. Hymns from the Vedic period described the god Agni as beautiful, glowing and quixotic; Indra as a powerful soldier attractive to women, and Soma half-male, half-female associated with the moon. These were a powerful triumvirate. From the third century BC the worship of the god Soma ceased while many of the other Vedic Gods became a part of the Hindu pantheon. Of these Surya had pre-eminence.

Surya

Sun worship had its origin as early as the neolithic period in India. While the sun was an important part of Vedic ritual its status was strengthened by contacts with Achaemenid Persia from the fifth century BC onwards. Achaemenian sun worship coexisted with and was absorbed into a coagulating deity drawn from Aryan and non-Vedic beliefs and practices. From the beginning of the first century AD the Sakas and the Kusans, North Indian dynasties whose origins were within the sphere of Persian cultural and religious influence, encouraged the cult of Mithra, which was associated with the worship of the sun. Their impact contributed to the growth in popularity of the sun cult from the fifth century in specific areas of North and Eastern India. A revival of sun worship in the eighth century was caused by the arrival in Western India of the Parsees, who were renowned for their ritual solar practices. Around the ninth century the Scythian tribes in Western India were also responsible for building a series of temples dedicated to Surya. His popularity was shortlived however and his pre-eminence in this area was not sustained.

According to Srivastava, the earliest known image of the sun-god in human form appears on a terracotta plaque from Patna that has been dated from the fourth to third century BC.[38] The sun started to appear in iconic form on certain coins issued by the Indo-Greeks and the Kusans. One of the earliest sculptures of Surya depicts a figure riding a chariot on a first-century BC railing on the Bodh Gaya stupa. A figure of Surya is also seen on a wall near the entrance of a cave at Bhaja from the Sunga period of the second century BC. Following the Kusan period images of Surya develop Hellenistic features.

Surya was and still is the sun-god and as such was considered as the source of light, warmth and life itself. In ancient legend the sun's daily progress across the sky was described as an eagle, flying bird or horse. Legend describes Surya's consort as a mare, who, overpowered by her husband's radiance, fled to the shade of a forest. While in the forest the sun-god was reputed to have come to her as a stallion while she studied meditation. Later legend describes how Visvakarma, the father of Surya's wife, reduced Surya's brilliant rays by cutting away one-eighth of his substance. Parts of the sun were believed to have fallen to earth as the disc of Vishnu and the trident of Siva.

Surya is portrayed with only one head and two or four arms and in each hand he holds a lotus. His emblems, such as the cakra, wheel, discus and lotus, incorporate earlier pre-Vedic aniconic symbols of the sun such as the swastika and the ringstone. Evidence of Surya's Western non-Indian origins is shown by his wearing Northern dress, a fashion among the Saka and Kusan rulers, consisting of a long, heavy cloak and high boots. Surya's horse-drawn chariot does however go back to the *Rg Veda*. He wears jewellery and his head is crowned with the same Kiritamukuta as Vishnu and is encircled by a halo. In South India he is shown in contemporary local dress with bare legs and feet while his charioteer Arjuna may occasionally be present as part of the image. The god Surya is often flanked by two female figures, who are shown shooting arrows. These are known as the dawn goddesses Ushas and Pratyusha.

The sun is still an important element of worship in Hindu ritual life and each morning the mantra which invokes the sun is chanted by priests. A particular verse dedicated to Savitar (one of the sun's names in its manifestation as the procreator, the principle of creation) referred to in the *Rg Veda* is still uttered three times a day by Brahmans and is called the Gayatri mantra.

Animals

As well as the worship of sacred beings in idealized human form, the divine is acknowledged in all living beings. Certain animals are shown particular reverence. Some of these were earlier cult deities which were later absorbed into the Hindu pantheon. Reverence for the boar in Malwa, the monkey in Sri Lanka and the snake throughout India are examples of this practice. Hindu story-tellers created legends around such creatures so that mythology and history are interwoven. Hindus understand them as a part of the illusion of the phenomenal world or 'maya'.

Hanuman, the monkey god, is given his chief role in the Ramayana where he is acknowledged to have assisted Rama in his victory over the demon Ravana, helped by his allies the bear Jambavan and the vulture Jatayu. Hanuman, although now popular throughout India, was held in particular reverence in Sri Lanka and Bali. His mantras are used with care, as he is seen as the trickster deity.

The boar, the lion (Narasimha), the fish, the dwarf and the tortoise were associated with and absorbed into Vaishnavite iconography as avatars. In the first millennium AD the boar was honoured and admired as a symbol of potency, and was adopted as the royal mark by the South Indian kings of the Chola and Vijayanagara dynasties. In relation to the lion avatar Narasimha, we see a long history of the tribal worship of a beast in the form of a lion in the Deccan and Orissa. Blurton suggests that Narasimha's tearing of the demon king's stomach may refer to tribal ritual sacrifices.[39]

There is a long history of the association of nagas (snakes) with ritual worship in India.

Figure 3.12 A seal from Mohenjo Daro, Pakistan. Harappan period, 2300–1750 BC. Drawing by Christopher Glanville RWA.

Evidence of this is given by an Indus valley seal which shows snakes protecting two worshipping figures who flank a seated cross-legged figure (Figure 3.12). The nagas as cult figures, the serpent rulers of the underworld, were represented as early as the second century BC. The usual portrayal of the naga had a human head and torso with a serpent-like form below the waist and a canopy of either five or seven cobra heads. In early Buddhist art the nagas appeared in human form submerged up to the waist in a river or lake with a group of snakes rearing above their heads. The replacement of the legs with a serpent-like tail was a later development. Snakes who emerge in the rainy season have always had a close relationship with water. Greek writers from the time of Alexander's invasion refer to India as the bane of snakes. The writer Aelian refers to a snake which was kept in a cave and worshipped; this provides literary evidence of the existence of actual serpent worship from as early as the fourth century BC.[40]

The nagas were frequently incorporated into temple iconography. Their presence is considered auspicious and believed to produce fertility, abundance and para-doxically protection from snakes. Belief in their powers of protection can be seen in the legendary account of the cobra who shielded the head of the meditating Buddha from the storm. The snake is also con-sidered to be a phallic symbol and is associated with prolific offspring and the fertility of the earth. Women desiring children set up snake stones (naga kals). Stones carved with entwined snakes are erected beneath sacred trees. These are particularly common in South India. When the snake stone has been carved it is usual to place it in a well for six months to imbue it with life. It is then invested with prayers and ceremonial and set up under a pipal or nim tree. Naga kals (Figure 3.13) vary, as some show a pair of cobras entwined and some show snakes with as many as seven heads. The most important serpent temples are in the south Kanara district on one of the highest mountains of the western Ghats, named Subrahmanya. The sanctuary contains an idol of Subrahmanya but

Figure 3.13 Naga Kal shrine, Tamil Nadu. Robert Elgood.

numerous serpents live in the sanctuary walls. An annual festival is performed from November to December, where people are brought to be cured of ailments, or for fertility purposes. Numerous devotees coil and wriggle like snakes around the temple, and some will even slither up the mountain. One of the devotees will become possessed by the spirit of the serpent and will dance and answer questions from the audience, as he will be believed to have the power to foretell the future. The body rolling for penance and for the fulfilment of vows is also seen in Tamil Nadu. One of the great festivals in honour of the snakes is called the Nagapanchami which is held during the first month of the rainy season early in August. Snake shapes are drawn with cow dung on both sides of the doorway, and flowers, sandalwood, turmeric, rice, beans and sorghum are offered to the painted serpents. Lamps are lit and waved and incense is offered to the snakes. In the afternoon people visit the anthills and snake charmers are seen with live serpents to which offerings are made. The worship of these snakes is largely performed by women, who gather together to tell the story of the festival of the nagas on the day of Nagapanchami. During the hearing of the story the women take a few grains of rice and on the conclusion of the story the rice is exchanged and placed on their foreheads. Different rituals make up a varied practice of the Nagapanchami festival which is popular in Bengal, Bihar, UP, Garhwal and Nepal.

The sight of entwined snakes is considered auspicious even today. The snake's characteristic shedding of its skin led to its being seen to possess the power of liberation. Its venom became associated with soma, the sacred liquid drunk during ritual Vedic sacrifice.

Naga displays the power of transmutation by turning fluids (the underground waters and in some cases milk) into poison and by transforming poison into the sacred knowledge that is an antidote for deprivation and ignorance (as snake venom in small doses is an antidote for a snake bite).[41]

Snake-worshippers search for the holes where they (the snakes) are likely to be found, and which more often than not are in the little mounds raised by the Kanats, or white ants. When they have found one they visit it from time to time, placing before it milk, bananas and other food which the snake is likely to fancy.[42]

Snakes are feared and revered even today; South and West India are particularly noted for the worship of snakes. This is most common with women who desire children, as snakes are believed to impart fecundity and to cure infertility. The most revered snake is the cobra. The image of the naga is represented either in purely animal or in a semi-human shape, and is always characterized by a snake hood. Shrines dedicated to the snake were often worshipped alongside sacred trees. There is a long association between the sacred tree and the snake with the belief that beneath the tangled roots of trees lie the subterranean waters, the haunt of serpents. The creation myth describes this formless darkness associated with the cobra from which life arises, as seen in the form of the waking Vishnu. The snake is believed to inhabit both this dark and formless world and the colourful human world. The snake is also associated with the idea of Kundalini or sexual energy (mentioned above). The favourite haunt of the cobra is the anthill; this has become associated in myth not only with the snake but with guarded treasure. This connection provides an explanation for the worship of the anthill which is seen not only as the abode of the snake but as the entrance to an underworld. According to Vogel, a further connection can also be made between the anthill and the rainbow, which is seen as Indra's bow or the exhalations of serpents. Abbe Dubois described how

An early example of a naga image is from Mathura, inscribed the fortieth year of Kusana reign of Kanishka. Further examples are from the Jataka of the naga Champeka from Amaravati and a Gupta image of the naga and nagini at Ajanta. The naga is shown depicted in three principal forms, the first being human, the second in its natural serpent form, the third as half-man half-snake.

Gods are frequently shown in art being carried or supported by a vehicle in animal or bird form. The animal forms on some of the seals of Mohenjo Daro may have inspired the vahana or vehicle of the gods or yaksha. Supporting dwarfs or animals are also seen in association with yaksha and yakshini on the columns of the Buddhist site Bharhut of the second century BC. In the Gupta period the yakshinis were supplanted by river deities who continued to be identified by their vehicles, the goddess Jumna on the turtle and the goddess Ganga on the makara or crocodile. Reference to the gods and their particular vehicles is given in several texts. The vehicle of the God Siva is the bull, while his consort Durga's is the lion. Parvati's son Ganesa is carried by the rat and the son of Siva and Parvati, Karttikeya, by the peacock. Vishnu is associated with the bird, garuda, and Sarasvati the goose. An analysis of these associated deities and animals suggests a reflection or reinforcement of some of the qualities perceived in or expected of the deity. For example, both the makara and the turtle are strongly linked to water symbolism, while the bull has strong connections with sexual energies or man's wild, uncontrollable nature.

According to the text the *Asvalayana Grhya Parisista*, the buffalo is the vahana of Yama, Varahi and Vaivasvati the daughters of the sun-god. The goat or ram (a common sacrificial offering) is the vahana of Agni (fire deity) and the ram is the vahana of Kuvera (*Agni Purana*), while the rat is the well-known vehicle of Ganesa. Vishnu's vehicle, the bird garuda, according to Banerji, literally means 'garutman', a name of the sun-god in the *Vedas*. The swan or goose was the vehicle of Brahma. The earliest representation of the swan associated with certain gods is seen on some of the Asokan pillars. Four parrots were also associated with Agni.

The frequent appearance of the bull on Harappan seals from as early as 2500 BC suggests its significance, and the bull is still revered as the vehicle of Siva (Figure 3.14). The buffalo, on the other hand, continues to be a valued sacrificial animal and is perceived as a demon with mythological associations with the goddess Durga. Other warm-blooded animals were revered. From Harappan times the domesticated cow has held pre-eminence. As early as 2500 BC the people of the Indus valley culture measured their wealth in the numbers of their cattle. Anything the cow produced, from its milk to its dung, was prized and sacred. Even today, Hinduism forbids the killing or eating of the cow, and makes domestic and ritual use of its products (Figure 3.15).

The deer hunted by most predatory animals was called mriga, literally meaning 'rover'(or forest animal). Brahma was known in Indian tradition to have been born

as a deer. The horse was not indigenous to India and had a long historical association with victorious foreign invaders. The horse was revered and respected, representing mastery, proficiency and success in battle. Horses were highly prized and horse sacrifice became associated with kingship.

Fantastic creatures also make up some of the complex imagery on Hindu temples. Composite beasts comprising sea- or river-dwelling reptiles (makara) were combined with land animals, such as the tiger. Tiger- or lion-like forms, frequently appearing on the outer walls of temples as part of the iconography, are called vyala (meaning vicious). These rearing beasts overshadow a small human figure which cowers beneath them and are said to represent man's uncontrolled passions and appetites. The crouching figure is believed to symbolize man's powerlessness in the face of them, his depiction aiming to remind man of the need to transform and master these forces. Other creatures of the water, the apsaras or of the air, supparnas, must not be forgotten. Suparna, meaning fair-winged, was originally a term used in the *Rg Veda* to describe garuda, the giant kite of the sun, the vehicle of Vishnu. The suparna later became a class of beings who were depicted with human torsos bearing offerings to the Buddha. In Hindu sculpted friezes the apsaras form part of the panoply around the heads of the major deities.

Maithuna figures

Maithuna (couples engaged in love-making) are a recurrent theme in temple sculpture.[43] The union of male and female was understood to be sacred and creative in the broadest sense by the ancient peoples of India. The eroticism and sensuality of the

Figure 3.14 Nandi, temple in Tamil Nadu. Robert Elgood.

courtesan figure in Indian art was intended to arouse, while the portrayal of couples performing the sexual act was intended to depict the union of male and female energies, abundance and fertility, and thus prosperity and auspiciousness. Maithuna couples were therefore deliberately placed on temples for specific protective purposes. According to Devangana Desai, these maithuna images are found at points of transition or thresholds and are believed to strengthen these structurally weak architectural junctures.[44] Desai sees complex yogic/sexual positions as a symbolic diagram of forces. Most of these sculptures are integrated in friezes which run around the temple on three sides.

Emblems held by the Gods

The sastric texts give detailed accounts of the required form of the major Hindu gods and goddesses. As part of these prescriptions there are references to their individual implements, ornaments, and their vehicles (vahanas). In some texts these matters are dealt with in separate chapters, while others list them alongside the descriptions of the deities. The various implements may well suggest or reinforce the deities' qualities and attributes. The origin of these emblems associated with the deities is, according to Bhattacharya, traceable to the Indus valley civilization and the *Rg Veda*. The symbolic interpretations of many of these implements are explained in the *Vishnudharmottara Purana*. Evidence for this may be seen in some images, such as the seal depicting a figure known as the proto-siva. Despite uncertainties as to the identity of this bull-headed image this figure does possess what appears to be a horned bull mask. It is interesting to note that in

the Vedic period a sula (horns) ritual called 'Sulagava' sacrifice was performed in honour of a deity.

As well as animals and birds, chariots also had symbolic significance. Symbolic interpretations, while inaccurate and subjective, contribute to our understanding of the gods. Prescriptive texts such as the *Silpasastras* by their injunctions added a further allegorical dimension to the images, and tried to give form to the ideal world.

Various kinds of objects are shown placed in the hands of Hindu images or deities. Objects are classified under several headings, such as weapons, implements, musical instruments, animals and birds. There was a wide range of weapons such as the cakra (wheel), gada (mace), danda (cudgel), khetaka (a shield either round or oblong in shape made of wood, metal or skin), dhanus and sara (a bow and arrow: the bow of Siva is called pinaka and that of Vishnu is called sarnga), ankusa (elephant-goad), pasa (noose or lassoo), khadga (sword), vajra (thunderbolt), and agni (fire).[45] An object such as the sankha, a conch shell, was sounded on the battlefield in ancient times to inspire fear. The tanka is a stonemason's chisel, while hala is a ploughshare.

Various kinds of musical instruments are represented in early and late iconography.[46] Other objects in the hands of the divinities included water pots (kamandalu), lotus flowers, rosary beads or mirrors. A characteristic vessel, an emblem of Siva and Parvati, is the cup made out of a skull. Despite the fact that animals are rarely portrayed carried in the hand, the figure of Siva in the Gudimallam Linga carries a goat or a ram. It is interesting to recall this image of Siva standing on a yaksha and the association of the ram with the yaksha. The multivalence, the diverse origins and

Figure 3.15 Cow carving in a cave temple, Mamallapuram, Tamil Nadu. AD 700–800. Robert Elgood.

compositions of these deities is sometimes expressed by these emblems. An example of this can be seen in the depiction of Balarama with a ploughshare, pestle and drinking vessel.[47] These symbols are reminiscent of his earlier form as a harvest and bucolic deity. The god Vishnu's association with the sun is supported by his link with the vedic Adityas, Vasudeva and Narayana and his vehicle Garuda and Vishnu's emblem the chakra.

Festival Images

The festivals of the Hindu calendar are accompanied by special images. These may be freshly painted on the walls of one's home,[48] or clay images bought in the bazaar or made for the community to which one has made a donation. Many of these images are taken in procession through the community during these festivals. Festivals

such as Divali give rise to the manufacture of small figures of Lakshmi for individual worship. For some festival occasions, particularly Dasara, sometimes known as Durga-puja, large, brightly coloured images are made, composed of straw, twine and clay on a wooden frame. The whole exercise is paid for by a civic or religious instituion. Bengal is famous for the images of Durga which are made for the autumn festival of Navaratri or Dasara, during which the goddess is worshipped in her many forms. On the final night the image is taken in procession to the river and sunk.

In many festivals, images in procession are paraded before the people in the streets. In Orissa, the Jagannath deities are pulled in chariots down the wide street of Puri. While this Rathyatra festival at Puri is famous, there are many such local processions. Sometimes the actual images from the temple sanctum remain in place and duplicate images are used in processions. Madurai demonstrates this practice, where special festival images of the goddess Minakshi and her divine consort Siva Sundaresvara are carried through the streets in a royal palanquin.

In the context of the village, folk tradition plays an important role. During festival seasons village people sometimes decorate the outside and sometimes the inside of their homes. For example, in the Madhubani district in North Bihar the women paint elaborate and intricate artwork on the clay walls of their homes, themes determined by the festival season or the domestic occasions requiring ritual. In the case of weddings they paint auspicious designs on the walls of the new couple's bedroom or for festivals they create intricate geometric mandala to designate sacred space in front of the doorway or the altar of the home.

Painted Images

As well as images carried in procession at festivals, two-dimensional painting is also produced in a secular and religious context. Two ancient literary texts exist which describe the origin of painting in India. According to the *Chitralakshana* of Nagnajit, on the premature death of a Brahman's son a struggle ensued between the god of death and the Brahman. This struggle was finally resolved by Brahma, who instructed the Brahman to draw a picture of the boy, into which he breathed life. On requesting more accurate instructions as to the correct method of drawing, Brahma said it was necessary before Vedic sacrifices to draw a picture of the altar (as the drawing was to be done in colour, the drawing should be known as 'chitra', a pun on the word 'chit' as in 'Chaitya' and 'chitya') 'and that the

Brahman should go to Visvakarma to learn the rules of painting'.

The second tradition is found in the *Vishnudharmottaram* (Part I, Chapter 129 and Part III, Chapter 35). Here it is said that when Nara and Narayana were engaged in meditation, in order to prevent distraction from several persistent apsaras, Narayana drew a picture of a beautiful damsel with the juice of a mango tree. The apsaras, on finding the beauty of that picture surpassing theirs, fled. From this picture arose Urvasi, the most beautiful of heavenly women. The great sage Narayana thus created the art of citra and taught it to Visvakarma.

Bhattacharya suggests that the first legend, with its reference to sacrificial altars, ascribes a religious motive to the origin of painting. The conveying of likeness in portraiture through the use of tree juices, and colours to drive away sorrow and other evils, are some of the other objectives in the execution of paintings.

According to the *Vishnudharmatorra Purana* (Part III, Chapter 43):

> A proper painting brings on prosperity, removes adversity, cleanses and curbs anxiety, augments future good, causes unequalled and pure delight, kills evils of bad dreams and pleases the household deity – rules of painting should also be applied to carvings in iron, stone, wood or clay modelling.

According to the *Silpasastras*, painting embellished homes and palaces. This literature also refers to citrasalas (picture galleries) which were a part of city life.[49] Evidence for the existence of drawings is provided by the fact that Buddha was reputed to have prohibited his disciples from possessing imaginative drawings of men and women.[50] Figures of women, widows and prostitutes, dwarfs, generals, foot-soldiers, archers and wrestlers are some of the images proscribed, and natural objects such as mountains, seas, forests, water, cities and villages, markets, drinking places, battlefields, burning ground, roads, dawn, moonlight, falling rain, etc. were some of the subjects of paintings enumerated by the *Vishnudharmatorra Purana* and the *Samr Sutra.*

The paintings referred to in Buddhist literature were made on cloth, canvas, boards, mats, fans, boxes and walls of houses.[51] Paintings on canvas in the form of scrolls were known as patas, a variety of which was the Charana chitra or Nakhachitra. From the Buddhist period up until the eighth century and even later, these Charana chitras have been mentioned in religious and literary texts. Even today, pata is known in Bengal (especially Kalighat). The Charana (literally conduct) chitra consisted of pictures of happy and unhappy destinies of men after death according to their actions in this life. They show the pious enjoying heaven or the sinners undergoing various punishments in hell in the presence of Yamaraja. Appropriate labels were attached to each picture. They were shown to the people in the form of portable galleries, along with songs. In the Siamese Buddhist text (*Saratha Pakasini*) these citras are said to have been shown to the people by wandering Brahmans. Known as 'nakhas', such patas were commonly shown along with explanatory songs at East Bengal fairs at the beginning or end of the year.

Several rules existed in relation to the practice of painting. According to Bhattacharya, one should not keep in one's own house the paintings drawn by one's own hand. Several kinds of figures, in sculptural form or in painting, were prohibited from being displayed in or drawn on the walls of residential houses. Some might be placed in the assembly halls of kings, but not in their residences. Almost anything could be drawn on temples. Several kinds of figures expressing particular rasas were prohibited in residential quarters. Images of gods with terrifying appearances were forbidden in houses. They could be worshipped in towns, villages and some even in forests. Images or paintings which had some defect were believed to bring disaster. Hence all texts refer to these defects.

According to Bhattacharya, quoting from the *Vishnudharmottarra Purana,*

> Improper juxtaposition of colours, figures which are inexpressive, or have not proper positions (poses), are devoid of any Rasa, empty to look at, devoid of life movement and having defective limbs are unfit for a chitra....Proper position, proportion and spacing, gracefulness and resemblance are good qualities of a chitra. One that seems as if dancing by its posture, or appears to look frightened, laughing or graceful, thereby appears as if endowed with life, as if breathing – these are the figures of the auspicious type.[52]

The *Vishnudharmatorra Purana* also lays down rules regarding the representation of the back view of figures, colours, brushes, and methods of producing light and shade. The qualities of paintings were seen as sweetness, variety, a well-prepared background (Bhulamba), proportion, similarity to what is seen (Sadrisya) and minute execution. A good painting is one which can be appreciated by every class of people.

In many Vaishnava shrines in Bengal, there is a custom of illustrating the stories connected with the early life of Vasudeva-Krishna through the medium of different colours of rice powder. A section of the shrine is set aside for this purpose on a raised platform where, these scenes are painted with extreme care, using the coloured powder. Such pictorial depiction is probably referred to in the *Silparatna* as dhulichitra.[53]

The portrayal of the most abstract and yet precisely measured images is seen in the drawing and painting of the yantra (Figure 2.2). This is not an arbitrary invention but a revealed image of an aspect of cosmic structure. The linear yantras are composed of simple geometrical figures (line triangle, rectangle, circle, etc.). Rekha is the actual process of drawing the yantra. As a process it evokes in sequence the forces which compose the network of the yantra. According to Mookerjee it is a key to the unfolding of the visionary images and the guiding principle for all ritual achievements. It underlies the formal disciplines of geometry, astronomy, temple architecture and even ritual dance and music.

Painting in later Hinduism, inspired by the illustration of Buddhist, Jain and Islamic manuscripts, began to depict the most popular stories of the gods. The most prolifically illustrated and the most popular of these was the Gita Govinda, the love story of Vishnu's avatar Krishna and his lover Radha. The potency of these images was found not in vital imagery or precisely drawn forms but in the effect of strong, dramatic and symbolic use of colour. The stories of Krishna were successfully told with poetical lyricism and linked with drama, dance and music. They had a didactic function in keeping alive in the minds of the devotees and their children some of the fundamental principles of the Hindu faith.

Sculpture ornamenting the temples was also not free from painted embellishment.

This is most clearly visible in temples in South India even today. Paintings in the outer niches of temples such as the Kailasanatha temple in Kanchipuram are still visible. As in so many of the Indian religious arts, painting and sculpture are not isolated phenomena.

Conclusion

The interrelationship between the pre-Vedic and the Vedic ritual requirements and belief in the sacred have gradually brought about these fantastic and yet life-expressive images. Abstract aniconic or lifelike human forms aim to contain and emanate a force which has the power of manifestation at will in different forms and moods. Despite and perhaps on account of this immense flexibility and fluidity, the search and aim of the devout Hindu is to escape from this phenomenal world of man and spirits and to reach union with Visvarupa, the absolute and single deity without shape, form, place or time. Each Hindu deity is however part of a complex of deities; the absolute is both the fabric and interconnection of this network of relationships and hierarchies. Belief in the potential of rebirth governs and inspires the need to follow the dharma or law of appropriate behaviour.

For the average Hindu whose life requirements are not governed by philosophical debate, the contractual relationship between devotee and deity is cemented by the image. The deity, who is believed to reside in the image, is propitiated by gifts and in return will provide favours and answer prayers. Popular Hinduism thus becomes essentially material and practical and images are in turn fundamentally utilitarian. The depiction of the sacred in male and female images operates both within orthodox Hinduism and in a tribal and a village context. Religious objects can be housed in elaborate monumental temples or simply placed in the open air. Not only images but forest groves, rivers, caves and mountains in India are invested with sanctity. India itself, 'Mother India', is the Goddess.

Notes

1 This belief is also followed in many other religious movements, notably the Buddhist and Christian celibate orders.

2 O'Flaherty 1973, p. 318.

3 Meister 1984, p. 41.

4 The same power is believed to exist in the berry of the Elaeocarpus ganitrus known as the rudraksa – which is sacred to Siva (Fuller 1992, p. 58).

5 Blurton 1992, pp. 20-1.

6 Gritli 1984, pp. 12-18.

7 See Maxwell 1982, p. 214.

8 See Blurton 1992, p. 84.

9 O'Flaherty 1973, p. 316.

10 See Blurton 1992, p. 91.

11 Danielou 1964.

12 O'Flaherty 1973, p. 317.

13 Blurton 1992, p. 110.

14 For further information on the snake see Chandra 1978.

15 Gonda 1993.

16 Panini, IV.3.98.

17 For more information on these stories see Blurton 1992, pp. 118-23. For Hindu myths see Zimmer 1946 or O'Flaherty 1975.

18 See Blurton 1992, p. 125.

19 See Doshi 1971, pp. 125-6.

20 Carstairs, *The Eastern Anthropologist*, nos 3 and 4, p. 180.

21 Blurton 1992, pp. 115 and 134.

22 See Danielou 1964.

23 See Shah 1985.

24 A recent study by Kinsley (1986) however suggests that the goddesses in local forms should still be seen as individual entities and that one should resist the earlier tendency to treat them as one overarching Goddess.

25 see Coomaraswamy 1971.

26 See Kinsley 1986, pp. 200-1.

27 Seth 1992, p. 53.

28 I am grateful to Naman Ahuja drawing my attention to the early Sunga terracotta female figurines who have five weapons in their hair.

29 *Rg Veda*, Vol. I, 32, Vol. II, 12, etc.

30 Kinsley 1986, p. 129.

31 Ibid., p. 19.

32 Ibid., p. 151.

33 Shulman 1985, pp. 307 and 339.

34 Ibid., p. 339.

35 For further information on tantra see Mookerjee 1985 and Khanna 1979.

36 See Fuller 1992, p. 45.

37 In Tamil known as 'ananku'.

38 Srivastava 1972, pp. 152-4, 258.

39 See Blurton 1992, pp. 123-5.

40 See Vogel 1926, pp. 1 and 2.

41 Sutherland 1991, p. 40.

42 See Dubois 1928, p. 648.

43 For further information on mithuna see Chapter 4.

44 Desai 1988.

45 See Banerji 1941, pp. 329 and 330.

46 Ibid., pp. 331-2.

47 Ibid., p. 335.

48 For example, the serpent image painted on each side of the doorway for the monsoon festival of Nag Panchami.

49 See *Vishnudharmatorra Purana*, Vol. III, p. 43.

50 *Cullavagga* V1 3

51 According to Bhattacharya (1947), the chitra is divided into the Bhaumika, Kudyaka and Urddhvaka with reference to their position in the house. The Bhaumika chitra meant decorations on the floors which might be painted using powdered or tinctured colours, inlaid with coloured stones and gems. The decorations on the walls were called Kudyaka, and those on top of pillars, beams and ceilings as Urddhvaka chitra. These classifications could be applied to painting as well as sculpture.

52 Bhattacharya 1947, p. 394.

53 According to Banerji 1941.

CHAPTER 4 Hindu Sacred Architecture

The *Oxford Dictionary* defines the term sacred as that space set apart for, or dedicated to, some religious purpose. The English word temple in this instance designates the Hindu sacred area. The word temple derives from the Roman 'templum' which referred to a square area fenced off for augury. In Sanskrit the temple is referred to by several names, one of which is 'vimana', literally meaning 'measuring out, traversing ... or chariot of the gods'. The temple itself was perceived as god's chariot, which is implicit in the name vimana.[1] The Hindu temple needed to conform to accurate prescribed measurements in order to be spiritually efficacious. It is a visual manifestation of the cosmos which reflects the Hindu philosophy of the universe as a macrocosm and man as the microcosm. The temple building is an analogy of both the universe and the human body. The temple is not solely an area for religious ritual but the very fabric is believed to represent and to be capable of becoming the divinity itself. Hindus believe it to be a transmitter and focus of divine energies wherein in the central darkness of the temple which is, from earliest times, consistently referred to as the womb chamber (garbhagrha), the regeneration or rebirth of the individual may occur. This darkness is believed to be a necessary condition for the transformation which is wrought in the devotee. The devotee is one who visits the temple, participates with inner vision and is not a mere spectator. It is this interplay between the potential divinity within man and the divinity within the architectural form which creates the purpose and the dialogue between the two. The science of the architecture of the temple is designed very precisely to create the conditions in which this synthesis is most likely to occur.

This chapter will explore the origins of the Hindu temple, examining early sacred sites and shrines associated with groves and trees in Indian tribal and village areas. It will analyse temple design and study the meaning and symbolism of its component parts. This will be followed by a study of the ancient sastraic prescriptions, the equivalent of building manuals. The relationship between sculpture and architecture will be considered both as regards the central icon and its potency and the function of the decoration of the interior and exterior walls of the temple. An analysis of the differences between northern and southern temples will be undertaken. Finally, ritual practice associated with the temple will be explored.

The principal reason for the construction of a temple is to house the deity. The presence and blessing of the divinity was considered essential for the well-being of the local population and the construction of a temple was a statement of the good order of society. A major factor determining temple construction was the ruler's need for legitimacy.[2] The rulers acquired the respect and recognition of the Brahmans, on which their legitimacy depended, by the construction of temples. A ruler's dharma, literally meaning 'duty', included the unwritten contractual obligation to build temples. By this means rulers acquired merit for themselves and prosperity for their subjects.

The Hindu temple was sometimes an institution with a legal identity of its own, representing the titular deity who acquired a status similar to a property owner.

> It could house a deity who on occasion would be regarded as the suzerain overlord by the reigning king and thus acted as a further source of legitimacy. Temple ritual imitated the daily routine of the household and the deity was treated at least as a feudal chief if not the overlord.[3]

Origin of the Temple

Sacred places

Hindus revere many forms and elements of the natural world. Rivers, the earth itself, trees, sacred groves, mountains and caves all constitute special places in the Hindu mind. Associated with these forms are the key elements of water, air, earth, fire and space. Rivers are associated with the goddess and water with fertility. Hindus identify the earth with the body of the goddess. They revere not only trees, which are sanctified and protected by railings, but even the shade under trees. The gods of Hinduism are said to be always attracted to mountains and caves and these natural forms are important in understanding the form which developed in the medieval Hindu temple. The fact that the terms Meru and Kailasa (the names of mountains in the Hindu epics) are synonymous with the temple demonstrates this connection, as does the actual superstructure, which resembles the mountain peak (and in South India the royal crown) and is called 'crest' or sikhara. The tiered effect and the curved shape of the tower of the Hindu temple enhances the effect of a mountain peak. This analogy became more complex in the multiplication of towers which suggested a mountain range seen in the development of the North Indian temple. The use of caves for sanctuaries and as places of religious focus pre-dates the free-standing temples as places of worship. It is interesting to observe that the most sacred part of the temple is the central shrine or garbhagrha, which in its unadorned form resembles the darkness of the cave or in human terms the womb.

Specific places in India became invested with sanctity and legend. For example, numerous myths recount how fragments of the dismembered body of Sati, Siva's first wife, fell to earth on to the soil of India. At these legendary places shrines, called pitha, which literally means where the goddess has taken her seat, were established to the goddess. They are often associated with places of outstanding natural beauty, at the junction of two rivers, near a cave or deep in a forest. The idea of a localization of the sacred in a particular place was also prevalent in Tamil Nadu, a concept which gradually contributed to the growth of sacred sites in other parts of India.

Sacred sites

It is customary for Hindus to make regular pilgrimages to sacred sites. In Hinduism human life is likened to a long journey of many stages, frequently visualized as a progression upwards through various stages of consciousness. These pilgrimage sites are referred to as tirthas, literally fords or crossing places, and are believed to act as places of inner spiritual transformation. The sacred sites are seen as places of transit, not ends to the human journey, but intervals on the road which offer joy, release and renewal. Hindus anticipate that pilgrimage to these sites will punctuate life's path with 'devotion', bhakti, and 'release', moksha. The *Mahabharata* speaks of hundreds of pilgrimage sites.

Originally these tirthas or pilgrimage places were on the banks of rivers, lakes or sea-shores. Water tanks found as early as 2500 BC in the cities of Mohenjo Daro and Harappa are believed to have had a ritual purpose. Water is indeed a prerequisite in the selection of sites for the later free-standing Hindu temples: 'The gods always play where groves are near, rivers, mountains and springs and in towns with pleasure-gardens.'[4]

If water is not available naturally or artificially it should be present symbolically. Three jars of water should be placed in the centre of the sacred site. Rivers and lakes, identified with the lotus, the symbol of renewal and enlightenment, are also celebrated for their healing powers. The antiquities scholar, the late Reginald Smith also indicated a link between underground streams and the location of Stone Age sites.[5] Further work on this subject has suggested a significant link between sites worldwide and a pattern of underground, blind streams and geodetic lines.[6]

Tribal Beliefs in Holy Shrines and Places

It is a widespread presumption among historians that the indigenous, pre-Aryan population of India contributed to the creation of what is now known as Hinduism. A continuity of images and ritual custom has been suggested by the possible link between the proto-Siva masked figure (Figure 2.3) from the Indus valley culture of 2000 BC, and the buffalo-horned masked dancers from the contemporary Maria Gond tribals from the Bastar district. The continuation of ritual beliefs and practices may also be seen in animistic beliefs such as the worship of trees and stones which remain a part of tribal and village custom. Underlying this mythology is the belief in a host of spirits which inhabit rocks and mountains, haunt trees or are associated with rivers, waterfalls, etc. Shrines to which offerings are brought are often constructed at these places. For all the tribes, whether major, like the Santal, Munda or Oraon or minor like the Birhor, Chenchu or the forest-hunting tribes of South India, the whole world is held to be full of spirits. Benevolent spirits are found everywhere, while malevolent spirits are believed to inhabit lonely places and graveyards. Because of this prevalence of spirits certain tribal groups house protective deities or associate them with certain images or shrines, to which they bring offerings or hold ritual ceremonies. Some tribes, for example, the Nagas and the Malayarayans in Kerala, regard stones as symbols of the deities. The wooden post associated with the Gond's tribal deity, known as Aki pen, is a square pointed post (munda) which is carved from teakwood and usually bears the symbols of the sun and moon. In India the tribal image generally consists of a simple pointed or vermilion marked stone or a set of a few wooden poles. Some terracotta pots on an earthern altar plastered with cow dung may also represent the tribal deity.

The shrines housing tribal images are usually of very simple construction, often associated with a large tree, a small plant or a pole, rock or water source near a tribal or village settlement. In some Santal villages the majhi-than (shrine) is a raised mud platform over which there is a well-kept thatched roof supported by four corner posts and a central post about five feet in height, but in other villages only the mud platforms and posts are permanent and the roof is covered with grass only at the time of the ceremony.[7] As in the sacred grove, clay figures of elephants and horses are kept in the shrine. As well as the sacred post and the round stones worshipped by several tribal groups,[8] the miniature dolmens of the Gonds may be an example of a possible continuity with much earlier pre-Hindu traditions of image worship. The dolmen resembles the megalithic village and way-side shrines and usually consists of three or four standing stones supporting a capstone.[9] Memorials to the dead in the form of small dolmens are common to tribal India. Dolmens are still being constructed by the Khasi, Munda, Oraon, Bhil, Kurumba and Malayarayan tribes.[10] These dolmens are not only memorials to the dead but commemorate the importance of the site which is marked by them. They may be said to serve a similar function as the Hindu temple insofar as they are believed to hold or restrain the presence of the invoked divinity.[11] It has been suggested that simple flat-roofed early Hindu shrines found in

India, such as temple number 17 at Sanci, the Vishnu temple at Eran, the Kankali Devi temple at Tigawa, may well derive from the tribal shrine or dolmen. Despite the evidence of the absorption of early ritual worship in chaitya shrines and sacred groves in present-day tribal and Hindu practice, Hinduism's principal root is in Vedic practice.

Vedic Altars and Sheds

During the Vedic period from 1500 to 600 BC, ritual revolved around human and animal sacrifice. Vedic priests were less concerned with beliefs and ideas than with precision in the performance and correct incantation of Vedic prayers. Responsibility for the ceremonial lay in the hands of a hierarchy of priests. The conceptual basis for Vedic sacrifice was that the human body was the symbol of the primordial man or purusa and in the enactment of his immolation the creation of the world was re-enacted. This burnt offering was conveyed to the gods, with the smoke of the fire (agni) thus functioning as a celebrant. This sacrifice required an encircled but open shrine. The sacrifice was conducted on open-air altars, which were constructed out of perforated bricks and conformed in shape and scale to a requisite formula. Despite the fact that the Hindu temple is covered and permanent, one may see links between the cosmic associations of the open-air sacrifice, the symbolic inner devotions in the presence of the flame and the symbolic sacrifice seen in the coconut or blood offerings in shrines or temples.

It is interesting to note that the summit of the temple tower is given the name vedi, the Sanskrit word for altar. A further link is seen by some of the names given to the temple, such as prasada, sadma and sadanam, which denote the act of sitting.[12] The method of corbelling and the trabeate arch used in the process of temple construction are also, according to Kramrisch, derivatives of the process of piling bricks on the altar.

Coexistent with Vedic open-air altars were the oldest known Indian sacred buildings which were both enclosed and roofed and are known to historians as sacrificial sheds. In Sanskrit these are called sadas meaning 'seat', the sacrificial operation being itself a sattra 'session'.[13] The sheds were constructed of wood and covered on all sides with mats, with a ridged roof and an easterly orientation.[14] These are thought to have been temporary enclosures and places for ritual initiation. Coomaraswamy suggests that man emerged from these enclosures following ritual initiation like an embryo from a womb.[15] The easterly orientation and the darkened enclosures of the sacrificial sheds are elements found in the evolved Hindu temple.

Shrines

Several ancient Indian texts suggest the worship and housing of deities from as early as the fourth century BC. According to Meister, in the text the *Astadhyayi*, Panini mentions a number of revered deities who received active worship and oblations. These included a number of Vedic deities (Agni, Indra, Varuna, Bhava, Sarv, Rudra Surya, Soma) and female deities, and point to a rise in bhakti worship with specific reference to Vasudeva and Arjuna.[16]

Ritual worship was also said to have extended to the Lokapalas and Yakshas. Meister suggests that reference to this ritual

worship of deities presupposes the existence of shrines. He supports this view by citing Kautilya's *Arthasastra* which was compiled in the third century AD, and referred to the placing of images within a fortified city of temples dedicated to the god Siva and prescribed that images of Durga, Vishnu, Kumara and Indra should be set in niches.

Early Buddhist relief carvings of secular and religious building from Bharhut, Sanchi, Bodh Gaya, Mathura and Amaravati show the frequent use of the vedika railings which surround trees and mounds. This railing was originally constructed of bamboo or timber but was subsequently built of brick or stone. These Hinayana carvings suggest that shrines were modelled on prevailing domestic structures and were commonly used in the worship of yakshas, nagas and other divinities as well as serving a Buddhist purpose. An early text describes Buddha relaxing on a dais, which consisted of a stone slab resting on four other stones, a most basic form of shrine. This simple dais (similar to the form of the Vedic altar) was often placed under trees and enclosed by railings. The Buddhist carvings show that despite some roofless shrines, others had large compounds, pillared pavilions and two or more storeys under a thatched roof.[17] These pavilions, apparently constructed of timber, were sometimes built around a tree.[18]

Evidence for the use of such structures for Hindu deities can be seen by excavation at the Gudimallam shrine (Figure 2.6) which reveals similar Vedic-type railings. Early Buddhist and Jain literature as well as Kautilya's *Arthasastra* also refer to various types of structures and their embellishments prevailing in the early centuries BC and in the Saka, Kusana and transitional periods. According to Meister:

Such evidence can conjure up a picture of a contemporary Indian city, with moat (parikha), rampart (prakara), bastioned and turreted gate houses, corner bastions, ornamental gates, and busy streets lined with private and public buildings, such as the royal palace shops and emporia.[19]

Jain texts of this period such as the *Rayapaseniya* detail the Kusana art of Mathura. The text discusses city gates, defences and quarters teeming with chaityas, stupas, theatres, lakes, lotus ponds, gardens and islands. It enumerates decorative ornaments, such as torana-salabhanjikas, ceilings painted with vegetal and figural patterns, pillar brackets bearing gandharvas and vidyadharamithunas, flags, umbrellas, festoons and arches embellished with garlands and bells.[20] It is interesting to note that all the designs mentioned in such Jain texts are present on Kusana sculpture and reliefs from Mathura.

Epigraphic evidence also supports this suggestion of the existence of small shrines dedicated to the worship of images as early as the fourth to first century BC. Meister refers to the discovery of significant inscriptions, one example being from 131 BC which revealed that a pillar was constructed to honour the supreme god Vasudeva. Other inscriptions refer to the installation of images in stone shrines. An inscription from Nandsa, Udaipur district, records the performance of Vedic sacrifices following construction of shrines to Brahma, Indra, Prajapati and Vishnu. An inscription recovered from the wall of a well at Ghosundi in Rajasthan records a royal donation for the construction of a shrine. It mentions an enclosing wall built around stone objects of worship 'for the divinities Sankarshana-Vasudeva who are unconquered and are lords of all'.[21]

A further example may be found at the ancient site of Vidisha where an inscription from the shaft of a column states: 'this Garuda column of the excellent temple of the Bhagvat was erected by Gautamiputra.'[22] Remains of an elliptical structure near this column may well have been the temple in front of which this column was erected. The elliptical building, if it was a temple, is a rare form, but perfectly illustrates at a very early date the philosophical belief that the form of the temple reflects the cosmos, since Hindu cosmology believes the universe to be ovoid.

Despite the fragmentary remains of the shrines to which these inscriptions refer, there is increasing architectural evidence of the form of these early shrines from the time of Asoka Maurya to the early Kusana period. Rock-cut shrines and foundations of other constructed shrines suggest that temples existed in circular (vratta), elliptical (vrttayata) and apsidal (capakara) forms. The Ajvika caves at Barabar, for example, from the Gaya district of Bihar, contain inscriptions referring to the rule of Asoka and his grandson and preserve both circular and elliptical hut-forms with domed or vaulted roofs.

By the third or fourth century AD, we see at Nagarjunakonda a rectilinear shrine with square cells, a type that ultimately virtually eclipsed all other forms.[23] The decorative elements found on these cave temples reveal the use of such elements as ribbed and vaulted ceilings which suggest a knowledge of wood construction. These features persist and develop throughout the history of rock-cut architecture, finding their apotheosis in the rock-cut temple of Ellura.

The ancient text the *Visnudharmottapurana*, which pre-dates the tenth century AD, contains references to temples dedicated to the major deities, but also refers to yaksha temples and to shrines to Kama, god of love. The absence of any surviving evidence of these lesser shrines and temples may indicate that they were made of perishable materials since it is likely that they continued to be used for active worship alongside the great monumental temples.

From the available evidence it is possible to suggest that the evolution of the form of the free-standing temple arose from a synthesis of pre-Vedic and Vedic practice. The pre-Vedic elements are characterized by a belief in the spirit world, exemplified by ancestor worship at the commemoratory tribal stones or dolmens and by the belief in the spirit-dwelling sacred enclosed pillar and the tree shrine. These elements are echoed in the Hindu free-standing stone linga and in the belief that the numinous and transient spirit may dwell in such an icon, and the rites and practices associated with fertility and regeneration. The Vedic elements may be seen in the dark womb-like structure of the inner sanctum of the Hindu temple which echoes the intimate darkness of the Vedic sacrificial sheds; and the piling of stones (similar to bricks) in the monumental form of the Hindu temple. The sacred fire which was believed to purify and ignite the Vedic sacrifice on the open-air altar is reflected in the symbolic fire in the Hindu temple, while the vedic sacrificial victim is echoed in the offering of the flame, the coconut and the devotees' symbolic inner sacrifice to the Hindu deity. The establishment of the Buddhist stupa and monastery as a central institution was in turn responsible for the growth of religious building.

Objectives

> Let him who wishes to enter the worlds that are reached by sacrificial offerings and the performance of religious obligations (*istapurta*) build a temple to the gods, by doing which he attains both the results of sacrifice and the performance of religious obligations.[24]

This ancient text implies that the ritual religious and sacrificial objectives of entry to the heavenly realms (svarga) are achieved by the building of temples. The temple provides more than just a meeting place and an area for the prayers of the faithful. Kramrisch suggests that, unlike the building of the Vedic altar, the Hindu temple has to be seen by the devotee. It is also itself an offering and a threshold or crossing place in life's journey. The Hindu temple aims to be a representation of the perfect universe and to be identifiable as such, as well as to contain and house the deity. The establishment of cult image worship in temples in the early medieval period entailed the abandonment of the old Vedic ceremonial as a separate ritual performance.

Temple Elements

While having variations in external form, Hindu temples share certain common components (Figure 4.1). The three main vertical components of every Hindu temple are the base, the covered sanctum (garbhagrha) and its tower or super-structure. The base of the temple is sometimes constructed on a raised plinth and often next to a water tank. The enclosed sanctuary or garbhagrha has usually three, but sometimes four entrances and a central icon. While the temple interior may possess

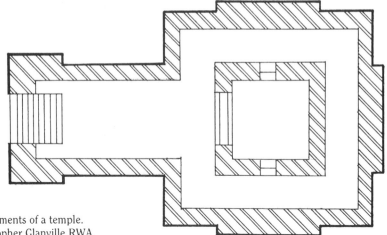

Figure 4.1 The elements of a temple.
Drawing by Christopher Glanville RWA.

a limited range of carvings, the exterior is usually covered with a numerous and complex range of symbolic sculptured reliefs. The superstructure, while the norm, does not appear to have been indispensable. Flat roofs illustrated in the reliefs of Bharhut show alternative forms such as an open pillared hall, rectangular or round, with a second storey. The tower however became the accepted form for the covering of the shrine or sanctum. It is built with a gentle curve in the north and a pyramidal form in the south. The tower became increasingly complex in the medieval period when various aedicules and miniature sikharas were added to its composition.

In addition to the simple covered and enclosed shrine, a temple may consist of additional carved and pillared halls surrounded by subsidiary shrines and buildings. The temple often stood in the centre of a broad, rectangular platform, on the corners of which were secondary shrines. These secondary shrines introduced the presence of the other gods of the Hindu pantheon within the world symbolized by the temple. The temple itself was sometimes so large that it became the

centre of an entire temple town with walls and gate towers, as, for example, at Srirangam, in Tamil Nadu.

In Hindu architecture the expansion of form is an overriding principle. Remnants of the temple's monolithic qualities have involved this outward movement and achieved a visual balance between action and repose, dynamic and static forms.[25]

Temple Symbolism

The temple's most simple function was to protect the deity manifest in the sacred icon. The covered shrine developed gradually from the open tree shrines, naga shrines and shrines to deities such as Vasudeva from as early as the first century BC.

As well as being a symbolic palace, the temple design was based on a mandala or geometric diagram of the universe. The Hindu temple was a three-dimensional form of this cosmic two-dimensional chart. The mandala is an attempt to express and contain the cosmic dynamic and the temple is similarly said to be a powerhouse of energies obtained with absolute certainty from the precise mathematical and geometrical formulae by which it is built. In more prosaic terms, the mandala with its central deity is paralleled by the central location of the icon in the sanctuary. This is also visualized as a king in his palace surrounded by his retinue. Subsidiary gods such as saints, planetary and local folk deities associated with Hinduism stand guard over the eight directions of space. In Hindu cosmology the centre of the universe is conceived of as the symbolic mountain of Meru and it therefore follows logically that the tower which surmounts the icon in the womb chamber resembles a mountain.

It has been suggested that another aspect of the architectural form of the Hindu temple incorporates the embodiment of time. In the more complex temples a multiplication and an 'expanding repetition' of shrines and aedicules echo ideas such as the cycles of growth and disintegration in Hindu thought. The cycle of life, birth, death and renewal is so central to Hindu philosophy that it permeates all aspects of Hindu art. The square is the fundamental form of Indian architecture but it must not be forgotten that the square presupposes the circle and results from it. Life, growth and movement are visualized in a circle, while the square is perceived as a mark of order, finality, and of perfection beyond life and death.

A further symbolic aspect of the temple and its functions is linked to the deliberate darkness of its interior and the ritual practices associated with it. As has been mentioned above, the darkness of the inner sanctum and the symbolic sacrifice of the worshipper and his offerings provides an environment for his transformation. Coomaraswamy suggests that the worshipper, consciously or unconsciously, re-enacts a ritual of symbolic self-sacrifice. This also involves darsan in both seeing and being seen.

> The sacrifice is essentially a mental operation both outwardly and inwardly, or in any case inwardly. It is prepared by the sacrificer's 'whole mind and whole self'. The Sacrificer is, as it were, emptied out of himself, and is himself the real victim. The true end of the cult is one of reintegration and resurrection, attainable not by a merely mechanical performance of the service, but by a full realization of its significance, or even by this comprehension alone. The Agnihotra, or burnt offering, may be ... an interior self-sacrifice, in which the heart is the altar, the outer man the offering, and the flame the dompted self.[26]

Coomaraswamy goes on to describe the symbolic ascent of the worshipper (following his immolation) from the sanctum through the tower and the finial at its apex. The resemblance of tower to mountain and sanctum to cave reinforce this powerful symbolic movement and aspiration. This powerful vertical axis of sanctum to finial is also perceived as forces of energy which radiate in ascending, descending and horizontal directions. The upward aspiration has parallels in Hindu goals of enlightenment and in the recurrent visual depiction of the path, aspiration and pattern of the universe resembling a tree supporting the universe in its ample branches.

The temple is not only likened to the universe or macrocosm but also to the cross-legged figure of man and to the body of the primordial man (purusha). The purusha's bodily frame is suggested by the temple's square plan; the womb, the garbhagrha; the door of the sanctum the mouth, while the outer walls express the many facets of personality. Man's spinal column, which in Hindu thought is the pathway for energy in its ascent to higher levels of consciousness or chakras, is paralleled by the temple tower. Coomaraswamy likened this theoretical exit or ladder from chamber to finial to the cranial foramen in man. Man's foramen corresponds to the circular aperture at the apex of the temple tower which is significantly closed by the solar form of the amalaka. It is customary among Hindus for the foramen, which is naturally open at birth and gradually closes, to be opened again at death when the skull is ritually broken prior to cremation. The gavaksha, the symbolic openings in the tower, refer to the deity's eyes or the pathways for the deity's emanations. The active manifestations of the deity which may be termed his arms are represented by the subsidiary deities placed at specific axes to the main image.

Characteristic Elements

The temples are characterized by certain common elements in their ornamentation and construction. By and large these temples have plinths, chambers and superstructures which have a hierarchy of mouldings, friezes and niches. The lowest mouldings begin with petals of the lotus flower just above floor level and are said to be binding. They include elephant courses, which suggest rain clouds and a sprouting waterpot moulding. Niches placed in these mouldings contain images of subsidiary incarnations such as the Saptamatrkas, Vishnu's avatars or sometimes narrative texts.

Above this level there is usually a frieze which emphasizes the central deity with attending deities on either side and guardians of the eight directions on the corners. Celestial maidens, composite animals and musicians emerge from the secondary offsets in the walls. The transitional cornice mouldings above the frieze sometimes carry narrative reliefs which depict scenes from the epics (*Mahabharata* and *Ramayana*) or the *Puranas*.

The door

Temple doors can be interpreted as the thresholds between the secular and spiritual worlds and passages through which people may be transformed or regenerated. Carvings, which include sculptured deities around, below and on the door lintels and jambs promote and reinforce this potential passage. The door to the sanctum has also been described as God itself. One is reminded of the reference in The Bible (John X:9) when Christ said of himself, 'I am the door'. The deity to which the temple is dedicated often appears in the lintel and presides over the dvarapalas or door keepers.

Protective tree spirits were carved on thresholds and doors in early Buddhist and Hindu caves and free-standing Hindu temples. By the sixth to eighth centuries AD these had been largely replaced by river goddesses. This may well have been intended to express a growing belief in lustration with water from sacred rivers, which was thought to transpose the divine essence to the image. The empowering of the image would therefore have been maintained by this symbolic ritual bathing. Even today the sanctity or divine presence is reinforced by the ceremony abhiseka, during which a liquid is poured through a hole in the roof of the shrine on to the image.[27] These river spirits were occasionally accompanied by celestial maidens, vegetal motifs, lotuses and dwarfs or Gana figures. According to Kramrisch, the images associated with the river at the temple entrance effect a ritual bath:

> The energy of the waters is so great that the bath itself confers Diksa, initiation: Ablution, transmutation, and initiation are effected at the entrance.... There inception of a new life is beset with dangers. The guardians of the threshold thus are the most enduring images of the door where perils must be warded off and contamination with the impurities of the world prevented.[28]

Symbolic doors also appear in the form of niches which hold aspects of the main enshrined divinity. In some temples the niches are sunk into the wall while in others they project like balconies.

Windows or gavakshas

The temple possesses solid but symbolic window-shaped forms which are called gavakshas. The term gavaksha means literally 'go' (cow), 'aksha' (eye). These architectural features are said to derive from the curves of light, flexible wood, such as bamboo or tree branches.[29] Visibly solid and without the slightest opacity, the gavakshas function not as apertures for the illumination of the temple's dark interior but to facilitate transmissions radiating from its central icon: 'God is the light as he is the door. He sends forth his splendour in the darkness of the Garbhagrha and upwards across the innumerable 'raywheels'.'[30]

The gavakshas are also described as windows through which the deity looks out. In some cases, for example, in the Parasuramesvar temple at Bhubanesvar, this is shown explicitly in the form of a lion surmounting the gavaksha which is a solar animal. From the tenth century onwards, the Kirtimukha mask surmounts the symbolic aperture of the sikhara or temple tower.

Kakshasanas

Kakshasanas, stone benches, have angled backrests and appear in temples in projecting porches of open mandapas and along ambulatory paths. The presence of these seats in the majority of northern shrines support texts, which suggests that the halls were intended not only as places of prayer for the approaching devotees but as stages for dance, music, drama and even as resting places for weary pilgrims.

Kirtimukha

Temple doors, walls, niches and windows are enhanced by symbolic adornments. Pre-eminent among these symbols, often as a repetitive motif, is an image known as the kirtimukha, (Figure 4.2). It appears on cornices and temple walls and at the socle or bases of temples. The kirtimukha is described as a fusion of man and beast, while its appearance shows a creature bulging with power, inflated with breath and modelled on a death-like skull. This face, or death-mask, is known as the devourer and symbolizes the passing of time, while its inflated breath suggests the vitality and power of the lion. In the guise of the lion it is known as Simha-mukha. In West and East India the masked face is known respectively as Grassamukha and Rahur-mukha, both of which refer to a devourer. The lack of the depiction of a lower jaw in the majority of kirtimukhas is

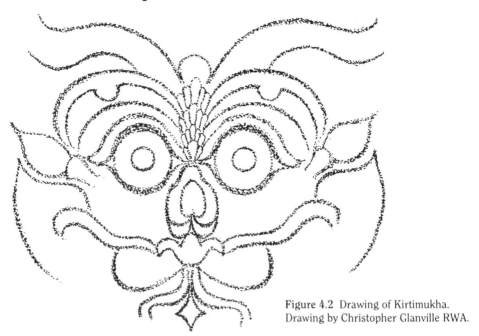

Figure 4.2 Drawing of Kirtimukha.
Drawing by Christopher Glanville RWA.

said to express the lack of the finality of death and the maintenance and cyclical progression of life. The motif becomes common from the early part of the fourth century AD and it has been suggested that the origin of the kirtimukha may be found in the Chinese T'ao T'ieh, the 'devourer' and in the lion masks from classical times. We may also see its echo in the gargoyle, a common feature of medieval Christian architecture.[31] The characteristic image of the kirtimukha faces linked by pearl garlands became extremely popular thoroughout North India from the tenth century onwards.

Vyala

Another motif which became popular in temples from the ninth century AD is that of a man riding a beast or lion (Figure 2.9). This beast is known as sardula or vyala and is said to represent the wild, uncontrollable energy of nature. This bestial form of the vyala or rearing lion frequently appears in medieval temple bhadra offsets. This mythical, sometimes composite, creature possesses a lion's body, while its head sometimes resembles the horned lion or kirtimukha. It may also have the trunk of an elephant, a parrot's beak, a goat's or even a human face. The vyala's first appearance was as an image carved on a bracket which supported an overhanging cornice. In the South Indian tradition it retained this location, while in the North the motif became integrated into the body of the temple and appeared in a limited number of locations. In the tenth century vyalas of equal stature with exterior niche images came to inhabit the vertical indentations that separate the offsets of the temple wall. Unlike the apsara, the vyala is never placed on any projecting offset.

The interpretation of the vyala is based on an understanding of the potential power and significance of the lion. Its form derived from Achaemenid Persia, where it was

Figure 4.3 Maithuna, Visvanatha temple, Khajuraho. Chandella dynasty, eleventh century.
Don Stadtner.

associated with royalty. It is invariably shown on the walls of North Indian temples with two male human figures, one riding and the other crouching below the animal's upraised paw. One or both figures bear swords or shields. The man who attempts to ride or to tame the vyala can be seen as a ksatriya warrior or royal knight. These images of man's attempt to subdue a lion with the sword may be interpreted as the mind's attempt to master or control his wilder physical, instinctive and emotional nature.[32] It represents both royal and metaphysical force. In the Chandella temples of the tenth century the man riding Sardula is interspersed with images of the apsaras and other goddesses. By the eleventh century, in North India, it became fashionable to replace these vyala forms with images of ascetics.

Maithuna

An increasingly prevalent motif in temple iconography from the first century AD was the erotic or loving couple known as the maithuna image (Figure 4.3).[33] These appeared on monuments such as the Sanci stupa and the door frames of Deogarh. They also appeared at Ajanta, Ellora, Karle, Aurangabad, Bhubaneswar, Mukhalingam, Rajm, Sirpur, Lalitagiri, Udaygiri and Baijanatha. Mithuna couples were most commonly found on thresholds and weak architectural junctures. This, together with evidence of ancient texts, supports the suggestion that they fulfilled a magico-protective function and were remnants of ancient non-Vedic fertility rituals.[34] The *Silpasastras*, *Puranas* and other authoritative texts implicitly recognized the auspicious (mangala) and protective-defensive (raksartham-varanartha) aspects of erotic depictions. Texts such as the *Agni Purana* and the *Brhat Samhita* also suggest that doors of the inner sanctum, or garbhagrha, should be protected by such imagery. Despite ritual offerings to the goddess to promote childbirth on an individual basis, texts which allow erotic images on sacred temples while discouraging their appearance on the walls of domestic houses provide evidence of the Hindu attitude towards the depiction of sexual coupling as generative of moksha (spiritual liberation), rather than fertility or pleasure.

The early depictions of maithuna couples were small, discreet and held to be purely magico-religious in function. An example of these types of images can be seen at Ellura in the interior of the Kailasa temple from the sixth to seventh centuries. These images are suggestive of folk cults rather than orthodox Brahmanic Hinduism due to their unsophisticated graceless appearance.[35] The form of these images pointed to the continuity of primitive and popular cultural elements or an 'other Hinduism' in Indian society.[36] The more dramatic and overt appearance of large and aristocratic couples, found in such sites as Aihole, Badami and Pattadakal, have been explained by the growing power and involvement of the aristocracy in patronage. This is also observed in the works of Sanskrit poets like Kalidasa, Subandhu, Bana, Harsa and others.[37] Gradually from AD 900, there was a profusion of a more consistent, blatant and sophisticated treatment of sexual depictions of the maithuna couple. By AD 950 maithuna was already represented in sculptural decorations of the temples of the western Deccan such as Mahakut, Aihole, Badami cave I,

Pattadakal, Ellora and so on.[38] Maithuna figures are seen on the Jain Parsvanatha temple of Khajuraho and the Buddhist temple No. 45 at Sanchi as well as Hindu temples belonging to the Saiva, Vaishnava and Sakta sects. Different regions of India display varied treatment in the placing and emphasis of the mithuna or maithuna figures. For example, the Sun temple in Modhera shows erotic figures on the plinth, shafts of pillars, lintels and kaksanas in a crude manner, while in Bhubanesvar and Khajuraho they are more bold and prominent. From the tenth century on in Central India, the carefully considered arrangement and handling of these figures on temples from Khajuraho represents a fully realized aesthetic in contrast to the earlier more archaic and inconsistent handling of the maithuna figures at the Kailasa temple in Ellura.

The presence of erotic motifs at Khajuraho was not an isolated phenomenon. Yet in certain temples at Khajuraho such as the Lakshmana, the architect seems to have been the first to conceive of the idea of putting erotic figures on an architectural juncture. The temple is dedicated to Vaikuntha-Vishnu and an inscription states that Vaikuntha assumed this conjoint form in order to kill the three demons 'who possessed one body' and were therefore difficult to destroy. This verse implies a belief in the greater power inherent in conjoined figures. The temples of Kandariya Mahadeo and Visvanatha also have complex sexual-yogic images at the wall junctures of the sanctum and the mahamandapa. To understand these images it is necessary to read beyond the outward superficial appearance of form.

On the Lakshmana, the Visvanatha and the Kandariya temples erotic figures are

Figure 4.4 Maithuna, Lakshmana Temple, Khajuraho, mid-tenth century. Don Stadtner.

placed by the architect on the wall junctures which join the garbhagrha and the mahamandapa.[39] Similar temples in West and Central India have no maithuna on juncture walls, although Meister has recently referred to the placing of conjoint figures of deities on the junctures of the Kumbhasyana temple at Chittorgarh dating from the eighth century.

Several scholars of Indian art have attempted to interpret the significance of the growing proliferation of these maithuna images. Scholars have noted the persistence of primitive pre-Aryan cults and practices with the ancient associations of the magico-protective function of sexuality and the influence of ideas of tantrism on pleasure-loving aristocrats. They also note the concept of the stimulation of generative powers expressed in the king/concubine relationship[40] and the use of punning or tantric sandhyabhasa (intentional language)

to express deeper, more abstract philosophical ideas.

One example of the continuity of these primitive beliefs is the association of hair-cutting and sexual intercourse depicted on temples such as Bhubaneswar, Konarak and Ratnagiri in Orissa and Bagali in Mysore. The offering of hair was a widespread practice associated with the Vedic royal consecration ceremony and was linked to the offering of heads and purification enjoined by medieval puranic literature.

Desai suggests that even obscenity served a function as a device for stimulating generative powers (aslila) (Figure 4.4). Obscenity was however confined to the lower architectural stratas of the Lakshmana and the Visvanatha temple, while the walls of the superstructure reveal exquisite refinements in gestures and sexual relationships. An example of both the depiction of generative powers and punning is given by imagery on the Lakshmana temple at Khajuraho, where on the outer walls of the platform there is a scene which shows a king and some soldiers indulging in various bestial and unconventional sexual acts. This frieze may reflect narrative and contemporary literature, which caricatured a comedy of orgiastic sex as a commentary on certain tantric sects.

Desai suggests in her authoritative work on erotic imagery that this was a result of a pervasive influence of tantrism which had begun to penetrate and inspire Hinduism more pronouncedly from the eighth century AD.[41] This, she suggested in her recent work on Khajuraho, was seen at different levels of tantrism associated with medieval sects.[42] She suggested that this influence was reinforced by the association of tantrikas with pleasure-loving aristocrats, while not being designed specifically for tantrikas. She suggested that courtly society was preoccupied with the glorification of pleasure (bhoga), far from the ascetic ideals of the Upanishadic era of asceticism. Medieval courtly drama and literature such as the *Kama Sutra* support this view of a more permissive group in society, yet this more 'secular' drama and text does not reflect the questions of mysticism and sacred power envisaged by 'tantrism', which are revealed in such imagery in the temples at Khajuraho.

Punning or hidden meaning may also be used to camouflage messages to the initiated or more intelligent. An example of this is the pun on the word scorpion at Khajuraho, where beautiful ladies remove scorpions from their legs. This expresses both the rain-making power of nudity and the scorpion. The Sanskrit Khajura was synonymous with both the scorpion and the town where the temples were built.

According to Desai, it was common practice for tantrikas to use sandhyabhasa with double or triple meanings in order to conceal their doctrines from the non-initiate. As Mircea Eliade says:

> In this 'intentional language' any erotic phenomenon can express a Hatha-yogic exercise or a stage of meditation, just as any symbol, any state of holiness, can be given an erotic meaning. We arrive at the result that a tantric text can be read with a number of keys: liturgical, yogic, tantric, etc. The commentaries especially stress the two last. To read a text with the 'yogic key' is to decipher the various stages of meditation to which it refers. The tantric meaning is usually erotic, but it is difficult to decide whether the reference is to a concrete act or to a sexual symbolism.[43]

At particular points of juncture, complex sexual, almost yogic positions are shown. In later works Desai suggested that these specific sexual acts may hide geometry that depicts a yantra diagram which itself expresses a profound cosmic union (Figure 4.3).[44] The west frieze on the south side of the Kandariya Mahadeo temple, for example, shows the interlocking figures with the man standing on his head. This, Desai concludes, may be a figural reference to an underlying yantra, with a compositional diagram of the meeting of two equilateral triangles.

> Some yantra-like geometry seems to underlie the head-down poses of the Visvanatha and the Kandariya Mahadeva, as the lines of their compositions would suggest. This reminds us of the Kamakala yantra given in the Orissan text Silpa Prakasa, assigned to the period between the ninth and twelfth centuries. The text points to the magico-protective and propitiatory aspects of sexual symbolism underlying this yantra....

To summarize: Images are used to protect and reinforce the devotee's passage towards and around the central image and to reinforce his communication with the divine presence through darsan, with the divine image emanating rays which also bathe the devotee by deflection via secondary images. Images are used to protect the enshrined divinity, the actual architectural structure and to generate prosperity and auspiciousness both in the temple and in the surrounding community. Narrative and deliberate figure groups also serve a didactic capacity in warning devotees and offer sectarian commentaries of disapproval or humour. From the medieval period not only Brahmanic prescriptions influenced the appearance of the temple but ancient rituals symbolized in the role of the devadasis, the surasundaris and erotic imagery actively contributed to the generation of this divine energy and achieved these protective and reinforcing objectives.

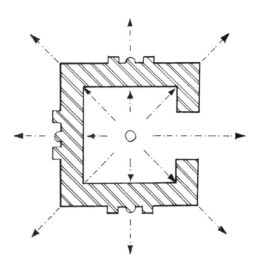

Figure 4.6 Radial plan of images. Drawing by Christopher Glanville RWA.

Deities

Sculptures of the numerous chief and minor deities appear on the walls of Hindu temples (Figure 4.6). These are placed in radial positions from the central deity, whose images are also carved on the central offset of the outer wall of the sanctum.[55] Deities such as Ganesa are usually placed near the entrance to the temple as the remover of obstacles. The placing of these deities also corresponds to the devotees' circumambulation of the temple which usually takes a clockwise direction.

Planetary deities, guardians of space and other astronomical deities are also deliberately placed around the outer and inner walls of the temple. The cosmic geography of the Hindus endows the earth with seven great insular continents, seven oceans, beyond which at each of the eight cardinal points are eight regents or protectors: Agni, Yama, Nairita, Varuna, Vayu, Soma, Ishana and Indra. These are accompanied by the following vehicles: ram, buffalo, sword, makara, antelope, horse, bull and elephant. These guardian deities or astadhikpalas are for the most part Vedic deities who devolved through the centuries into subsidiary protective identities.

Dancing figures and accompanying musicians, together with the bell and chain motif, symbolic of the ringing of the bell to evoke and awaken the deity, are also part of the temple repertoire.

Demigods and spirits

Hindu cosmology conceives a universe which abounds with spirits and demigods (devatas). The temple therefore reflects this vision, and several secondary figures such as the gandharvas, literally fragrances, are to be seen in this category. They are often

113

shown playing music on the vina, singing the praises of heroes or recounting ancient tales. They are essentially celestial beings, while the ganas are dwarf-like creatures whose role is to protect the temple. These creatures are part of Siva's retinue. Ganesa, who is their leader, is also known as Kubera, lord of the ganas. Other spirits such as naga deities are shown as part of the temple pantheon; they are half-snake, half-human and act as defenders of the underworld. Other temple guardians are known as yalis, which are a combination of creatures such as dragons, elephants, lions and horses, and are depicted with roaring open mouths and bulging eyes.

Amalaka

The amalaka is the crown and summit of the North Indian temple, surmounted by the finial (stupika), with the vase (kalasa) as its most conspicuous part. It is a characteristic feature of North Indian Hindu temple architecture.

Etymologically, the amalaka is perhaps derived from the root 'mal' meaning 'hold or gather', perhaps suggestive of its ring-like form which surrounds the upper part of the temple. According to Coomaraswamy, it is also analogous to man's cranium. If written with a short *a* it literally means purity or stainless. If written with a long *a* it is Sanskrit for the fruit of the emblic myrobalan, phyllanthes emlica, whose shape it recalls. The following myth associated with the myrobalan tree reinforces the fact that it is sacred not to one god but to all three, Vishnu, Brahma and Siva:

> Once when all the gods and sages (rsi) had assembled at the Tirtha of Prabhasa, Devi, Siva's Sakti, wanted to worship Vishnu and Lakshmi who is Vishnu's Sakti wanted to worship Siva. Deeply touched, their eyes welled over with tears of joy. Where tears fell to the ground, Amalaka trees grew up, 'since they were born from tears and all the gods and sages saw Brahma, Vishnu and Siva in the Amalaka tree'.[56]

As well as the shape of the fruit of the myrobalan tree the amalaka resembles both the ring stone and the ribbed wheel. In the *Vastu-sastra* the amalaka is also called anda, the egg, which is itself identified with the sun. It is the crown of the summit, while also functioning as the sheath or ring around the pillar or tower of the superstructure of the temple. The amalaka also signifies the celestial world: 'It is the architectural symbol of the celestial world; viewed as sculpture, it is a three dimensional shape of the filaments of the lotus or of a halo with its rays.'[57]

On some sikharas, for example, in the temple complex in Baroli in Rajasthan, the small figure of a man is portrayed climbing the sikhara towards the amalaka. It is the figure of a warrior, a ksatriya, or the king, who gains a footing high on the superstructure ascending to heaven. In South Indian temples the shape of the amalaka is replaced by the domical cap stone to form a little palace or prasada.

As well as the solar symbol, the moon often appears at the threshold to the temple entrance.

Makara

A mythical creature called the makara is frequently carved on brackets and in friezes. The makara is an aquatic beast which resembles a crocodile and is associated with rivers. It is shown with large teeth and is often portrayed with no lower body as though emerging from water (Figure 4.7). In the Hoysala period it was portrayed in varying combinations with the peacock, pig, lion, crocodile or fish. The makara acts as the vehicle to the goddess Ganga and is a symbol of time the devourer.

Animal and vegetal friezes

Friezes of animals, such as the elephant, lion or horse, birds such as the goose, and vegetation, abound in the evolving forms of the Hindu temple. Vegetation such as the vine scroll and lotus and the stylized flame weave over the surface of the temple. Innumerable variations of the vine scroll or patralata are to be seen.

The lotus mouldings, the water pot friezes and the vine scroll all serve to bind the base of the temple and to link it with water symbolism, thus rendering the ground fertile and the building potent. Lotuses, with or without sprouting foliage, abound in various forms in all the temples. Lotuses can also be shown as growing foliage, or, in a more abstract form, in a diamond and circle pattern. Small lotus ceilings also appear in temple halls. A common pattern is the circle and diamond frieze, the diamond sometimes being flower-like.

Elephant friezes may be interpreted as Indra's rain clouds, but elephants are also known as the treasure keepers of darkness (the symbol of ignorance). Friezes of free-standing lions are sometimes joined by a necklace of pearls. This may refer to the legend where lions break into a storehouse protected by elephants and scatter the hidden pearls of wisdom. This legend implies that the lion may be both guardian and assistant in the process of divine illumination.

Figure 4.7 Drawing of Makara.
Drawing by Christopher Glanville RWA.

Royal and secular scenes

The temple decoration shows a variety of royal, courtly and secular scenes. Scenes which depict royal celebration, entertainment or war are often depicted on the lower mouldings.

Mythological friezes

Friezes of narratives are part of the fabric of sculptural decoration in the Hindu temple. These narratives relate the mythology and dance themes of the great *Mahabharata*, *Ramayana* and the *Bhagavata Purana*.

Prasada

As has already been mentioned, an ancient text refers to the temple which is usually called the prasada (seat or palace) as the purusha (perfect man): 'The Prasada should be worshipped as Purusha. It is both, His house and representation.'[58]

Ancient texts or manuals called Sastras draw and describe the structure of the Hindu temple and cosmology in the form of a square diagram called the 'vastupurushamandala', which literally means vastu (building); purusha (man); mandala (diagram). Meister describes this diagram as a man offered for sacrifice who is: 'pinned as sacrifice to the earth by a series of divine entities distributed within a grid of usually sixty-four or eighty-one squares'.[59]

According to Meister, this was based on the earlier Vedic construction of open-air brick altars, which were constructed on this precise division. As mentioned above, the temple is believed to be a symbolic representation of the primordial man. The square plan and the partitions may be an analogy for the man's frame; the tower, his spine; the door, his mouth; the amalak his head, pierced like the foramen at death to receive the finial from above. The image is visualized as the life of the soul, concealed in the darkness of the cave or womb. The outside with its many images, is seen as the manifestation of purusha and is believed to radiate through closed doors and windows.

Hamsa or goose

The rythmic pattern of breathing in and out and which is another expression of life is given tangible expression in the shape of the goose whose name is the mantra Ha,

the outer breath, and Sa, the inward breath. The goose is carved on the base of the prasada or on the ceiling of the mandapa. The goose symbolizes the bird, which is said to fly from earth to heaven, linking the realms of the deities with that of heaven. The hamsa is also the vahana of the god Brahma, symbolizing knowledge, a means to the end.

Purna-kumbha

The idea of fullness, expressed in Vedic hymns: a full pot expresses this concept. It is such a central element and symbol of Hindu art that no ceremony can be performed without the installation of an auspicious vessel. The vase of plenty is placed both on the top of the temple as the kalasa and frequently appears in the decorative scheme both outside and as an integral part of the inner columns (Figure 4.8). This pot is often decorated and overflowing with bunches of lotus buds and flowers. Before construction a pot is also buried as the ritual foundation of the temple.

Text and Theory of Temple Design

Sastras

The earliest evidence for Hindu architectural theory lies in the sastric texts. These oral traditions which represented theoretical suggestions rather than exact prescriptions were collated and compiled from the first century BC and outlined many ritual practices. The sastras described the correct and most auspicious way to perform a large range of activities such as warfare, cooking, making love (the most famous being the *Kama Sutra*), playing music,

identifying the fabric of the temple itself with the deity and setting out to dissolve the boundaries between man and the divine. This is achieved by the Hindu philosophical belief that the temple, man's body and the sacred mountain and cave represent aspects of the same divine symmetry. The prior insemination of the site and the diagram drawn on the ground which consists of precise measurements permitting the realization of the underlying cosmic ideas are believed to contain and control a forcefield of energy. Literature refers to the temple as prasada, meaning the platform of God, or devagriham, the house of God. This expresses Hinduism's belief in God's willingness to manifest among man. The reference to the inner sanctum as the garbhagrha or womb chamber also expresses the birth and essence of the divine presence. The relationship that develops between forms and their meanings within the Hindu temple is essentially the link between earth and heaven.

Practical Building Methods

Before the construction of a temple, ancient ritual required the ploughing, sowing and watering of grain seed to test the fertility of the ground to see if the site was suitable. After the third, fifth and seventh nights the germination of the seeds was examined. When the ritual was completed the ground was again ploughed. The preparation of the chosen site also included rites of consecration, the placing of a foundation deposit, such as a pot, through to rites for the placement of the final anchoring stone crown or sikhara.[63] The ritual for the insemination of the temple site has remained unchanged to the present day.

Astronomy and astrology were determining factors in the temple's construction. The plan of the temple is strictly orientated to the cardinal directions, usually on an east–west axis. The architect first draws the ground plan or diagram which forms the spiritual and actual foundation of the subsequent process of construction. As mentioned above, correct measurements and knowledge of the correct drawing of the vastupurushamandala based on a square forms the first part of the science of Hindu architecture.

Engineering principles are simple, the most common architectural form of temple construction being the combination of vertical columns and horizontal cross-beams which, it is suggested, originated from an earlier form of wooden construction. The stability of the building's elevation was achieved largely by the sheer mass of columns and the weight of the cross-beams, and the additional supporting brackets and iron clamps. Doorways are usually spanned by a lintel, while ceilings are constructed of stone slabs. Roofs are built with overlapping stone courses. The arched niches are a result of carving rather than complex construction. By the fifth century AD, free-standing temples were usually made of stone, occasionally of brick, with the stone blocks sometimes transported over large distances. Elephants, rollers and sleds, barges and manpower were the means used. When the stone arrived at the site the blocks, roughly hewn, were placed in position by rope pulleys on scaffolding. Earthern or timber ramps were used to place the heaviest blocks.[64] Whether an Indian temple is built of wood, brick or stone, the work is done with precision. Bricks and stone are carefully laid and joined. Frequently they are kept in position without any cement. The stone is sometimes bonded with bronze dowels or copper cramps. Plaster and cement mixed with other substances such as conch shell powder (the conch being the emblem of Vishnu) or white earth (kaolin) is sometimes used. The earliest occurrence of lime mortar was in the brick foundation of the Vishnu temple of Besnagar.[65]

Before the craftsmen begin work they perform certain traditional rituals during which they revere and make offerings to their tools. Objects of daily use such as the axe, the line and the hammers are worshipped with offerings of incense, flowers and unhusked rice.[66] During the carving some artisans would wear amulets to ward off accidents. Indian craftsmen even today consecrate their tools at the autumn festival of Dasara, on the day which is sacred to Visvakarman, their tutelary deity.[67]

According to Biardeau:

Whether one installs the divinity upon a diagram drawn on the ground with coloured powders or whether one invokes it in an imaginary setting, one always begins with the invocation of God within.... [In temple ritual] especially in those regions where tantrism is most vital...every gesture, every ingredient, every formula, every movement through space bears a symbolic meaning which the initiate alone is capable of perceiving.[68]

Positive and Negative Forces

Hinduism perceives that the universe contains forces of energy which can be both creative and destructive. The spirit world is visualized as a hierarchy of demons, spirits of the underworld and an ascending range of halflings, spirits, female, male and animal deities. The daemonic is believed to be capable of damage and destruction, and means are employed to protect the devotees and the community at large from their influences. Ritual consecration in the form of mantras, specific images and building procedure offered protection against any weaknesses. As in many of the ceremonies on a village level, rituals were undertaken to improve security, to acquire prosperity or for the good health of the worshipper. The temple itself is largely closed, but the doorways or thresholds are considered to be particularly vulnerable and in need of support. The gavakshas are closed and act as symbolic windows, while secondary openings or windows are echoed in the symbolic niches, which display aspects of the divinity of the temple. Certain images such as the mithuna or erotic images, seen to encompass life and renewal, are carved at weak junctures, such as between the central sanctum and the adjoining mandapa, and are regarded as protective and potent.

Not only is the temple protected from harmful influences by deliberately placed sculpture, but it is also believed to be capable of transmitting beneficial divine forces. These forces are believed to radiate from the central icon and to be transmitted through the intermediary of carefully chosen related deities. This forcefield is believed to act on the community and to create harmony in the immediate vicinity of the temple.

Placing of Images

As has been mentioned above, the position of each image is significant. The outer walls of the Hindu temple are covered with multiple and repeated images. This ornamental imagery will be shown to have general and specific purposes. Ornamentation (alankara) on the temple is believed to be auspicious and to promote prosperity.[69] Desai cites Gonda, who studied the semantic development of words and demonstrated that the words alankrita and alankara not only denote the idea of adornment but that of preparation. Desai suggests that alankara, as well as fulfilling an aesthetic function, holds magical properties.[70] She suggests that adornment, in the form of collyrium for eyes, jewellery and elaborate costume, can be perceived not just as decorative and beauty-enhancing but as protective. In a similar way the *Silpasastras* and *Puranas* emphasize that ornamentation or alankara on the houses of gods and men brings good fortune.

The actual sculpture on the temple walls is either applied directly or carved on separate slabs, which are set in place after construction. Darielle Mason in her study on the significance of the placing of sculpture on sacred Indian architecture concluded that architects and patrons of seventh- to thirteenth-century temples showed a concern not only with dynastic glorification and human pleasure but also with the 'balance and grace necessary for properly housing the divinity'.[71]

The pre-eminent function of the temple was and still is the housing of the principal image. The representations on the walls of the central shrine or garbhagrha derive from this central enshrined image and are reflections of the active manifestations of this deity, close family divinities or the deity repeated in iconic form. These secondary images become direct links or channels of radiation from the central image and paths for communication with and manifestation of the deity with the world of man. The central figure on the bhadra or offset on the back wall of the temple opposite the door is an aspect of the principal icon. If the central icon is missing this figure often reveals the temple's dedication. Deities in this position are frequently shown in a frontal and symmetrical manner.

As has been mentioned above, in the first free-standing temples of the Gupta period images initially appeared only on the central niches of the exterior walls. From the early eighth century they began to appear first on the corners (karnas) of shrines and then on the intermediary offsets (pratirathas). From the mid-eighth century a set of eight guardians of the directions of space appeared in a standard order, orientation and placement on the karnas of the sanctum exterior. These guardians were originally elemental deities of the Vedic pantheon who became subsidiary to the major gods such as Vishnu and Siva and performed a protective function. Mason suggested that in the early eighth century they were a mixture of Vedic gods and other deities. In about AD 725, they were placed at each corner of the temple. She suggested that these images acted, as in a pre-ordained sequence within a set, as guardians of the corners and to give direction in space (compass direction). She concluded, however, that while narrative order could sometimes play a part in the placing of deities, greater importance was given to the axial connection with the deity in the interior.

Artisans

For the building of the great temples, the carving of the sculptural decorations, the making of religious icons and religious painting, varied caste groups were involved. Early Buddhist texts supply us with a considerable amount of information regarding the social position of the craftsmen in early Buddhist times. The most striking features are the hereditary nature of the craft and the importance of the elder or master craftsmen. In early Buddhist times caste was less crystallized and not so rigidly tied to craft. The Jataka *Alinachitta* refers to an entire village of carpenters. In the Mauryan period craftsmen were said to have been valued, and the emperor Asoka initiated the employment of stone workers to shape and erect monumental stupas and columns. In the Gupta period blacksmiths, goldsmiths and carpenters enjoyed higher status, with goldsmiths settling in the rich areas of the city.

Architects, artisans and workmen were engaged in groups or guilds. These guilds preserved their tradition orally, and were by and large extensions of family units, where techniques were handed down from one generation to the next. Traditions and techniques were jealously guarded, while the guilds united both the family and the individual craftsmen into a single corporate body. These guilds served the great temple sites, fixing rules of work and wages and setting standard prices for work completed, their regulations having the force of law. The guilds had judicial rights and could expel a rebellious member. The headman of the guilds was sometimes appointed by the king. Owing to the irregularity of patronage in a certain area, guild members frequently travelled from one region to another in order to work on different projects and this in turn gave rise to the spread of architectural and artistic traditions. A thirteenth-century palm leaf manuscript detailing building operations of the contemporary Surya temple at Konarak in Orissa provides evidence of the organization of the architect and his workforce. This was similar to the European guild system and may be typical of the organization of the construction of other temples throughout India. The Orissan manuscript lists the workmen, their salaries and rules of conduct and provides an account of the various building operations, though oral transmission was more usual in order to preserve the guild's trade secrets. The manuscript records such details as the early vocational training of children and describes the guilds as extended family units, which went so far as to ordain who could be married to whom and who could even act as guardians of widows and orphans. Sometimes, individual members or whole villages would seek work with distant patrons, thus giving rise to the transmission of architectural and sculptural style. It was not unknown for wealthy guilds themselves to make charitable donations to temples. Evidence from this inscription also reveals that craftsmen were recruited from villages and small towns in Orissa, and gives a detailed description of a group of masons from Madurai in Tamil Nadu, from where they had been brought by the local ruler. The guilds also had the potential to become wealthy in their own right and inscriptions exist which record their charitable donations. An example of this is silk weavers from Lata (Gujarat) who built a splendid temple of the sun at Mandasalur, or ivory carvers from Bhilsa who donated part of the railings and gateways of the great stupa at Sanchi. Sometimes whole villages and small towns were engaged predominantly in one type of activity.

Hindu craftsmen were also known to work for patrons of different religious persuasions. This suggestion is supported by evidence from several Jain temples which include Hindu iconography in the sculptural decoration. A strong Hindu flavour and detail can also be seen in Indo-Islamic architecture. No religious restrictions were imposed on the guild members in the professional sphere of their work. According to Nath, guilds of Hindu artisans of Rajasthan, Gujarat and Malwa who were employed on the construction of the mosques could conduct the same preparatory ritual in their worship of Vastu Purusha at the time of laying the foundations of the mosque as they would if they were constructing a Hindu temple. This clearly showed independence from the wishes or control of their patron.[72]

Brahmans are involved not only in laying down and transmitting theoretical guidelines but also in the practical task of performing the ceremonies for the removal of obstacles, the consecration and purification of the site, the tracing of the initial ground plan, the setting of the crowning finial of the superstructure and the installation of the image or symbol of the deity in the shrine. They are also responsible for the preservation of the sanctity of the site. The work of the architect, artists and sculptors in the construction of these large projects requires a close relationship between priest and project.

A hierarchy existed in the group of artisans constructing a great temple. The most important individual in the erection of a temple was the chief architect (sutradhara) and the superintendent of works.

> The Sthapati should be fit to direct (sthapan) the construction and should be well-versed in all Sastras, the traditional sciences, perfect in body, righteous, kind, free from malice and jealousy, a Tantrik and well-born; he should know mathematics and the Puranas, the ancient

compendia of myths etc. painting and all the countries; he should be joyous, truth speaking with senses under control, concentrated in mind, free from greed, carelessness, disease and the seven vices famous having firm friends and having crossed the ocean of the science of Vastu.[73]

The assignation of work to the artisans was on the basis of paid contracts. The four classes of craftsmen were the architect (sthapathi) who was assisted by the surveyor (sutragrahin), sculptor (taksaka) and builder-plasterer-painter (vardhakin). There were fine divisions of labour, such as stonemasons who cut stone and sculptors who were responsible for the fine chisel work. Specialists carried out particular jobs such as:

> laying out the axes of the building, marking out the plumb and square lines which regulated the carving, grinding the polishing materials, carving the bands of friezes and mixing the coloured pigments for paintwork. Leading master-craftsmen worked on the principal images of the sanctuary and its outer walls.[74]

The leading master craftsmen worked on the principal images of the sanctuary and outer walls and the design and composition of panels in the great temple, may well have been inspired by a single artist. The majority of remaining craftsmen and builders would be responsible for the execution of the building. The work was assigned by contract, each of which had a different leader, with payments relating to the contracts. The heads of the whole project did not have individual contracts but were responsible for coordinating the various stages of the entire project. The sculptors were engaged in small sections of the building and women were employed for cleaning and polishing stones.

Workmen settled in camps around the building site, and the domestic arrangements for the cooking and distribution of food were highly organized. Even the maintenance of law and order was provided by officials who would settle disputes. Fines were imposed as punishment for delays in delivering materials or completing the work. Doctors were also present to look after the sick alongside barbers, and oilmen were employed to prepare torches and lamps. Work ceased during the rainy season and holidays were granted if a royal patron visited, had a son, or once an important part of the building was completed.[75]

The relationship between artists/ craftsmen and the Brahman priests was crucial. The priests advised and gave guidance to the workmen, performed ceremonies for the removal of obstacles or when some accident required atonement. They also conducted important consecrations, purifications of the site, the initial tracing of the ground plan, the setting of the crowning finial of the superstructure and the installation of the principal image or symbol of the divinity in the sanctuary.

Stylistic Variety of the Hindu Temple

The external differences between northern and southern styles of temple architecture are considerable (Figure 4.9). Certain sites such as Pattadakal, situated midway between North and South India, juxtapose and combine the characteristics of both styles of temple building. On the Papanatha temple, for example, the southern elements of pilastered wall with eave and surmounting parapet are combined with northern niche pediments and superstructure. Certain other sites in the Deccan show a similar juxtaposition of the two styles.

Evidence of early timber architecture from Buddhist rock reliefs from the second century BC reveals that the coalescence of architectural features into distinct 'northern' and 'southern' styles had not occurred in the centuries immediately preceding the Christian era. The earliest extant freestanding structures show no transitional architecture and the preserved brick and stone temples clearly display features of the two broad styles. In the ancient texts or sastras such as the *Brhatsamhita*, the temple is known as prasada and the northern style of architecture as nagara, while in the south it is known as vimana and the southern style as dravida. The former is characterized by the frequent appearance of the amalaka, and the stone slabs or pidaha which surmount the roofs of the early stone shrines. The southern temples, on the other hand, visually resemble the secular palace or prasada, the seat of the enthroned king or deity, with a pyramidal tower and more dramatic gopuras or gateways. Despite some common terms, each temple style has its own distinct technical language.

Despite frequent invasions from outsiders such as the Muslims from the eleventh and twelfth centuries AD and the sacking of such great temples as Somnath, Mathura and Benaras, the north reveals several significant examples of early free-standing temples. A good early example of the northern style is the Gupta temple of Deogarh. The most distinctive feature of the North Indian type of temple is the gradual convex curve of the mountain-like tower over the square sanctum known as a sikhara (Figure 4.10). The link between sanctum and tower in the use of niches and

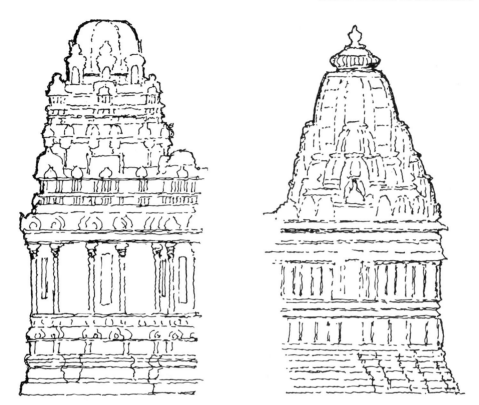

Figure 4.9 The characteristic features of southern (left) and northern (right) temples. Drawing by Christopher Glanville RWA.

offsets is also characteristic of the North Indian temple.

South India was not subject to the same degree of architectural devastation and demonstrates a continuous development of building over the period from the sixth to sixteenth century AD. The pyrimidal towers, crowned cap stone and barrel-shaped roofs are characteristic of the southern style (Figure 4.11). The gateways of the South and North Indian temples are also substantially different, with the enlarged gateway being the most pronounced feature in later South Indian temples (Figure 4.9). This southern gateway had a tower-like superstructure capped with a barrel-vaulted element. A more recent development in the southern temples from the thirteenth and fourteenth centuries is their scale and a continuation in the colouring of the sculptural ornamentation.[76] Sacred complexes of the Nayaka period with their enclosure walls, one within the other, and their towering and coloured gopuras are urban units in their own right. Such temples employ immense numbers of staff and bring large quantities of money into the local economy.

The distinct differences in stylistic architectural and decorative features exhibited in different dynastic and geographic groups are due to several factors, including the availability of raw materials and the influence of climate. Hard and crystalline rocks, for example, prevented detailed carving, whereas soft

Figure 4.10 Kandariya
Mahadeo temple, Khajuraho.
Eleventh century.
Pat Barylski.

and sedimentary stone permitted great precision. Friable and schist-like stones, such as those employed by the Hoysala architects in the twelfth and thirteenth centuries, gave rise to the carving of mouldings created by sharp and angled incisions. Brick-building traditions survived: Hampi shows an extensive use of brick even in the vimana towers, for example, in the Vitthala temple in a region where stone was plentiful. Techniques of moulding and carving bricks also doubtless influenced the style of temples in these areas. Climate also had an impact on the style of building: 'in general the hotter and drier the climate, the flatter the roof; open porches provide shaded seating, and pierced stone screens are utilized to filter the light.'[77]

A further factor in the growth of style and the choice of architectural forms is the innate conservatism of the architects and craftsmen, and their faithfulness to textual prescriptions. Repetition was another feature of architectural choice. In the northern style of temple:

The rythmic projections of the temple plan carried into the vertical elevation were created by multiplications of the original central wall projection with which early temples were

Figure 4.11 Muvarkovil
temple, Kodumbalore.
Early Cola, ninth century.
Robert Elgood.

provided. The southern style temples created their rythmic wall systems by the repetition of projections that framed recesses, pairs of pilasters marking each change in the wall plane....Essential to both temple styles was the principle by which forms were repeated on different scales so that shapes which were large and indicative of structural context became small and ornamental; these diminutive forms were sometimes combined with the originals from which they were derived. Such stylistic diminutions were at the root of the complex and subtle rhythmic proportional schemes by which the elevations of Hindu temples were organized.[78]

Patronage of the temples, chiefly inspired by royal devotion, gave rise not only to the fostering of a dynastic style but also to the transference of style by victorious monarchs bringing artisans from one region to another.

In India today the categories of 'northern' Nagari and 'southern' Dravida may still be applied to sacred building activity. In South India there has been no distinct break in architectural tradition, and modern temples are built in a style that is a direct continuation of that perfected under Vijayanagara and Nayaka patronage. In the north, the forms still broadly followed the temple style seen under the patronage of such dynasties as the Chandellas, Kalingas and Solankis from the tenth to thirteenth centuries AD. The simple village shrines perhaps preserve best the tradition of reverence; for example, modest wayside shrines sometimes sheltered by no more than sticks and leaves.

Ritual Practice in the Temple

The ritual practices of Hindu worship derive from oral prescriptions which became codified in ancient texts such as the *Brahmanas* or the *Agamas*. Continuity can be observed in the principal Hindu rituals which follow a more or less standard pattern due to the Brahmanic belief that only correct ritual action brings efficacious results. The Brahman priests serve the temples and perform regular devotions (Plate 5). They are regarded as the purest and highest group within the caste structure of Hindu society, which justifies their direct access to the deity. Strict rules of intermarriage are observed to preserve this genetic purity. Before worship, certain rites and ritual bathing reinforce this preoccupation with purity. Devotees and other individuals who wish to approach the deity are also first required to purify themselves by bathing. Ritual worship involves a series of contractual relationships by the devotee with the deity, whereby they make offerings in return for spiritual or material gain. There is a widespread belief that this offering is made more effective by appearing before the deity at a sacred shrine or temple and performing the ceremony with the priest's mediation and prayers.

The priests retain an intimate relationship with the deity in their frequent ritual devotions and, as the representatives of the community at large, do not require a congregation. The welfare of the community is believed to depend on a ceremony, to maintain the divine presence and the right relationship between priest and deity. It is a widely held belief that devotees can witness this ritual and with priestly mediation, through prayer and contemplation, acquire spiritual merit, inner transformation and ultimate release or moksha. The outward forms of ritual act as an indispensable support for some who are still on their religious path, but can be dispensed with by those who have already reached enlightenment.

An account of a fifth-century traveller who witnessed certain extreme temple practices supports the suggestion of the Indian scholar Coomaraswamy that this ritual derives from the Vedic sacrifice and, like it, seeks to lead the worshipper from this world to another reality:

> These idols are sometimes of the height of sixty feet. The modes of praying and of sacrificing among them are various. They enter the temple morning and evening, having first washed themselves in pure water; and sometimes prostrating themselves upon the ground with hands and feet held up, repeat their prayers and kiss the ground, at others offer incense to the gods by burning spices and the wood of the aloe. They also present feasts to their gods, after the manner of the ancient heathens, which are afterwards distributed among the poor to be eaten. In the city of Cambaita the priests, standing before the idols of their gods... urge them how acceptable it is to the gods that they should quit this life for their sake. Many present themselves who have determined upon self-immolation having on their neck a broad circular piece of iron, the fore part of which is round and the hinder part extremely sharp. A

chain attached to the fore part hangs suspended upon the breast, into which the victims, sitting down with their legs drawn up and their neck bent, insert their feet. Then on the speaker pronouncing certain words, they suddenly stretch out their legs, and at the same time drawing up their neck cut off their own head, yielding up their lives as a sacrifice to their idols. These men are regarded as saints.[79]

Contemporary ritual worship is believed to involve a symbolic offering of self.[80] The philosophically highest aim of Hindu ritual, as well as the acquisition of spiritual merit, was liberation from the worldly circle of existence. Devout Hindus hold a widespread belief that this release is achieved by man's inner transformation. Self-sacrifice, literal or symbolic, was one of the methods of purification. The transformed rarified inner presence achieved by the worshipper was believed under certain conditions (conforming to the principle of the blending of like with like) to have the potential to blend with the unknowable and indescribable creative source or deity. This interpretation explains the extreme rituals of self-immolation referred to above. A further contribution to this inner transformation was darsan. Darsan literally means 'seeing', implying vision and understanding. Eyes are seen as thresholds or doorways to the soul, and are believed to act as transmitters as well as receptors of light and energy. Eye contact between the worshipper and the deity is believed to open his soul to divine emanations from the numinous presence in the icon. The intimacy of darsan between the deity and the individual devotee enables the communicant to participate at any stage during or after the major priestly ceremonies of worship.

The actions of the priests developed out of domestic rituals. Underlying the care and correctness of each action is a belief in the potential for the ritual to transmute in an almost alchemical way the elements involved in the ceremonial.

The other aim of puja or ritual worship which is less esoteric and philosophical is the propitiation of the deity. This requires the evocation, reception and entertainment of the god or goddess as if the divine personage was a royal guest. This reflects the ancient association of royalty with the divine. There is also a belief, which has been particularly popular outside India, that the ruler's power is an extension of the divine law.

In the temple, entrance to the sanctum is restricted to the Brahman officiant who is responsible for the daily care of the temple. As mentioned above, the lay worshipper can visit the temple and conduct his personal ritual either during or independently of the priestly regular celebrations. While temples vary in their layout, there are certain standard features of worship. The devotee will often stop at a water tank outside the temple for cleansing before entering the temple. The worshipper makes a clockwise walk around the principal shrine before approaching the main sanctum. This circumambulation takes in the subsidiary shrines. Before actually approaching the icon in the sanctuary the worshipper should offer prayers to an image of the deity which is on the outside wall of the sanctum at the furthest point from its entrance. In front of the sanctum the worshipper comes to a vestibule which, unlike the mandapa, is walled and often columned. The worshipper may make offerings to the vehicle of the god which is often placed here. When the devotee passes through this chamber after worship he or she rings the bell which hangs from the ceiling of the vestibule. At the sanctuary threshold in some temples, for example, in the Kandariya Mahadeo temple at Khajuraho, there is a further chance to circumambulate the shrine or garbhagrha. In these temples a dark passage leads the devotee around the outer walls of the inner sanctuary. This is usually small and dark, with a number of images on either side of the inner ambulatory. The inner wall of the sanctum is bare however, with the exception of the Pallava temples, which have a Somaskanda panel at the back of the shrine. The interior of the shrine is often lit only by oil lamps. There is darkness in the interior shrines, a sense of wonder, sounds of chanting, and a trumpet announces the anticipation of the elephant. At the end of a long corridor of columns tiny lights burn in the distance, luring one along the approach to the central shrine. The secrecy and mystery is enhanced by the dark and the smoking incense. The length of the passage from the outer door to the inner sanctum assists the sense of journey, marking the spiritual transformation of the worshipper.

The actual rite of puja begins with the priest expressing his intention to worship the god. He washes the sacred idol with sanctified water, and anoints it with milk or oils. This both purifies and transfers the spirit of the sacred waters to the image. The deity is then fed by placing food, sometimes in the form of cooked rice, ghee, vegetable oils or fruit, on or in front of the idol. Finally the idol is again washed and dressed in a carefully prescribed manner, often with richly decorated red fabric. Beautification and adornment are part of honouring and preparing the deity to see and be seen once he or she has awoken. The idol is finally

garlanded with flowers, and sandalwood and red paste anoint and cool the deity's brow. This process is often performed behind a curtain. The priest then rings a bell and intones prayers to summon the deity. Various mantras, sacred syllables known as bijas and mudras or symbolic hand gestures are also used to draw the power of the deity into the image. Special care is taken on the part of the priests to follow the correct prescribed prayers, particularly with regard to their intonation. Incense is lit in front of the deity to purify the air. The drawing back of the curtain reveals to the devotees a darkened smoke-filled atmosphere where the priest with a circular motion illuminates the image with a small flame. Caught in wondrous anticipation, the women sometimes pat their cheeks in awe at the moment when the curtain is drawn back after the image is prepared for the ceremonial. The image may be blackened and its form indistinct, it may glow with rubbed saffron, or shine with the overlaying of gold or silver leaf or with silken cloth and brilliant flowers. The flames which illuminate the image and the dark shrine enhance the mystery of the space. The deity is almost invisible, more a presence than a clear outline of form.

The devotees stand aside from the direct view of the deity so as not to impede the vision of the other worshippers further back. The priest, having reverentially passed a flame clockwise in front of the deity, brings the flame from the inner sanctuary. The incandescent intensity of the flame fills the vision of the worshipper. The priest then offers the flame to the devotees who place their hands over it and then over their eyes, in the belief that by so doing they may symbolically and actually transfer the divine essence through the flame to their own eyes. In the flame's reflection both deity and worshipper are one; the deity becomes the flame, the vision of which enters the mind of the devotee. The flame being essentially formless enables the worshipper to make eye contact with the deity on a personal level with something divine as well as essentially formless, while the image gives the worshipper some sense of a numinous presence. This darsan and the reciprocal seeing and being seen is the culmination of worship. The final sight of the deity and the absorption of the radiation of the deity's presence as tangibly sensed contribute to the arrival at the final goal for the worshipper, the identification with the inner place where the dark unconscious may be illuminated and the experience of the ultimate unity of god and man realized.

After the ceremony the priest may present some of the devotional offering as prasad to the devotee. The devotee will partake of a substance that has itself become transformed through its ingestion by the deity. Finally, the priest will draw back the curtain (if one exists) and close the door, as the deity is once more considered to be asleep. This formula is repeated with minor variations during each temple ceremony, both at Saivite and Vaishnavite temples. Ideally, just as every puja should be preceded by a preparatory ritual of purification, so it should be completed with a sacrificial fire ritual. This involves kindling a fire, invoking the deity in the fire and pouring oblations on the flames (a rite known as homa) and making offerings to the temple's guardian deities around the fire. This is carried out in conjunction with acts of worship during certain very important rituals but otherwise is omitted. The distribution of powder and ash completes the ritual.[81]

For the lay devotee a variety of motives lies behind ritual worship. Desire for a multitude of everyday needs such as children, good health, cure from sickness, wealth, prosperity or the removal of fear are some of the objectives. A contract is essentially made with the deity where offerings are exchanged for desired results. The expression of devotion and reverence, known as bhakti, which is nearer the offering of the self, must also not be ignored as an impulse in the Hindu's feeling for the divine. These visits to the temple supplement daily prayer at the household shrine.

Certain occasions are cause for a more congregational approach to worship, such as the public performance of sacred song and dance to glorify the god or the recital of ancient texts. Other ceremonies occur at regular intervals and are treated as festivals. Every important temple has regular festivals which consist of processions and the enactment of popular myths. Khajuraho, which is not often visited for active worship, becomes alive in Sivatri when it is visited by many hundreds to celebrated the marriage of Siva and Parvati.[82] These festivals and ceremonies go on for many hours; hundreds bear witness and partake in the event.

Processions have a particular significance, an event where the image is carried around the town or village in a mobile temple. Devotees have the opportunity of directly presenting flowers, fruits and other offerings to the god or goddess being carried in procession. This image is generally not the same as that which is housed in the temple but is identified with, the representation of that god. These festivals are popular and often coincide with the planting or harvesting of a crop. They provide opportunities for the mingling of mythology and folklore expressed in performances of music, dance and theatre as well as for the manufacture of temporary images of clay or earth for special ceremonies.

The practical running of the temple takes place in offices which are often situated in a large temple complex on the inner face of the compound wall. This sometimes includes accommodation for pilgrims. Storehouses exist for precious items, such as water vessels, lamps, incense burners and lustration spoons, and the elaborately ornamented clothes of the deity. Instruments may also be stored there such as the double reed shawm, nagasvara or shahnai and processional chariots, or rathas.

Conclusion

This chapter has explored the development of the Hindu temple. It explains the temple's debt to pre-Vedic beliefs, rites and customs and also to the Vedic ceremony. The chapter also analyses the temple's symbolism and component elements, and the rules governing the architectural form. Variations in the outer appearance of the northern and southern styles of temple building are also explored. A belief in the temple's efficacy and the fact that it both represents and could, under certain conditions, become the deity itself, is also emphasized. The chapter stresses the importance of the mediation and role of the priest in maintaining the temple's power and concludes that the Sanskrit chanting, conducted by the priest, is an essential element in this necessary dialogue. It has shown that the deity is believed to reside in the temple as long as this priestly service continues.

Devotees, while receiving religious merit, are not essential to the ceremony of worship. The devotees' desires in visiting

the temple and approaching their deity were seen to be varied, ranging from a desire to acquire merit, to achieve ultimate release from life and become one with the deity; to the making of contractual promises and offerings for worldly profit, health or good fortune. An essential component in understanding the ritual of worship is seen in the act of transformation of the animal, vegetal offering or man's own inner self-sacrifice. It is an essential requirement for this offering to be made with sincerity of feeling, a clear mind, and the correct intonation and gestures.

Despite the temple's visual complexity the dark, unadorned, square inner sanctum which houses a numinous sacred icon is the essential and common element. In wealthy temples, regular paintings and sculptures continue to be produced together with recitations, music and dancing. These performances act to both glorify and amuse the deity, and to educate and entertain the devotee. The daily worship of the Hindu does not require a temple. Coexistent with the worship at modern-day orthodox temples, daily offerings at shrines dedicated to local village or tribal cult deities are still considered valid, and the practice is widespread. Many homes, however small, have a shrine in some part of the house, yet even in large urban communities in India the temple continues to be a religious and economic focus. The temple is a complex weave of philosophical symbolism and Brahmanic theory, but one must not forget the behavioural aspect of religious practices associated with the temple in the rites and festivals, the institution of the devadasis and erotic imagery which reinforce the seminal role of sex and fertility, which in turn explains many of the mysteries of Hindu iconography and ritual.

Notes

1 The sun temple at Konarak is a good example of this; it is also implied by the wheels on the sides of the temples at Darasuram and Chidambaram.

2 See ch 5.

3 Thapar 1966, p. 37.

4 *Brhat Samhita*, Vol. LV, pp. 4-8; *Bhavisya Purana*, 1, Vol. CXXX, pp. 11-15.

5 The late Reginald Smith, former keeper of the Department of British and Roman Antiquities at the British Museum, suggested that ancient Stone Age sites were located in places which conformed to a radiating pattern of underground streams (cited in Underwood 1972, p. 14).

6 For further information on 'geodetic lines' and the 'earthforce' see Underwood 1972, pp. 18-20.

7 Vidyarthi and Rai 1976, p. 255.

8 Haimendorf 1979.

9 According to Kramrisch 1946, (Vol. 1, p. 152, fn. 60) the circular prasada should also not be overlooked. These, according to Kramrisch, have their prototypes in the circular shape of some of the Vedic hearths. Stone circles or their wooden equivalents are also prototypes of the round shape of certain Hindu temples. See also Underwood 1972, p. 91.

10 See Mookerjee 1987.

11 A similar process is enacted where the orthodox Hindu marks his body with the symbol of the deity on his forehead.

12 Chaitya, ayatana and prasada etymologically and originally are piled up seats or altars, sanctuaries in the open and also within an enclosed space. Ayatana means a resting place or support and as such a seat, the place of the sacred fire, and the abode of the divinity.

13 See Kramrisch 1946, Vol. 1, p. 40.

14 Ibid., p. 158, fn. 74. Gabled or pent roofs are also seen in Malabar and gabled temples are found in Kashmir and Nepal.

15 Coomaraswamy 1977, p. 4.

16 See Meister 1988, p. 3.

17 Ibid., p. 6.

18 This double-level hut was engraved on a bronze plaque from Sohgaura inscribed in the Mauryan Brahmi script showing a form that continued at Sanci, Bodhgaya and Mathura, and these have a parallel in a tribal hut in contemporary India.

19 Meister 1988, p. 5.

20 Ibid., p. 15.

21 Banerji 1956, p. 91.

22 Ibid., p. 92.

23 Meister 1988, p. 13, Plate 8.

24 *Brihat Samhita*, Vol. LV, p. 2.

25 Michell 1977, p. 93.

26 Coomaraswamy 1977, p. 6.

27 In any replacement of an icon, the sacred waters from the lustration of the old image are collected in vessels, around which a knot is tied, and the liquid used to transfer the divinity to the new image.

28 Kramrisch 1974, Vol. I, pp. 315-16.

29 For a further detailed description see Kramrisch 1974, Vol. 1, p. 319. The gavaksha is also defined according to the 'vacaspatya' as that by which the rays of the sun - or the waters - penetrate and pervade.

30 Ibid., p. 320.

31 The gorgoneion, an awful monster's grizzly head sent up by Persephone from Hades is a cognate head, with glaring eyes and protruding tusks (Odyssey 1X: 633 f.).

32 A warrior, his sword of knowledge drawn, crouches below and seizes the tail of the beast, or he proffers the shield of dispassion, the protective weapon by which nature is held in check. For an example of this, see Lakshmana Temple, Khajuraho bracket of Mandapa pillar.

33 The sanskrit term mithuna refers to a pair, while the term 'maithuna' refers more specifically to copulation, especially in compound terms such as maithuna bhoga.

34 I am grateful to Naman Ahuja, who drew my attention to the large number of Sunga terracottas which exhibit explicit mithuna imagery.

35 Chatham, in Meister 1984, pp. 164-5.

36 This term was used by the Indian scholar A.L. Basham (1968, p. 82) to describe a conglomerate of rites and practices which answered the needs of lower castes and women who were unable to participate in the exclusive Brahmanical rituals. It also fulfilled the needs of men and women whose emotional and instinctive demands were also not met by intellectual philosophy.

37 Desai 1985, p. 199.

38 Desai, in Meister 1984, p. 144.

39 Ibid., p. 147.

40 See Shulman 1985.

41 Desai 1985.

42 Desai 1996, p. 52, fn. 12.

43 Eliade 1958, p. 250.

44 Desai, in Meister 1984, p. 153.

45 Ibid.

46 Ibid.

47 *Brhadaranyaka Upanishad*, Vol. IV, Part 3, p. 21.

48 Punja, 1992.

49 Ibid.

50 Desai 1985, p. 202.

51 Desai, in Meister 1984, p. 147.

52 Desai 1996.

53 See p. 35.

54 Desai 1985, p. 111.

55 See also pp. 120-1 for the placing of images.

56 *Brhaddharma Purana*, Vol. X11, pp. 1-35, cited in Kramrisch 1946, Vol. 2.

57 Ibid., p. 352.

56 *Silparatna*, Vol. XVI, p. 114.

59 Meister, in Mason 1993, p. 95.

60 It is also suggested by Underwood (1972) that other fields of energy which he terms 'geodetic lines' (which at present cannot be proved by science) and underground streams may have a bearing on the selection of sacred sites. Certainly termites are sensitive to the underground water sources in the location of their mounds high above the water table. It is interesting to note that termites orientate their mounds to the rising sun, and are revered in certain Indian villages. Lord Siva dwells in an anthill at the Tyagaraja temple at Tiruvarur in Tamil Nadu. He is called Valmikanatha.

61 Tadgell 1990, p. 42.

62 Michell 1977, p. 71.

63 Kramrisch 1946, p. 15; see also *Vishnu Samhita*, Vol. XII, pp. 36-42.

64 Michell 1989, pp. 70-1.

65 See *Archaeological Survey of India Annual Report* (*ASIAR*) 1913-14. Brick temples frequently have a thin layer of a clay mixture as an adherent between the bricks. The brick temples of Sirpur were covered by a thin layer of white plaster while the bricks were carved (*ASIAR* 1909-10, p. 11).

66 *Vishnudharmotarra*, Part III, Chapter XC, p. 29.

67 Huyler 1992.

68 Biardeau 1981, p. 150.

69 Desai 1985, p. 110.

70 Ibid., fn. 200.

71 Mason 1993, p. 126.

72 Nath, in Dallapiccola 1989, p. 200.

73 *Manu Samhita*, Vol. VII, pp. 47-8.

74 Michell 1977, p. 57.

75 Ibid.

76 There is evidence from early temples that the colouring of sculpture was common; this can be seen in the Kalaisanatha temple at Kanchipuram.

77 Michell, 1977, p. 89.

78 Ibid., p. 92.

79 The Travels of Nicolo Conti in the early part of the fifteenth century. Hakluyt Soc. 22, 1857, p. 27.

80 Coomaraswamy 1977.

81 Fuller 1992, p. 66.

82 Punja 1992.

CHAPTER 5 Royal Patronage of the Religious Arts and Its Historical Development and Objectives

Introduction

Patronage as part of religious devotion has been a feature of a variety of sects and classes in India throughout history. For a thousand years until the third century BC, Aryan kings acquired the divine powers on which their temporal powers rested by means of sacrificial offerings, rather than by the patronage of temples and images. The sacrificial ceremony took place in the open air on a simple altar within an enclosure, and therefore did not require the building of temples or the making of images. From Brahmanic times royal patronage involved the investment in ritual sacrifices to achieve certain pre-ordained results. It was widely believed that the king was transformed from being an ordinary mortal through the rajasuya ceremony, during which he was imbued with spiritual power through a symbolic ascent with the smoke from a burnt offering on the sacred fire to the abode of the gods. This ceremony gave the king a mandate and placed him above society. The Vedic view assumed a sharing of cosmic power between gods and men in a cycle of exchanges, transubstantiation and contractual obligations. The priests were

essential intermediaries in this ritual sacrifice or yajna.

The king's powers required frequent renewal. Kings in ancient North India were essentially dependent on their priests, the ritual officiants to whom they gave donations in order to guarantee the desired outcome of the highly complex and costly prescriptive action. This gift (dana) donated by the patron of a sacrifice to the priestly officiants was not a fee, but a present guaranteeing the fruition of the sacrifice. The priest's function was also to secure boons and to ward off evil from his client. The priest actually accompanied the king in battle, sharing his chariot with the express purpose of affording him spiritual protection. His prayers, literally the uttering of his voice, ensured the king's safety, victory in battle and timely rainfall, all of which contributed to the prosperity of his kingdom.

One of the most important of the cosmo-regal rites during the Vedic period in which the priests officiated was the great horse sacrifice or asvamedha. This was believed to strengthen the potency of kingship and to enhance welfare and fertility and extend the king's claim to the land covered by the grazing horse. The king was referred to in the *Rg Veda* as the 'protector of the people'. From as early as the Brahmanas, Brahmans claimed a share in dharma, the source of the king's authority, and were called the 'protectors of the state'. In South India, where in the period 200 BC to AD 300 Brahmanic authority was not as powerful, the evidence of the king's divine authority was demonstrated by military success. The booty obtained by raiding provided evidence of divine approval,[1] while his generous distribution of the captured wealth cemented spiritual and temporal allegiances.

Those people who were not members of the Brahmanic or Ksatriya castes were excluded from Vedic rituals. They therefore resorted to other means to fulfil their spiritual and material desires. Their rituals included the worship of local cult deities such as yakshas and nagas. These were believed to reside in sacred places, simply identified by the placing of a post, railings around a tree, a pile of stones, or even a termite mound. These spirits were propitiated by offerings of food and liquid and by rituals which included the use of images.

From 500 BC an imperial administration under the Mauryan dynasty arose in East India, a result of and reaction to the expansion of the Achaemenid and Alexandrian empires in the West. In the third century BC the Mauryan emperor Asoka promoted Buddhism as the imperial religion, constructing monumental stupas as spiritual foci and erecting free-standing stone columns on which were chiselled religious edicts. He revitalized an earlier burial mound to create a religious focus for prayer and power. Despite royal interest in the early stages of Buddhism in India from the third century BC, it was more usual for the major monuments and stupas to have been the result of the collective investment of ordinary people. They were inspired by Buddhist teaching to renounce wealth in exchange for spiritual merit. Particularly susceptible to this idea were monks, nuns, pilgrims and many pious women. The monasteries required the laity to sustain them. This Jain and Buddhist monastic concept was in contrast to the Upanishadic ideal of the solitary holy man begging alms for himself. Sanchi, for example, dating from the first century BC, was raised through small donations from the residents of various towns such as monks, nuns, lay worshippers, householders, housewives, and members of professions such as merchants, bankers, surveyors and masons. Each paving stone, crossbar, rail pillar, coping-stone or sculpture was inscribed by individual donors with their names and occupations. Wandering monks collecting contributions were believed to have been responsible for the encouragement and growth of this form of patronage. Pilgrimage resulted in the accumulation of substantial wealth at religious centres and on the back of this came increasing trade to serve the needs of the community.

The rise in settled monastic communities led to the construction of more permanent stone buildings and a concurrent rise in the development of guilds and the numbers of artisans. The stupa was believed to act as a centre of power and its construction acknowledged a calling upon the Buddha for protection. In India, the earliest phase of permanent stone image making and architectural patronage occurred under Buddhist and Jain patronage. From the first century AD, devout Hindus also made use of architecture and imagery as an integral part of their religious practice. The emphasis shifted from the performance of sacrificial offerings to the building of religious monuments, which were believed to bring religious merit. This was of primary importance in the rise of community investment in religious art and architecture. It has been suggested that the Jains were among the first to use images for spiritual ends during the regular seated gatherings of lay devotees. Perhaps these religious portraits served to remind disciples of the spiritual virtues of their teachers, known as tirthankaras.[2]

Comparable collective patronage was also responsible for the construction of the Hinayana Buddhist rock-cut monasteries of West India. The great hall at Karle, for example, contains 27 donative inscriptions from monks, nuns, traders and a carpenter and perfumer. From a total of several thousand caves in West India, only two caves at the site of Nasik were excavated by royalty. However, kings supported these monastic complexes by granting villages for their upkeep. Such widespread community involvement during this period suggests general economic prosperity. Following his conversion to Buddhism, the Mauryan emperor Asoka abandoned the royal cult of sacrifice which had been at the core of the king's spiritual existence. He replaced it with the Buddhist tradition of acquiring merit through gift giving to monks and monastic communities, and donations to the stupa which became a monumental focus for lay aspirations. The essential feature of this practice, known as the renouncer tradition, involved material giving for the acquisition of spiritual aims, and the rejection of worldly possessions. The Buddhist texts refer to the 'Mahadanas' or great gifts and were opposed to the Vedic animal sacrifices which they designated

'Mahayajna'. Imperial rulers turned the bestowal of gifts into formal ceremonies which became a central feature of ritual activities. For their part the Buddhists absorbed earlier local cult practices of offerings to tree and naga shrines into the worship or honouring of the signs of the Buddha.

Response to this can be seen in the medieval Hindu sutra literature, where prescriptions of ritual action are given. Slaughter is replaced by the symbolic offering of vegetal substances into the sacred fire. Gift giving to Brahmans became one of the prime duties of the king. The earlier rituals of the householder which had been considered secondary to the cosmo-regal sacrifice now became more significant as the kings abandoned their ancient rites. The great revealed or cosmo-regal rites which had been performed inside the sacrificial enclosure lost their pre-eminence and gave way to those performed outside it.

> The great gift ceremony of Buddhism became the central ceremony of the imperial kingdoms of ancient India, and so long as the Aryan states were included within it, they were confined to the performance of vegetarianised, simplified domestic forms of Vedic sacrifice.[3]

The old rituals were not forgotten however, for after the decline of Buddhism at the end of the seventh century AD and the weakening of the imperial centre, the regional rulers again reverted to horse sacrifice as they acquired independence. From the second century BC there was a gradual revival of Brahmanic authority and royal interest in the empowering and legitimizing attributes of sacrifice. The Sunga king in the second century BC sponsored two horse sacrifices, and inscriptions attest to similar Satavahana, Ikshvaku and Pallava Vedic ceremonies.

Alongside formulations of the sacrifice in the sutras, texts as early as the *Mahabharata* began to transform regional Vedic deities whose icons became honoured in a similar manner to the honouring of the symbols of the Buddha. During the Gupta period statues were placed in domestic shrines and in small temples which were less lavish than the Buddhist structures, and daily domestic rituals were conducted by Brahmans. These had their roots in the long established practices and everyday needs of Vedic society and reinforced the authority of the Brahmans as the mediators between the population and their gods. However, image worship was still not seen as the core part of devotion. Following Buddhism's banning of sacrificial ceremonies and despite the prevalence of the renouncer tradition, there arose a revival of dependence on Brahmans who continued to perform the major ceremonies of initiation and wisely acted to absorb the renouncing aspect which had become perceived to be vital to kingly success. Hindu rites replaced Buddhist in central cults.

The ceremony that came to replace the Vedic cosmo-regal sacrifice was referred to in the *Puranas* as the 'great gift' (mahadana). This giving took a number of forms; for example, hiranya-garbha, literally meaning birth from a golden embryo, and tula purusa or the weighing of the king against gold. This latter ceremony was first performed by the Rastrakuta king, Dantidurga in AD 753. From the fifth to seventh centuries Hindu kings no longer saw the necessity for the old cycle of exchanges with the elemental gods and approached the deity for grace rather than with the expectation of contractual obligations. According to the

scholar Dirks, the great gifts in the Pallava period took the form of large endowments of land and wealth to learned Brahmans and temples.[4] This new personal relationship with the gods arose in part because of a new belief in divine benevolence towards man expressed on both sides in terms of human emotions instead of ritual duties. It also expressed the new concept of the king's descent from the Puranic gods Vishnu or Siva. Early evidence of this changed attitude appears in the *Bhagavad Gita*. One manifestation of this direct relationship between the individual and the gods was the appearance of the emotional bhakti devotional cults, which began in South India and later spread to the north. The Vedic fire rituals were subordinated by the central Puranic ritual of image on a central altar.

Gradually, however, the need for Vedic ritual to supply and renew the divine power of the warrior king became supplanted by the need to secure legitimacy by identification with the deity and to be empowered through devotion and ritual bathing. This is most clearly seen from the Ikshvaku, Pallava and Rastrakuta periods. The Kusana kings (first century AD), of foreign origin brought the idea of divine descent, a new concept in India and claimed to be 'the sons of God'. They were occasionally depicted in sculptured portrait form in the shrines.

As part of this changing relationship between men and the gods, the medieval Hindu royal ceremony continued the Rajasuya Vedic royal consecration ceremony. In Sangam literature, the early Tamil kings were credited with performing this ceremony. Ritual lustration became the crucial element in the transmission of the divine and served to both purify the king and also to fertilize the king's symbolic marriage to the earth. Marriage became an antidote to sacrifice; marriage, like sacrifice, was an event during which mortals and deities interact, and in the royal consecration symbolically expressed the taming of the goddess (earth) by her marriage to the god. The visual association of Lakshmi on a lotus lustrated with elephants is seen as early as the second century BC portraying this ceremonial and expresses through the elephant the themes of royal authority and fertility. Certain myths associating Lakshmi with Indra also reinforce the idea of Lakshmi and ritual fertility.[5] It also incorporated ancient pre-Vedic ideas regarding ritual bathing and purification and perhaps also subsumed the divine liquid known as Soma. It is significant that in the course of history Sri-Lakshmi has herself been associated in some texts with the god Soma. In attending the god Soma she was seen to bestow royal authority; her association with Soma is also linked to the fact that Soma was lord of the plants and vegetative growth. For centuries this sacred intoxicant had been imbibed by the Brahmans during sacrificial ritual and was associated with fecundity and procreation. Soma disappeared with the old ceremonies taking with it its precise ingredients.

The essence of Hindu religious evolution from the second century BC to the third century AD may be summed up as follows. In temple ritual the adoption of ahimsa resulted in the practice of symbolic sacrifice substantially replacing sacrificial violence. Hinduism incorporated the renouncing tradition and absorbed the 'folk' belief in placatory offerings and the worship of personal gods. Most importantly, Hinduism accepted the folk belief that spirits or devas have the potential to reside in a structure

or image, under the right conditions. The creation of tangible visual images as an alternative to the abstract verbal descriptions of the elemental gods of Vedism provided dramatic new possibilities for patronage and devotion.

Section I of this chapter will explore what were the principal forms of artistic patronage and will then examine the relevant historical evidence. Section II will explore the identity of the principal patrons and their motivation for patronage. It will however limit the study of patronage to the monumental stone temples, sculpture and painting. The folk tradition, with its patronage of the minor arts including wayside shrines, terracotta figurines, textiles, wall and hand painting and metal vessels will be explored in Chapter 6. It is important to note that this division between the 'monumental' and the 'folk' traditions is an artificial division, the result of an attitude in Indian and Western scholarship over the last two hundred years. It is becoming increasingly apparent, as this book also indicates, that there is much more interrelationship than was hitherto believed.

Evidence of patronage is mainly to be found in the form of inscriptions. The climate is not conducive to the preservation of manuscript records. Land grants and eulogistic and commemorative inscriptions on stone tablets or pillars and copper plates do exist however. On some inscriptions the date, names of the architect, the author of the inscription and the engraver may be given. The opening invocations are generally to a deity such as Siva or Vishnu. The verses usually praise the royal patron or record the donor and his family before detailing the nature of the gift which was usually money or agricultural land. This was intended to build or sustain the temple. Other sources of information for patronage include inscriptions by pilgrims to holy sites, and memorial inscriptions which refer to departed relatives or warriors who died, and occasionally the self-immolation (sati) of widows.[6] Michael Willis has written that the study of religious and royal patronage in North India has been difficult due to the standard, repetitive formulae of the epigraphical inscriptions, and the fact that many of the temples have been subsequently ruined and are therefore unidentifiable. In South India by contrast, from the seventh century AD, many temples bear inscriptions of a rich and varied kind together with prasasti and eulogies. North India suffered from sporadic Muslim raids and at the end of the twelfth century a permanent Muslim state was established. This resulted in a sudden decline in the endowment of temples and the making of images in north India. Despite this however, the Jains continued to invest in large-scale temple construction in remote areas such as Gujarat. South India remained free from Muslim attack for a further century and patronage of Hindu temples continued unabated.

Forms of Patronage

The nomadic Aryan peoples did not encourage the building of permanent secular or sacred buildings nor the commissioning of images. They did however construct altars (vedi) and erect sacrificial posts (yupas). From the earliest texts however, there are references to the mention of wooden vessels such as buckets and large sacrificial ladles. Referring to the making of offerings, the *Upanishads* state that purtadharma, which involved the building of temples, water tanks and such works, was meant for fools who go to the lower worlds; and that tapas or spiritual penance was held to be the highest virtue.

By the time of the *Puranas*, however, there was a fundamental change of attitude and purtadharma was now held in the highest regard. This took the form of housed images, continued payment to Brahmans and the building of grand temples. These temples housed religious icons and water tanks and were ornamented with decorative sculpture. Other forms of artistic patronage included religious painting, music and dance, and the offering of a range of ritual items such as bells, swords, lamps, textiles and jewellery to the temple gods. Other gifts could be in the form of sandal paste or flowers, cash donations, thrones, parasols, crowns and clothing for the deity, palanquins and temple chariots.

In many temples records exist of exact amounts of money provided for the work on a sculptural panel or for the upkeep of the buildings. As temples became larger, more costly and elaborate, public subscriptions or additional taxes were sometimes introduced to provide a further source of revenue.[7] Donations from royal patrons and private individuals towards the running of the temple and its upkeep were received in the form of money, valuable objects such as jewels, livestock or income from grants of land, including whole villages and their inhabitants.

Donations were sometimes given in gratitude for the intercession of the gods or for the fulfilment of a vow. Two other important requirements of the temple were music and dancing. For example, in the Minaksi temple at Madurai, Vedaparayana Brahmans and otuvar were responsible for the sacred hymns and the devadasis for music and dance. The devadasis were gifted to the temple as young girls and were dedicated to the god. This wealth acquired by the temple served not merely its construction but also the expenses of administration, puja, festivals and payment of temple servants. Rulers instituted festivals and ordered the routes for the progress of processions. The cost of the festivals and the expenses of daily worship six times a day were largely borne by the temple from the income of land owned by it.

The Historical Development of Royal Patronage

Kusana dynasty: first to fourth century AD

The Kusanas were a tribe from the northwestern province of China who established an empire in North India from approximately AD 120. They brought the idea of divine descent, a new concept in India, claimed to be 'the sons of God' and placed their portrait sculpture among the icons in the shrines. The distinct feature of Kusana art was the emphasis on the divinity of the emperor. Evidence of this is seen both on coinage based on Near Eastern and Greek prototypes, and in surviving shrines, such as Mat near Mathura and at Surkh Kotal in Afghanistan which were found to include royal portrait sculpture. The term devaputra, 'son of God', was used to refer to the kings themselves. The inscription on one of the statues in the shrine at Mat gives the ruler the title 'Great king, king of kings, son of God the Kusana scion, the shahi'.[8] The inclusion of the title 'shahi' betrays the king's Iranian origin. The Kusan ruler Kanishka was a tolerant, perhaps pragmatic ruler who permitted and apparently encouraged the patronage of the religious

arts from such diverse faiths as Buddhism and Zoroastrianism. This religious co-existence gave rise to an interrelationship in the sculptural styles of Buddhist, Hindu and Jain art from Mathura and Gandhara from the first century AD. The standard iconographic formulae for Jain, Buddhist and Hindu figurative sculpture was established during Kanishka's reign and figure sculpture became commonplace from this period. Despite this interest in royal portraiture much of the religious art and architecture was still not a direct result of royal gift but continued to be dependent on communal donations. The decline of Buddhism in North and East India was marked by a corresponding decline in trade and a decrease in the patronage of Buddhist monasteries. This coincided with a gradual increase in royal patronage. Kusana art flourished for approximately two centuries, until it was eclipsed by the new style patronized by the Guptas, who seized power in the north as late as AD 445.

Satavahana dynasty: first to third century AD

In South India from the first to third century AD, the Satavahanas were largely responsible for the patronage of Buddhist cave or stupa sites. Amaravati, the most famous of the Satavahana Buddhist sites, was the result of royal and communal patronage. It was a thriving economic centre which benefited from international sea trade.

Ikshvaku dynasty: third to fourth century AD

The successors to the Satavahanas in the south, the Ikshvakus, ruled from the second quarter of the third century AD for about a hundred years. The Ikshvakus who were patrons of both Buddhist and Brahmanical faiths were the first to worship Karttikeya, whose name is derived from Krttika, the Sanskrit name for his birth star, otherwise known as Skanda. A local deity, Murukan, was specific to Tamil Nadu and is known and worshipped in the villages to this day. Murukan was absorbed into orthodox Hinduism as the warrior god Karttikeya. Karttikeya incorporated some of the Tamilian sangam warrior hero tradition and legend described him as the brother of Ganesa. The Ikshvakus are important in providing fragmentary evidence of the beginnings of free-standing temple structures. During this period Hindu nobles appear to have increased their patronage and involvement in temple activities. Princes and queens were certainly involved in the construction of temples for Karttikeya and other gods.[9] As we will see below the princesses were also supportive of Buddhism.

Chantamula was the founder of the dynasty and was a devout Hindu and worshipper of Karttikeya. Epigraphic records suggest that Chantamula himself was a monarch with indomitable determination who involved himself in the performance of Vedic sacrifices. In accordance with Vedic practice he was probably more interested in the traditional ritual ceremonial than in the creation of permanent shrines.

The golden age of this dynasty was during the rule of Chantamula's grandson Vasishthiputra Ehuvala Chantamula, a devout Saivite. His son, prince Haritiputra Virapurushadatta by his queen Kapanasri, claimed himself to be mahasenapati (son of Karttikeya). He was also given the title Haritiputra (son of the goddess Hariti),

a practice adopted from the fourth century by the neighbouring Cutus, who had a close marriage allegiance with the Ikshvakus.

Ehuvala was succeeded by his son Rudrapurushadatta, who had a memorial raised in honour of his mother. Inscribed memorial pillars were common at the time and were erected in honour of soldiers who fell in battle. This practice of erecting memorial stones remained popular in India until comparatively recently.

Extensive archaeology in 1956 at Nagarjunakonda, prior to the flooding of the site as part of a hydel system, revealed a well-planned capital with considerable emphasis on bathing establishments in the form of ornamental water tanks, wells, underground drains and paved cisterns. The baths generally consisted of an oblong cistern, a well and a soak-pit, sometimes even connected with open or underground drains. Dice were played using game boards on the casing slabs of the bathing ghat. There are the remains of temples, some on the banks of the river Krishna. Half a dozen provide inscriptions which indicate their affiliation and date; five of them were dedicated to Siva and his son Karttikeya or Devasena (another name for Karttikeya). There was only one dedicated to Vishnu and one to the mother goddess. These temples are particularly important for the study of Hinduism because they are the earliest remains of Brahmanical temples known in the south. Haritiputra Virapurushadatta built the Pushpabhadrasvamin temple at Nagarjunakonda on an apsidal plan, near the river and adjacent to the other Siva temples. These were found to have been apsidal or oblong, the shrines being constructed of brick, the mandapa of stone and one even included the use of wood.[10]

Square shrines were also evident at this time. The excavated Pushpabhadrasvamin temple revealed a provision for the flow of abhiseka water through the pranali which confirms literary evidence on current practice at that time.[11] The importance of lustration may well derive from earlier cults associated with the cult of the goddess as seen in the early Gaja Lakshmi image from the Bharhut stupa of the second century BC. The generous provision of ceremonial baths also points to ideas of purification and the importance of ritual bathing. This may echo ancient practices involving the large water tank at Mohenjo Daro in the Indus valley culture, though these matters remain conjectural and the link unproven. The intermarriage of the Ikshvakus with the Rastrakutas may explain the growing significance of ritual bathing as part of the royal initiation of kings during the Rastrakuta period.

Evidence of the importance of an earlier matriarchal society is revealed in the Ikshvakus period. This can be seen in the continuation of the old matronymic practice (the use of the mother's name) and in the pre-eminence of female patrons;[12] and in the large stone image of the mother goddess found in Nagarjunakonda. Further evidence of the strength of the cult of the goddess may also be suggested by the discovery of terracotta female figurines and a pot formed in the image of a squatting female, as well as the two temples to the goddess.[13] A matriarchal culture, a goddess cult, the pre-eminence of noble or female patronage, the emphasis on ritual bathing and a prolific number of water tanks and ceremonial baths seem to be characteristic features of the patronage of the Ikshvaku dynasty.

The decline of the Ikshvakus coincided with the rise of the Pallavas from the mid-fourth century AD, when the Ikshvakus may well have been reduced to subordinate vassals.

Gupta dynasty: AD 320–650

In the Gupta period kings continued to show more interest in the traditional Vedic ritual than in temple building. Inscriptions however reveal a concern with self-promotion through edicts on pillars or coins rather than through identification with sacred monuments. The idea of great temple complexes had not yet been established. The relationship of interdependency between king and Brahman was reinforced. Gupta kings were concerned with the acquisition and maintenance of earthly power rather than in giving away wealth by the patronage of building in order to gain spiritual merit. This period however was a time of great economic prosperity. The increased prosperity of the aristocracy gave rise to a flowering of literature and the visual arts. The Gupta monarchs continued the Kusan attempt to depict the king as God and revived Sanskrit, the hieratic language of Brahmanic ritual. Narrative poems, dramas, inscriptions and coins portray idealized figures of kings who were said to rival the gods in their physical and spiritual prowess as well as their skill in art.

Stone was used infrequently for the great Hindu temple complexes before the fifth century AD. The earliest North Indian temples have been assigned to the patronage of the Gupta kings but this is uncertain due to their fragmentary inscriptions. The two earliest extant temples of this period are at Sanchi and Tigawa. They are simple flat-roofed sanctuaries with entrance porches. No image is preserved in these sancturies nor are there dedicatory inscriptions. Other examples are the fifth-century Siva temple at Bhumara which has a fine ekamukha (single-faced) linga, a sixth-century Dasavatara temple at Deogarh, which has superb friezes depicting scenes from the Ramayana and Krishna legends, and the temple at Nachna which can also be attributed to this period on stylistic grounds, although there are no inscriptions to support this attribution.

Evidence of one royal patron in this period is provided by an inscription on an early fifth-century Jain cave temple at Udayagiri, dedicated to the Gupta ruler Kumaragupta. It is significant that this temple with its royal inscription is dedicated to Jainism which has a tradition of spiritual gain in return for material gift giving. Another inscription dedicated to the Gupta king Buddhagupta can be found on the neck of the great fifth-century boar (Varaha) image at Eran. However the scarcity of these royal inscriptions suggests a limited royal interest in the patronage of sacred architecture and images.

Architectural expression in North India during this early period was in the form of free-standing stone buildings, the construction of brick architecture (for example, in Ahichhatra, Pawaya and Bhitargaon) and rock-cut architecture was also undertaken. A sculptural panel in a cave in Udayagiri, west of the ancient capital of Vidisha, has as its subject the rescue of the goddess Bhudevi by Varaha. This panel has sometimes been interpreted as an allegory of the unification of North India under the Gupta ruler Chandragupta II.[14]

The personified river goddesses Ganga and Yamuna feature regularly as the guardians of shrines by this time. They are said to represent purification and to act as the bridge between heaven and earth. This sacred bridge links the earth to those realms from which the river Ganga arose. These water images supplanted earlier Yaksha, Yakshini or the Panchika, Hariti guardian figures. The earliest known depiction of the image of Durga also dates from this time and can be seen on the outside of the Gupta temple of Deogarh. It has been suggested that this signifies the revival of the cult of the goddess and her defeat of the buffalo demon, the defeat of the male-dominated hierarchical religion of the male Vedic Gods. During the Gupta period Vaishnava worship encouraged patronage of monuments dedicated to Puranic deities, but these appear to have been inspired by princes or nobles rather than kings.

Gurjara-Pratiharas of Kanauj

Few buildings have survived from the sixth and seventh centuries, a period of political disintegration and invasion, in North India. The death of the local ruler Harsa in AD 647 gave rise to political disintegration, leading to division into states and a variety of styles. The most significant ruler to emerge in this period was Yasovarman of Kannauj (AD 720–50). Despite his historical importance little architecture can be assigned to him, although he is reputed to have built a temple at Harischandranagari (Ayodhya). His successor is credited with building a temple to Mahavira at Gwalior.[15] By the beginning of the eighth century in North India the Pratihara dynasty had become the dominant power in the region.[16] A column found in Maddodara eight kilometres from Jodhpur is believed to mark the Pratihara capital. Inscriptions recording the rule of the Gurjara-Pratiharas have been found in an extensive area of North India, in the states of Rajasthan, Haryana, Gujarat, Uttar

Pradesh, Madya Pradesh, Bihar and West Bengal and even in Bangladesh, but remains of buildings are scarce.

Fragmentary inscriptions on buildings during this period leave responsibility for temple construction in considerable doubt. Inscriptional evidence suggests that princes continued to take an active interest in the construction of temples and that the kings remained detached, not committing themselves to any overt association with temple patronage. The early text known as the *Vishnudharmattora Purana* suggests that despite the lack of royal claim to temples at this time the king's permission needed to be sought before construction could commence.[17] In addition, historical evidence in the form of new entries in the *Puranas* from the sixth century AD onwards, as has been already mentioned, suggests that the kings supported ceremonial danas or gift giving to the Brahmans. The *Puranas* also emphasized that the purtadharma which involved funding the building of temples, water tanks and works of public utility was the most meritorious religious act.[18]

However, in conformity with past practice the Pratihara kings appeared to have been more concerned with ensuring Brahman support for their authority than with identification with specific temples. Records demonstrate that the imperial Pratiharas were patrons of Brahmans and notable temples but there is no evidence to suggest that they patronized the actual construction of temples or images, though they may indeed have done so. Such evidence that exists shows that they were active in providing land grants. Surviving Pratihara copperplate inscriptions record gifts of villages to Brahmans. In several instances the kings made grants for the religious merit of their parents, an ancient practice.[19]

These records contain royal genealogies and references to deities who were the object of each monarch's special devotion.

Temple style continued in the Gupta tradition. A Surya temple at Mankheda, without inscription and attributed on stylistic grounds to the late ninth century, is one of the best preserved monuments of the Pratihara period. Gwalior possesses the most ambitious project of the Pratihara era, the 'Teli Ka Mandir', which despite its destruction has been carefully restored, but it too is devoid of any inscription. Temples ascribed to the ninth century are found in Rajim, Mankheda, Jagat and Osian to name but a few, but all lack dedicatory inscriptions. The Pratiharas were subject to rivalry from the Rastrakuta dynasty, which was growing in strength and ultimately eclipsed their position.

The obstruction of trade in the ninth to tenth centuries led to an accumulation of surplus wealth by the feudatories, who invested it in conspicuous consumption and the erection of increasingly large temples to proclaim the glory of the patrons. The temple became increasingly linked to the king and to the manifestation of power. Temple building during this period became more significant in its legitimizing and empowering role, so that temples acted as sacred centres of the dynasty. Buddhism and the concepts and manifestations of imperialism separated, and the former largely disappeared, while the regional sacrificial rites and the honouring and worship of idols became predominant. The *Puranas*, compiled from the seventh to eighth centuries AD, contained chapters on vastu and silpa and the artisans were expected to follow strict canons as regards the choice of site, design and construction of the shrine. Temple construction therefore attracted a greater proportion of royal revenue and became more complex and dramatic. There was a strengthening of the ties, dependency and identification of king and temple. This period is also richer in epigraphic records, which shed considerable light on post-Pratihara patronage. After the decline of the Pratiharas in the tenth century, Central India was divided by a number of independent dynasties which lasted until Muslim military incursions extinguished them.

An outstanding example of this connection between king and temple is seen in the Paramara period of the eleventh century in the Udayesvara temple (Nilankanthesvara) dated 1080. An inscription on the eastern porch proclaims the donor to be the king Udayaditya. In the Malwa region the Paramaras continued to hold power.

Chandella dynasty in Central India

Rivalling the Udayesvara temple is the great complex of temples built under the patronage of the Chandella dynasty from the tenth century on. As early as the ninth century the Chandellas had become prominent in Central India, using Khajuraho as their capital. The Chandellas first appeared as a notable power when Harsadeva supported Mahipala (c. AD 912–43) in his bid for the Pratihara throne. His successor Yasovarman (c. AD 925–54) took Kalinjar, an important fortress and centre of military power. They are perhaps the best known regional dynasty owing to the number of temples which survive in Khajuraho (ancient Khajuravahaka). This site was adorned with numerous water tanks, Hindu and Jain temples, lakes and gardens which were created by the Chandellas, their chiefs and merchants from

AD 900 to 1150. Tradition records the existence of 85 temples of which only 25 have survived. The shrines built by royalty and the aristocracy are situated in the western area near the Sibsagar lake (again this may refer to the importance of water in the Hindu ritual ceremonial), while those erected by the Jain merchants are to the east of the village of Khajuraho. The Khajuraho monuments are the culmination of central Indian style (Figure 4.10). Long inscriptions attached to some of the important temples in Khajuraho give an idea of the patronage in the town. Most of these inscriptions have been moved from their original positions however.

The Chandellas sought to glorify their origins as a means to elevate their previous tribal origin. Connection has been made between the Chandellas and the tribal Gonds and Bhars. The Chandella records equated kings with gods and epic heroes. They depended upon the Brahmans for the legitimation of their social status. In order to acquire merit and attain popularity, gift making and the building of water tanks, temples and other charitable works served an important function.

The Lakshmana temple at Khajuraho is an early temple symptomatic of the building activities of the Chandella kings. The inscription in this temple is on a stone slab in the porch. It gives a detailed description of how Yasovarman forced the Pratihara king Devapala to surrender an ancient and celebrated metal image of Vishnu-Vaikuntha which was set up in the Lakshmana temple, a building expressly constructed for the purpose by Yasovarman. This inscription also records that Yasovarman's conquest of the fort of Kalanjara marked a step towards sovereign power. It was specially built by the father of Dhanga to enshrine the Vishnu-Vaikuntha. This temple reveals a well-planned and integrated scheme. Its inscriptions glorify the royal patron and his family but fail to mention an architect. Thus this temple was a symbol of Yasovarman's victory and power.[20] The inscriptions also vow to protect Brahmanas, cows and to support the three Vedas.

The Lakshmana temple was the first at Khajuraho to place carved erotic figures on architectural junctures. There is considerable debate as to the purpose of these figures, but a factor which influenced the form and decoration of some of these temples was the absorption of tantric ideas and the increasing power of tantric sects in certain regions of India from the fifth to tenth centuries AD. Architectural junctures are structurally and esoterically weak, and the intention was probably to employ tantric concepts of sympathetic magic to guard these areas. According to Desai, a sect called the Pasupatas were invited by the kings of various regions such as Gujarat Dahala in Central India, Mysore, Orissa and Kashmir to head temple organizations. The power of the tantric sects increased because kings are thought to have valued their arcane knowledge on diverse subjects such as alchemy and aphrodisiacs which was placed at the service of the ruler and his state.[21] Pun and allegory were highly valued not only in plays such as the *Prabodhacandrodaya*, written by Krishna Misra, the Chandella court poet, but also in architectural decoration. Knowledge of several meanings of words was highly valued[22] and reflects the parallel taste for multivalent architectural decoration. An extreme example is *Rajhavapardaviya*, which tells through *double entendre* the stories of the *Ramayana* and the *Mahabharata*.

Dhangadeva, who ruled at Khajuraho between 950 and 1002, built the temple of Visvanatha in the western area of the town at the end of his reign. It has an inscribed slab placed in the porch[23] which praises the Chandella family, the kings Yasovarman and Dhanga and also the architect (sutradhara), Chhichha, who is described as well versed in the science of architecture. Praising the temple's entrance way, the poet described it as created by the architect Visvakarma himself. The inscription also tells of Dhangadeva's dedication to the temple of two stone lingas, one of which was specifically said to have been decorated with a large emerald.[24] The choice of an emerald suggests an awareness of a statement in the *Puranas* that an emerald or jewelled linga was an appropriate donation on the fulfilment of a desire. Inscriptions tell of the king's longevity (over a hundred years), and it would appear that he constructed the temple towards the end of his life when he had attained political status and fame.

Chandella inscriptions usually make a passing reference to their Pratihara overlord, yet the temple Visvanatha, built in 1002–3, fails to refer to him, and this supports the belief that the Chandellas had ceased to be tributaries and became independent. Dhangadeva was known as 'the lord of Kalanjara fort'. He conquered Gwalior and his territory extended from Gwalior to Vidisha and from Varanasi in the north to the Narmada river in the south. He was one of the leading powers of North India and the first independent ruler of the Chandella dynasty to resist the overlordship of the Pratihara kings of Kanauj.[25]

Dhangadeva's longevity and the stability of his rule was conducive to the flourishing of the arts. He is described in an inscription of AD 954 on a temple built by his father Yasovarman, which praises Dhanga

as a source of munificence, bravery, discernment (viveka) of arts and dalliance (kala-vilasa) of intelligence, majesty and might, accomplishing his purposes, by means of such conduct, all at once created in the minds of well-disposed people the belief that the Kali-age had out of season come to an end.[26]

During his rule, the Jain merchants of Khajuraho were active patrons of temples. The Parsvanatha temple was built by the Jain merchant Pahita who was, according to the temple inscription, respected by the king Dhanga.[27]

According to Desai, the religious leanings of Dhangadeva may have inclined towards the Saiva Siddhanta sect, worshipping Siva in the form of Sadasiva. Two unique images of Sadasiva Chatushpada (with four legs) found in Khajuraho support this assertion. A syncretic image combining Siva, Vishnu and Brahma placed on the superstructure of the Visvanatha temple is of significance, since such an image was considered to be a 'support' for meditation on Sadasiva.[28]

Inscriptions in Khajuraho also reveal that Dhanga performed the tulapurushadana ceremony, weighing himself against gold and distributing it to the Brahmanas. He also established dwellings for pious Brahmanas well versed in the six acts (shar karma) and who practised 'ever-enduring sacrifice', and he donated land, grain, money and cows to the Brahmanas. The Visvanatha temple inscription refers to a royal priest Bhatta Yashodhara, who according to a copperplate of Dhanga, was a follower of the Vajasaneyi sakha and received the gift of a village from the king.

Dhangadeva died before the dedicatory inscription on the Visvanatha temple was engraved, according to legend while meditating on Rudra. The Matangesvara temple is believed to have been erected in his memory. It has a roof of the conical type that is appropriate for a hall rather than a shrine and follows the requirements of funerary temples, like the Bhojpur temple, possibly built in memory of King Bhoja.

The Chandella temples from Khajuraho demonstrate the degree to which the patronage of temples is used to proclaim the power and legitimacy of the rulers. The reference to the seizing of an icon demonstrates the appropriation and extension of authority through belief in the power of images and also the use of emeralds to signify the fulfilment of desire. Evidence of a temple erected in memory of Dhangadeva provides evidence of a temple's potential to function in a funerary capacity.

Gujarat

The earlier temple at Mount Abu dating from the eleventh century was founded by Vimala and is dedicated to Adinath, the first Jain tirthankara. The Jain brothers Tejpala and Vastupala from Gujarat were famous for their keen patronage of art and architecture. Epigraphy and literature credits them with building numerous monuments. Tejpala built the temple of Neminatha (1230) at Mount Abu and the temple of Mallinatha (1231) at Girnar, both temples being dedicated to Jain tirthankaras. Inscriptions at Mount Abu state that the temple was built for the welfare of Tejpala's wife and son at a cost of 125,300,000 rupees and their portrait sculptures can be seen in the temple.

148

Orissa

From the fifth century AD, parts of East India were absorbed into the Gupta empire and therefore adopted the western Gupta architectural style. However, while western Gupta buildings were made of stone, in the eastern part of the empire most of the building was in brick, the structures being decorated with plaster and terracotta. The first stone temples in Orissa appear later and date from the seventh to eighth centuries. The earliest known patron of architecture in Orissa was Sasanka, a devotee of Siva, but little is known about his patronage. The Sailodbhavas dynasty which ruled until the second half of the eighth century initiated the building tradition which is largely found in Bhubanesvara. From the rule of Sasanka in Orissa until the thirteenth century Saivism (especially Pasupatite) was favoured. The seventh- or eighth-century Parasuramesvara and Muktesvara temples are fine examples of the formative style of the period but do not possess any dedicatory inscriptions.

The grandest architectural monument of the period is the Saivite Lingaraja temple, yet here too there is apparently no dedicatory inscription to link it with patronage of a specific king. The enormous expense of building these fine temples points to the probability of royal patronage. However, the absence of donative inscriptions suggests that the idea of promoting the aspirations of kingship by temple building had not yet taken root in the region.

From the thirteenth century, when the Ganga dynasty replaced the Sailodbhavas, inscriptions appear which give a clearer picture of the intentions of the patrons.

Vaishnavites by preference, they were responsible for the Jagannatha temple at Puri, the Ananta Vasudeva temple in Bhubanesvara and the magnificent sun temple at Konarak. The Ananta Vasudeva temple was dedicated in 1278 by Chandradevi. Chandradevi was a daughter of Anangabhima III during the rule of Bhanudeva I of the Ganga dynasty. In form, the temple resembles the Lingaraja temple but includes Vaishnavite sculptures.

The sun temple at Konarak possesses no contemporary dedicatory inscription,[29] but a later inscription and important textual evidence discovered by Alice Boner reveal that Raja Nrsimhadeva I of the Ganga dynasty initiated construction of the temple at the age of 18 at the suggestion of his mother while he was still a prince.[30] His reason for starting work on such a temple was said to be his successful campaign as commander-in-chief of his father's army. He apparently used the booty from his campaign (perhaps to atone for the violence and bloodshed) to construct this monument. The eventual enormous cost of the temple meant that additional finance from the royal treasury, and other contributions were needed to finish the work. It is believed that the project took 20 years to complete.[31]

It is apparent that the date of consecration for this temple was carefully chosen because of its auspiciousness, falling on the sun-god's birthday.[32] Additional plausible reasons why the prince chose to build such an extravagant monument to the sun on this site have been suggested. The site of the sun temple had already been dedicated to the sun-god in an earlier temple. Furthermore, the wife of Nrsimhavdeva whose name was Sitadevi was the daughter of a Paramara king of

149

Malwa. The popularity of sun worship and sun temples in West India in this period is well known. Sitadevi is referred to in inscriptions and in the *Baya Cakada* text as a major patron of the Sun temple. The queen gave her first-born son by Nrsimhadeva the solar name Bhanudeva, which literally means 'light god', the first time that a solar name had been used by this dynasty.[33] Clearly the influence of the queen was a strong factor in the king's decision.

Pala dynasty in North-east India

The Pala dynasty ruled North-east India from the eighth century. Taranatha, the Tibetan historian writing in the seventeenth century, claimed that Pala artistic style was established by Dharmapala and Devapala, the second and third Pala kings, and was the creation of two craftsmen, Dhiman and Bitpalo, father and son, none of whose works were known and whose historicity has not been verified. It is suggested by Huntington that in spite of Taranatha's emphasis on the Pala king's patronage of Buddhism, the art of this period is not properly a court art produced for the ruling families. Some inscriptions do however link monarchs to patronage of prominent monasteries. It is probably correct to say that the greater part of production reflects active Buddhist and Hindu lay communities.

The early Pala art was chiefly Buddhist, but during the later Pala and Sena periods Hinduism overtook it in popularity. By the end of the twelfth century the arrival of Islamic raiders brought destruction to many important Buddhist and Hindu monuments. Today, many of the religious buildings of this period have simply vanished. Buildings were constructed using brick not stone and wood, bamboo and thatch was extensively used. The more durable black chlorite stone sculptures have survived. So too have fine bronze and silver religious images which date from the twelfth century and were both valuable and portable, and therefore escaped the destruction wrought by the Muslims.

The Deccan and South India

In Maharashtra the Vakatakas were succeeded in AD 520 by the Kalachuri dyanasty, who were a major force in the Deccan region until they were superseded in about AD 600 by the western Chalukyas. The Kalachuri fostered religious movements, principally Pasupati Saivism. Although there are as yet no inscriptions or documentary evidence to tie the Kalachuris to monumental architecture, it is clear that a number of caves were excavated during this period in the western Deccan. The prime example is the great cave temple on the island of Elephanta off the coast of Bombay. An inscribed stone found on the island might have revealed information on the dedication, date and patronage of this site but this was regrettably lost by the Portuguese. Stylistically, the temple can be dated to AD 540–555. Among the interesting sculpture in the Elephanta temple is a large Sadasiva sculpture of Siva with five faces; another depicts Siva with flowing hair into which flows the river Ganga in female form.

The Deccan is an area of India where early stone architecture is better preserved. The capital of the early Chalukyan rulers was at Badami. According to George Michell, stylistic contacts with the Pallavas of Kanchipuram are suggested by inscriptions at the Badami site. A dedicatory inscription is found in Cave 3 dated AD 578 referring to its excavation during the reign of the early Chalukya ruler Pulakesin I. This is a large rock-cut monument with the most remarkable sculpture. By the seventh century the tradition of free-standing temple architecture was firmly established and from the first quarter of the seventh century the Chalukyan kings claimed the prerogative of building temples. The Meguti temple (AD 634), a north-facing Jain temple, bears a dated inscription ascribing it to the early Chalukyan ruler Pulakesin II. It is significant in being one of the earliest dated temples of India showing royal involvement.[34] Early Chalukyan buildings at Aihole, Badami, Mahakuta and Satyavolu comprise the largest group of Hindu temples in the Deccan at this time. The town of Aihole contains examples of Hindu and Jain temples which date from the sixth to the twelfth centuries AD.

In the mid-eighth century two queens of the Chalukyan king Vikramaditya II built temples to Siva at Pattadakal to commemorate the victory of their husbands over the neighbouring Pallava ruler. It was a site under which there had already been construction by the Satavahana dynasty from as early as the third to fifth centuries AD. The neighbouring temples to Virupaksha and Mallikarjuna are almost identical. Pattadakal served as a site for the coronation ceremonies of the early Chalukyan rulers. It was situated on the banks of the Malaprabha river at a point where the water flows auspiciously northwards towards the Himalayas, the magic centre of the universe.

Alampur is another important site under the control of the early western Chalukyas during their expansion. While the original name of these temples is unknown, a sixteenth-century inscription from the site calls them the Nava Brahma temples. Perhaps the most beautiful of these nine Brahma temples is the Svarga Brahma temple. This has an inscription above one of the dvarapalas stating that the monument was constructed in honour of the king Vinayaditya's queen during the late seventh century (AD 682–96) by one of her sons. It has been suggested that the use of the North Indian style of building for this temple may reflect the victorious expansion in the north in the way that the southern style of the Virupaksha temple and Mallikarjuna at Pattadakal may be related to the success of Vikramaditya II in the south.[35]

Rastrakutas

Control of the Deccan was taken by the Rastrakutas from the western Chalukyas around AD 750. Although the Chalukyas had founded a great kingdom, the Rastrakutas under Govinda III (794–814) exceeded them, reaching as far north as Kanauj and the sacred Ganga and bringing territory in central and lower western India under their control. Under the Rastrakuta rulers there was a resurgence of rock-cut architecture. The activities of the dynasty were mainly concentrated at Ellora. The most ambitious monument at Ellora is the great Kailasanatha temple. Regrettably, the purpose for the creation of such an extraordinary monument is unknown, but later Jain caves are constructed at Ellora. Most scholars believe that the major portion of the building, including the central temple and Nandi shrine and gateway, belong to the reign of the Rastrakuta King Krishna I, who ruled from AD 757–73. However, according to Huntington, it was planned by his predecessor Dantidurga, since the excavation next to Kailasanatha temple Cave 15 bears an inscription.[36] Dantidurga was the first to perform the Mahadana ceremony.

Inden suggests that the rajasuya ceremony which involved ritual bathing was central to the Rastrakuta ceremonial. Architectural decoration supports the literary evidence of the significance and importance of ritual lustration with large panels of Sarasvati and Abhiseka-Lakshmi flanking the garbhagrha in an early style.[37]

Pallavas

While the Chalukyas were gaining control in the Deccan, South India was dominated by the Pallavas who, by the late sixth and early seventh centuries, were established over an area extending beyond India to China and South-east Asia. No architecture or sculpture survives from before the Pallava period except the first century BC linga at Gudimallam.

It has been suggested that a tradition of using stone for the construction of funerary monuments in the south had given rise to a reluctance to use it for temple architecture.[38] The first monuments known to us are the seventh-century cave temples at Mamallapuram (Mahabalipuram), Mandagappattu and Tiruchirapalli. These rock-cut and monolithic temples are the earliest examples of monumental architecture in South India, and are simple combinations of columned mandapas and shrines excavated into granite boulders. An unusual development of Indian architecture is observed in Mamallapuram in the form of rathas. These are seventh to eighth century monoliths: large boulders carved like buildings on the exterior but, with the

exception of the Draupadi and Ganesa, rathas have no interior space.

Mamallapuram was the port of the Pallava rulers of Kanchipuram and was of great importance in the seventh and eighth centuries. With its natural rock formations and susceptibility to foreign influences through its important trading port, Mamallapuram was particularly open to the development of new architectural forms. It has been suggested that the sudden flowering of stone architecture was due to the strength of its rulers and the religious prominence of bhakti cults in the region giving impetus to artistic developments. Most of the monuments here are associated with two rulers, Mamalla I (AD 630–68) and Rajasimha (AD 700–28).

The earliest surviving monuments of the Pallavas belongs to the reign of Mahendravarman I (AD 580–630), whose rule coincided with that of Pulakesin II of the neighbouring early western Chalukyas. Originally a Jain, Mahendravarman was converted to Saivism by the saint Appar, as is clear from the Saivite dedications on monuments associated with him. The cave temple at Mandagappattu is linked to this ruler and is called the temple of Laksita in its dedicatory inscription.[39] Mahendravarman himself, the royal patron in the epigraph, is referred to as vichitrachitta (clear minded). The cave in the inscription is called a brickless, timberless, metalless, mortarless mansion, implying that former buildings were constructed of these materials and that Mahendra was the initiator of a new architectural tradition. This lends weight to Dirk's suggestion that there was a new emphasis in the Pallava period on large endowments to Brahmans and temples, which contributed to the growth in temple building and the power of the priesthood.[40]

The most famous phase of Pallava art was during the reign of the king Narasimhavarman I who is popularly known as Mamalla I. A successful and expansive ruler, Mamalla I seized Badami from the Chalukyas in 642. It is to Mamalla that credit is largely given for developing the existent seaport which took his title as Mamallapuram. Extant sacred architecture from the Pallava patrons of Mamallapuram range from cave temples to a single shore temple. The earliest cave temple is the Varaha Mandapa, believed to have been commissioned by Mamalla I. In the Varaha cave shrine it has been suggested that the sculptural panels of Hindu deities in the caves have a double meaning, referring both to mythology and to the actual achievements of the king. For example, it is suggested that the images of Varaha (the boar) and Trivikrama (the striding dwarf) actually symbolize the Pallava king's defeat of the Chalukya Pulakesin and the avenging of defeats to the Pallavas under his father. Dual allusions were popular in the Pallava period and are known from inscriptions and art. The other reliefs of Gajalakshmi on the left and Durga on the right suggest ideas of prosperity and victory. In the Durga relief the seated figure in front of the image of Durga is about to cut off his head in a ritual sacrifice. A further cave temple which contains an image of Gajalakshmi is the Adivaraha temple. This also possesses fine inscribed portraits of the royal patron and his father. The father is seated on a throne while the son, in deference to his father stands with his two queens modestly by his side (Figure 5.1).

The Trimurti cave shrine at Mamallapuram has fine carvings and gives special emphasis to Durga. The shrine also possesses a raised water tank in front of the cave (Figure 5.2). This is an early example of a feature which becomes characteristic of Pallava and subsequently early Chola monuments.

There is no dedicatory inscription on the famous rock-carved relief at Mamallapuram known as Arjuna's penance. Considerable controversy surrounds the identity of the patron of this magnificent monumental sculpture but it is generally believed to have been executed in the reign of either Mahendravarman I (AD 600–30) or of his son Mamalla (AD 630–68). A sheer, massive boulder with a vertical central cleft provides the stage on which a cast of gods, kings, semi-divine beings and animals dramatically converge on the cleft which is the focal point of the composition and the centre of its ritual purpose. The cleft represents the sacred river Ganga, falling vertically from the heavens as though out of the serene blue sky above the rocks summit to the earth below. A tank concealed on the hill above this boulder allowed water to be released down the cleft to complete the allegory on sacred occasions.[41] In its passage it lustrated naga and nagini, the serpent gods associated with water and fertility who signify their devotion. On one side Arjuna stands in meditation, while across the stream is the four-armed Siva bearing the weapons that Arjuna hopes to win. Below them is a Vishnu hermitage before which saints, deer and a lion peacefully coexist, while chelas practise religious austerities close by. The water from this sacred river originally filled the tank at the bottom which is now dry but which presumably served this sacred site as a place for ritual ablution and possibly royal consecration.

153

Figure 5.1 Narasimha Mamalla I, patron of the Adivaraha temple, Mamallapuram. Pallava dynasty, mid-seventh century. Robert Elgood.

As elsewhere in Indian iconography, the religious theme of the descent of the holy river Ganga and Arjuna's penance are believed by some scholars also to have a political symbolism. A later inscription drew an overt parallel between the Pallavas and the descent of the Ganga purifying the world; and Arjuna may symbolize the Pallavas seeking victory over the Chalukyas.

Also attributable to the reign of Mamalla are the five free-standing rock-cut monoliths called rathas (carts), whose purpose is unknown but which resemble shrines. It has been suggested that these unique stone monoliths resemble earlier,

Figure 5.2
Trimurti temple,
Mamallapuram.
Pallava dynasty,
early eighth
century.
Robert Elgood.

but now extant, domestic wooden or thatched architecture. The third-century Amaravati stupa has similar architectural forms carved on decorative stone panels. A study of these panels suggests that some of the buildings depicted are secular and others, because of the clear images of devotees, are sacred shrines. All appear to be derived from wooden architecture. It has been suggested that the rathas, as their name states, may be symbolic temple chariots. From the tenth century it became common to carve wheels on the base of temples.

The Dharmaraja ratha at the southern end of the site possesses inscriptions and a portrait of Narasimha which is regarded as evidence of the patronage of Narasimhavarman Mamalla I. Other epigraphs inscribed on this building refer to later kings.[42] Further royal symbolism can be seen in the panel of Siva and Uma with Skanda, a popular Pallava image, referring to the Pallava royal family. The portrait shows Narasimha in a stiff pose,

indistinguishable from the accompanying carvings of deities which decorate the building except for some details. His necklace, dress and the longer arms and fuller shoulders which were believed to be kingly qualities are depicted on the monument (Figure 5.3). It is noteworthy that the figures of other royal portraits of the Pallavas are shown in more relaxed poses, and it may be that the style reflects the fact that the king was dead and had assumed the less lifelike pose of the gods. The statue of Narasimha is placed on the south side of the structure, the side which is usually devoted to Yama, the judge of the dead. The existence of later South Indian Chola inscriptions indicating specific funerary monuments called Pallippatai which were erected for royal personages provides some support for the argument that this ratha is indeed a royal funerary memorial.

The Shore temple at Mamallapuram is thought to be a result of the patronage of Narasimhavarman II Rajasimha, who

Figure 5.3 Portrait of Narasimha Mamalla I, on the south side of the Dharmaraja Ratha, Mamallapuram. Pallava dynasty, early eighth century. Robert Elgood.

ruled from AD 700–28. Similar inscriptions are found at the Rajasimhesvara (Kailasanatha) temple at Kanchipuram, which are known to be from the reign of this king. Inscriptions dedicate the Shore temple to Narasimhavarman, who built the monument and named the deity in it and the temple after himself. He called it Rajasimha Pallavesvara, a practice that became popular in South India.[43] It is interesting to note that the earliest part of the temple was originally an open shrine facing the sea, in which still lies the dark image of a sleeping Vishnu. At the eastern end of the Shore temple complex a smaller

shrine dedicated to Siva was built by Rajasimha's son, Mahendravarman III. He also called the deity after his own name, inscribing it Mandresvara.

The growth of economic power through trade and the redistribution of booty led to greater settlement in towns such as Kanchipuram. At Kanchipuram, the Pallava capital, the Kailasanatha temple portrays Gajalakshmi and extremely fine carvings of Siva and Parvati. The interior walls of the colonnade around the courtyard are covered with carved panels which relate the history of the Pallava kings through coronation scenes and military campaigns, showing elephants, horses, footmen and soldiers. The Pallava king and his son are likened to Siva and his son. Inscriptions on pillars of this temple also reveal that Vikramaditya II, the early western Chalukyan king, was so impressed when he visited this temple that he did not carry off its treasures as spoils of war.

The Pallava kings portrayed themselves through myth and actual naming in order to identify themselves with the gods. This deification was intensified by ritual lustration.

> The growing importance of temples can be seen as a reflection of a stimulus to the elaboration and consolidation of local communities, making their rulers sufficiently honorable (or powerful) to make possible (or necessitate) their incorporation into royal relationships in hitherto unprecedented ways.[44]

This no doubt inspired the building of cave shrines and temples. Temples developed from an earlier tradition of stone funerary architecture, in contrast to the usual secular and shrine construction using bricks and mortar, stucco and wood.

Figure 5.6 Lion tank, Gangakondacholapuram, Tamil Nadu. Mid-eleventh century. Robert Elgood.

apparent play on both the name of the god and Vishnuvardhena's victory over the Cholas. By the thirteenth century the Pandyas had superseded the Cholas as South India's major power. By the fourteenth century the Muslim threat was making itself felt in the Hindu kingdoms; only under Vijayanagara rule were the Deccan and the south able to resist the foreign invasion and protect their culture from destruction.

Rayas of Vijayanagara

Vijayanagara, meaning city of victory, was the largest and most powerful Hindu capital in the Deccan between the fourteenth and sixteenth centuries. Within two decades the kingdom extended across the Deccan from sea to sea and at its zenith encompassed an area that included the former territories of dynasties such as the various Chalukyas, the later Cholas and the Pandyas. The primary objectives of the kings who founded these kingdoms was to resist Muslim force and encourage a Hindu revival. They sought to do so by investing in large-scale monumental architecture and carved decoration. Religious buildings were decorated with sculptures and paintings and refurbished.

The most important patron of Vijaynagar was Krishnadevaraya (1509–30). He was a patron of literature and is credited with numerous building projects, including the temple Vitthalasvami. Attributed to the reign of Krishnadevaraya are monolithic images measuring up to about 6.5 metres in height. A new departure in architecture was the placing of an independent goddess shrine, on a smaller scale than the main temple, to the north-west of the principal shrine. This, Huntington suggests, is a logical culmination of the growing importance of the goddess in the south, where as early as the Pallava period the Trimurti cave shrine at Mamallapuram allowed a separate area for devotion to Durga. The most obvious characteristics of this period were the enormous Gopuras or gateways, pillared mandapas, kalyana mandapas (marriage halls) and temple chariots.

Nayaks

Upon the collapse of Vijayanagara after the battle of Talikota in 1565, the Nayak princes who had been their viceroys took advantage of the power vacuum and asserted their political independence. Art under the Nayaks represents a continuation of traditions fostered by the Vijayanagara kings. Four branches of the Nayaks ruled at Madurai, Tanjore, Gingee and Ikkeri, thus establishing separate centres throughout the once unified Vijayanagara territories. Many of the important artistic works of the Nayaks may be attributed to the promotion of Tirumalai Nayak (1623-59). His capital was Madurai which he supplied with new temples, expanding and adding to what was already present. One of the most outstanding creations is the great temple of Madurai. His contribution was seen in the construction of many temples in the area of Tamil Nadu such as Tiruvannamalai, Srirangam and Kumbhakonam.

A temple such as Madurai, which cost so much to build, fulfilled an even greater role than the smaller, less complex temples referred to earlier. It was a focus of life and a major influence in the economic and social lives of the people. It was indeed almost a city itself and needed continuous staffing. It was no longer merely an offering or gift of thanks from the king in his wish to acquire punya (religious merit) or to proclaim his authority and wealth, but had become an institution in its own right. As a religious institution it gained greater power in its own right than any individual.[51]

A pillared hall at Madurai bears life-sized statues on the pillars including portraits of the Nayaks of Madurai and Tirumalai himself. Tirumalai is portrayed in a number of statues at the temple which reveal him in a naturalistic way. This tradition of royal portraiture has been seen in the south since Pallava times.

Analysis of the Patronage of the Hindu Religious Arts

The confusing and fragmentary historical evidence provided by surviving art and architecture from the third century BC to the seventeenth century AD over the whole of the subcontinent nevertheless produces certain broad trends in patronage, and this gives us considerable information on ritual practice. One may speak with some confidence of trends because Hinduism should be seen as an eclectic and coagulating faith. Tolerance of diversity is often a short step from conciliatory absorption and the lack of dogma and existence of common elements contributed to the gradual move to synthesis.

From 1500 BC in Brahmanic times, as has already been established, there was interdependence between kshatriya warriors and Brahman priests. The kings and warriors invested in ritual sacrifices conducted by the Brahmans in the belief that these had the potential to give them divine empowering, sanctification and purification. The renouncing of materialism and the spiritual aspirations of Buddhism and Jainism led to a change in the nature of patronage. Buddhist and Jain lay devotees offered alms to monks and invested in religious art and architecture.

Who Were the Patrons?

Communal patronage

The rise of devotional Hinduism from the third century AD created a need for enshrined images, and this, together with the renouncing tradition of Buddhism which had made such a vital contribution to sacred architecture, led to a growing proliferation of images, rock-cut and free-standing temples. This patronage of Buddhist and Hindu shrines can be seen in the Kusana and Ikshvaku periods from the first to third centuries AD. The religious art of, for example, Bharhut, Sanchi, Karle, Kanheri, Junnar, Amaravati and Nagarjunakonda was patronized by the mercantile and commercial class, artisan and craft guilds as well as the royal families. Communal patronage found among lay Buddhist and Jain devotees in religious art from the merchant classes continued, alongside the growing involvement of higher caste princes, nobles and to a lesser extent kings. Under the inspiration of puranic Hinduism the sculpting of images and the building of temples became the new form of patronage. It is possible that the earliest images were, like the early secular palaces, made of wood.

In the Gupta period in North India, poets such as Kalidasa spent considerable time eulogizing the godlike qualities of the Gupta kings, but despite this royal aspiration, Hindu kings were slow to lay claim to temples until about the sixth century AD. Studies of available inscriptional evidence suggest that patronage was not generally the sole prerogative of kings until the tenth or eleventh centuries.

In the Kusana and Gupta periods, princes and nobles seemed to have invested in shrines while portrait sculpture, resembling religious icons, were placed in temples. This practice may well reflect the growing popularity for the creation of permanent statues. The acquisition of power, however, still seemed to be better served by giving to priests for ceremonials, rather than in acquiring religious merit by building shrines, a practice hitherto associated more with Jainism or Buddhism, where sacred monuments were identified with the acquisition of merit. Kings familiar with open-air rituals and impermanent wooden secular palaces must surely have associated stone temples and shrines with Buddhism. Inscriptional evidence suggests that building shrines was an activity of the princes or wealthy merchants in the urban centres of the Satavahanas and the Ikshvakus in the first to third centuries AD.

Following the breakup of the Gupta empire a period of instability and aspiring leaders created a need to counter the problems and uncertainties of authority and to reinforce kingly legitimacy. This new dynamic of kingship is expressed in patterns of royal endowment, not only to Brahmans and poets but also it would seem to temples.[52] However, lack of material evidence obscures whether or not kings were actually responsible for commissioning temples in the seventh and eighth centuries. The attitude was undoubtedly changing and in South India considerable evidence indicates that the royal Pallavas were responsible for temple building. In North India, however, the moment of change is obscure and there is disagreement due to the fragmentary remains of most temples as to whether or not the Pratihara kings were responsible for their construction. Inscriptions in Pratihara temples reveal a continuance of the earlier patronage of people from various sections of society. From AD 650 to the tenth century, religious art was supported by feudatories and military chiefs who could own and donate land to religious institutions, and to a lesser extent by the kings. They were constructed

by members of the royal family, feudatories, rich merchants and religious acaryas. Among a large number of inscriptions, surprisingly only a few are associated with the kings.[53] Yet according to the *Vishnudharmottara Purana* the king's permission was required.

> An image is to be established in the age of strife in an imperial city, built beforehand, by that king who has defeated kings in battle and no other. Another may, however, establish one, O Yadava, after he has obtained permission (anujna) of the king. The establishment of a permanent image (sthira) in a house-hold shrine (grhya) also requires the permission of the king.[54]

Kings

One of the earliest inscribed and dated temples in South India refers to King Pulakesin, a Chalukyan king who was responsible for the construction of the Meguti temple in AD 634. It is significant that this early temple was not Hindu but Jain. The Jain belief in the acquisition of merit by temple building probably underlies this association and it is likely that the monarch was himself a Jain. Another Jain temple in the north, an early example of a royal Gupta patron of the fifth century, is at Udaygiri, dedicated to the Gupta ruler Kumaragupta, but this is undated. From the seventh century there is growing evidence of royal patronage of religious buildings in South India and to a lesser extent in the north. Under the Pallavas in South India from the sixth century, kings claimed descent from the Puranic gods and demonstrated their kingly power by the redistribution of their booty to Brahmans, temples and lesser chiefs. Royal patronage from North India is particularly evident from the tenth century, with inscriptions compiled by Brahmans which attest to the greatness of kings and to their genealogy to reinforce their power and legitimacy. The gods were brought down to earth and given a solid platform. These temples acted as the kings' powerhouses and became the focus of political and economic generation. Impetus was given to this development by the *Puranas* which claimed that purtadharma, was a spiritually worthy activity held in high esteem. The conscious identification of the king as God's representative on earth reached its apogee in the mid Chola period during the reigns of Rajaraja I and Rajendra I.

Women patrons

The historical evidence shows the extent to which women's religious patronage has had an impact on the development and growth in the popularity of image making. Considerable evidence exists as to the importance of female patrons from as early as the second century BC. The earliest known seated images are from Kankali Tila in the region of Mathura and these are inscribed with the names of female Jain devotees. Evidence of women's patronage is also seen in inscriptions found on early Buddhist religious sites and on early Jain and Buddhist images. Women had an important ritual relationship with local cult deities, notably in the pre-Vedic worship of yaksha and naga shrines; and the terracotta votive offerings associated with these shrines may reflect the common female practice of making offerings for wish fulfilment.

The continuation of an earlier matri-archal order under the Ikshvakus is seen by the continued use of the convention of matronymics. This naming system had been elaborately developed by the Satavahanas in the second and third centuries AD. According to the modern scholar Mulk Raj Anand, in the third century AD the Ikshvaku queens of Nagarjunakonda were respons-ible for the patronage of shrines and temples.[55] The patron of a memorial pillar to the mother of king Rudrapurushadatta which was discovered at Nagarjunakonda is unknown. However, we do know that the son of the Ikshvaku queen Kapanasri patronized the Puspabhadrasvami temple which has a very early transitional form. Evidence of a goddess cult is shown by the remains of temples to the goddess and by excavation, which revealed several miniature terracotta figures of female images and a female squatting image which resembled a purna-kumbha or filled jar decorated with flowers and foliage.[56] The matronymic practice, however, was more or less discontinued from the fourth century AD.

It appears that ritual bathing became more significant at this time. Certainly the facilities for ritual ablutions substantially increased. As has often been stated that in India, water has always been associated with fertility and, through its identification with Lakshmi and the river goddesses, regarded as feminine.[57] Perhaps as a vestige of the matriarchal system, men, who were ritually married to the earth, were seen to require the infusion of female procreative power. Ritual bathing may well have been perceived as the means by which the marriage of king and earth could be rendered fertile and fruitful, fertility and the bringing of rainfall being one of the king's duties.

Early Chalukyan kings of the Deccan claimed descent from the goddess Hariti and adopted her name, which supplanted the earlier use of the matronymic. High caste families from the fourth to sixth centuries AD refrained from appending their mothers' names, but the middle and lower strata of southern society did not fully abandon the matriarchal system. Hariti, from being associated with pestilence, became transformed into a benevolent goddess at the same time as the emergence of Brahmanism in the Deccan and the discontinuation of the matronymic from royal names.[58]

The Chalukyas constructed an increasing number of small shrines and temples, many of which were built by queens. The Chalukyan queen Mahadevi Khanduvula declared in an inscription that her marital happiness and offspring were due to the grace of the goddess Lajja Gauri. Early images of this goddess, who is portrayed with legs apart and the head of a lotus, are in Aihole, Badami, Mahakuta, Siddhanakolla, Jalihal, Alampur and Panchalingala and more than half a dozen survive at Ter, a site linked to the Chalukyas. One of the earliest representations of this cult deity was found at Nagarjunakonda, but there is no evidence of temples being dedicated to this goddess.

As has already been noted, further evidence of female patronage was the Virupaksha temple at Pattadakal, perhaps the most outstanding example of early western Chalukya temple construction. It was built during the reign of Vikramaditya II (733-44) by his chief queen Loka Mahadevi[59] and dedicated to Siva Loketesvara. In the mid-eighth century Loka Mahadevi and another queen built temples to Siva at Pattadakal to commemorate the victory of their husband over the neighbouring Pallava ruler. The neighbouring temples Virupaksha and Mallikarjuna are almost identical.

In Orissa, later inscriptions refer to queen Sitadevi's involvement in the building of the sun temple of Konarak. Queen Sembiyan Mahadevi, the Chola queen of Gandaraditya (949-57), who outlived her husband, was also an important patron. Her religious devotion was said to have inspired her patronage of the arts. Inscriptional evidence reveals her to have been an active patron during the reigns of both sons over the period from 969 to the first part of the reign of the great Rajaraja I (985-1014). Under her influence numerous older brick temples were rebuilt in stone and sculpture began to take on a more stereotyped appearance. This possibly reflected North Indian style which, due to a more faithful adherence to textual prescription, had changed in this manner by the tenth century (Figure 5.4). A sculpture on the side of the early Chola Nageswara temple shows a possible portrait of a queen or princess alongside other lifelike images.

Willis refers to the patronage of queens in North India during the rule of the Gurjara-Pratiharas. Inscriptions refer to queen Jayavali from Buchkala, daughter of Jajjuka of the Gurjara Pratiharas, who built a temple.[60] In Kaman (ancient Kamyaka), queen Vacchika, the wife of king Durgadaman, built a temple. Other temples were built as memorials to queens to increase the fame and religious merit of their consorts and sons. The Lacchukesvara Mahadeva temple at Rajor was built by a prince, Mathanadeva, in memory of his mother Lacchuka.[61]

A further factor in women's pre-eminence in unorthodox village rituals was their ritual purity. The domestic is itself perceived as pure and undefiled.[62] Women were also largely responsible for offerings to local cult deities, such as the snake and tree shrines.

Nobles and officers

Nobles, officers and the lower castes also made significant religious donations in North India. Stelae depicting nobles provide evidence of their involvement in the patronage of temples,[63] as on occasion do memorials recording the deaths of warriors and the self-immolation (sati) of their widows. An inscription near Kotah records the establishment of a temple by a prince in the ninth century and explains that its purpose was to bring spiritual merit and fame to the donor. The inscription also gives the date and the name of the author of the inscription and the temple's architect.[64] Evidence of patronage by the officer class can be seen in two inscriptions on the Chaturbhuj temple at Gwalior which state that it was established by Alla, the warden (kottapala) of Gwalior fort in the last quarter of the ninth century.[65] Alla was the son of Vaillabhata from Lata, who had served the Pratihara king Ramabhadra as a frontier commander during AD 833–6. Alla also became frontier commander and was sent to Gwalior by Mihira Bhoja. Alla built the Caturbhuj temple to Vishnu for his own and his wife's religious merit. The accumulated evidence suggests that officer patrons made only brief mention of their sovereigns in the dedicatory inscriptions and had considerable autonomy.[66] Their wives too on occasion emulated the example of their queens and endowed temples. An example of this can be seen at Gwalior, where an image of Siva and Parvati bears an inscription which states that it was commissioned by Rjuka, the wife of Sri Rudra, a Pratihara feudatory.[67] Another

inscription of unknown provenance records the activities of Yasomati, the wife of a commander in the service of a Guhila prince who built a temple to Vishnu.[68]

Inscriptions also suggest the patronage of artisans and other members of the lower classes who had been forbidden participation in the Brahmanic priestly ritual. Even from the early Buddhist period the decoration of monuments had reflected lower caste preoccupations with such iconographic elements as snakes, lustrating elephants, yakshas and yakshinis, lotuses and trees.

In medieval India collective gifts were sometimes made by social groups or a series of individuals. These are recorded in complicated inscriptions. How complex these arrangements might have been is shown by an inscription from Pehowa. This records that two horse dealers met at Prtthudaka and agreed to pay a proportion of their buying and selling price to four temples at Kanauj.[69] Endowments commonly included villages, fields, houses, shops, cash and even garlands and oil for the lamps of the temple.

Ascetics

A further factor in the construction of temples in North India from the tenth to the eleventh centuries is seen in the growing role of ascetics. Willis refers to an inscription which reveals that a Cahamana clan had a temple constructed by a Simharaja who provided the funds, while the custodians of the shrine were a line of Saiva ascetics or acharyas who supervised the building of the temple. The ascetics organized the hiring of craftsmen, and paid them with the funds provided by the patrons. Evidence of ascetics involvement in temple building and in the life of temples in general is graphically provided by the reliefs on temple walls, for example, on the walls of the Lakshmana temple in Khajuraho (Figure 4.3). With the passage of time the ascetics became a vital part of the temple and indirectly benefited from the revenue offered to the deity.

Temples as patrons

Temples acted not only as patrons and employers but also as charitable institutions. Some had hospitals for the sick and some had special feeding houses which gave free food daily to the poor,[70] particularly during festival time. Temples also acted as custodians and teachers of knowledge, adding to the intellectual life of the region. Ancient texts were compiled and copied and sometimes translated into regional languages. Schools with resident students were founded and maintained. Their dance performances had a vital and didactic role in the ceremonies and festivals. This process is still alive today. For example, the Venkatesvara temple at Tirumalai in South India, reputed to be the richest religious institution in the country, has an active cultural programme. Funds provided by the temple help to support a local university, publishing house and museum.

Aims and Objectives of Temple Patronage

As has been shown, divinity was a crucial concern of kings. The Vedic concept of the absorption of divine powers and of being renewed by transformation in the ritual fire as divine remained the goal in medieval India, but the means changed. The king having become associated with the temple through patronage, in time was identified with the god within the building. The power

of the king and the power of the god became virtually indivisible, manifested through the temple. The divine empowering of the Brahmanic king had been necessary to reinforce his pre-eminence over the other kshatriya warriors and over the Brahmans on whom in so many respects his office depended. To achieve his initial identification with the god, the king still depended on the royal consecration ceremony. Gradually during the Kusan period however, statues of the king were carved and placed in shrines beside stone images of the deity. From the third century AD, visual evidence, particularly in the south, shows the importance of ritual bathing in ceremonials and by the seventh century it had become an essential part of royal consecration. This, together with the acquisition of merit through gift giving, brought about widespread construction of temple water tanks.

One of the chief motivations for sponsorship of religious art in ancient India was the fear of death and its consequences. The desire for a favourable rebirth and ultimate escape from the circle of existence inspired the Buddhist and Jain patrons to acquire punya or religious merit. The patronage of temples by Hindu kings was believed to bring political and economic benefit in state matters and also to ensure favourable status in a future birth.[71] In medieval Hindu India the patron also had an eye to this world, with visions of the prestige attached to the funding of grand architectural monuments which helped his acquisition of power and legitimacy.

Merit

One early manuscript states: 'Let him who wishes to enter the worlds that are reached by meritorious deeds of piety and charity build a temple to the gods.'[72]

The later *Silpaprakasa* manuscript which contained instructions on the method of temple construction stated that such a patron 'will always have peace, wealth, grain and sons'. The acquisition of merit is here linked to prosperity in this world, to be acquired by gift giving. As stone replaced wood as the fabric for the new religious art that was everywhere appearing by the fifth century AD, so too the ancient ritual texts which had been memorized for generations began to be written down. It also coincided with the Puranic injunction encouraging purtadharma, the building of temples as the highest form of religious devotion. Despite the initial patronage of nobles, ladies and merchant classes, the growth of ever grander temple schemes involved an outlay of resources largely beyond the scope of ordinary people and became increasingly the exclusive preserve of royalty.

From as early as the fifth century we see an inscription in a Jain temple referring to a king seeking spiritual merit; and in the Chalukyan period from the early seventh century we again see the investment of kings in Jain temples. A number of early South Indian kings were Jains, a notable example being the early Pallava king Mahendra. Evidence of this patronage and gift giving is shown in an Ajanta Buddhist inscription, where the patron of Cave 17 was recorded as having built the cave for his parents and for the Buddha. As we will observe, kings from the tenth century kept a jealous guard on the patronage of these monuments, due to their association with legitimacy, prestige, spiritual merit and power in direct relation to investment. The concept of dana or sacrificial offering was ultimately transmuted in Hindu temple ritual to a symbolic offering of self described as bhakti or devotion. Despite the eulogies of praise in the Vedic hymns, the non-verbal visualization and identification with the deity and the intimacy of supplicant and deity became crucial to the aspirations of the Hindu patron.

The idea of acquiring punya or religious merit rests on the fundamental concept of and belief in karma (action), reincarnation, and ultimately moksha (liberation) from the cycle of existence. This has already been suggested as the single most prominent motivation for religious patronage.

Legitimacy and the acquisition of spiritual power

As has been mentioned above, the acquisition of temporal and spiritual power was in ancient Vedic India achieved by sacrificial rituals. The *Mahabharata* refers to the ceremonies of Yudishthira's royal consecration (rajasuya) and the horse sacrifice (asvamedha). This made the kings dependent on the Brahman priests who were responsible for such ceremonies.

The rise of Buddhism and Jainism prompted a new motivation for religious investment, where devotees primarily sought spiritual merit rather than power. This engaged a variety of patrons in the form of merchants, queens, princes and nobles in the building of Buddhist stupas and subsequently Hindu shrines in North and South India from the third century AD. The economy of classical India supported this, with much of the resources controlled by the bankers, merchants and other urban dwellers.

From 200 BC to AD 300 the Brahmans, although highly respected, experienced a temporary lessening of their authority, until they assumed a legitimizing role in the medieval period. This reduced influence was in part owing to the immigrant dynasties such as the Indo-Greeks, Sakas and Kusanas who had less inherent regard for the caste hierarchies. Despite this temporary decline the Brahmans, due to their essential role in domestic rituals, gradually reinstated their authority. The priests shifted the emphasis from yajna (sacrifice) to devotional worship. A few great kings such as the Satavahanas from South India patronized the traditional Vedic ceremonies but by and large the priests were preoccupied with more domestic ceremonials.

In North India from the third century AD in the Gupta period, the king's legitimacy was enhanced by travelling bards who sang of the king's military victories and generosity. In exchange for the poems these poets were given jewels, chariots and elephants, but rarely land.

> Specifically, legitimization of the king in this society came from compositions that spoke of his generosity and bravery and it was only later that the brahmanas, who could fabricate divine genealogies and connect the king to transcendent ideals, were called upon to authorize the king's power.[73]

In ancient India in the south, sangam literature paints the chieftain as a glorious hero whose rule is dependent on his own generosity and bravery in battle.[74] This did not come from the Brahmans but from the king's possession of his drum, tutelary tree and staff which were themselves protected and sacred objects.[75] The king's aim was not only land ownership but glory. In the medieval period bhakti literature extols the king like the earlier sangam poetry. From the first century AD the southern rulers such as the Satavahanas, the Ikshvakus, the Pallavas, the Rastrakutas and the Cholas,

though subject to northern Brahmanic influence sought a broader form of legitimacy than their predecessors; and from the third century AD the king actively sought Brahmanic support. When the economy of ancient India collapsed, the money of the merchant classes reverted to feudal chiefs who instead of reinvesting used it in massive temple-building projects. The prevailing ethos encouraged them to invest in stone and spiritual stock following the popular practice of the Buddhist and Jain communities.[76]

In the south, the Pallavas were the first to promote sovereignty and legitimacy by claiming descent from the Puranic gods and displaying royal power by large gifts of land and wealth to Brahmans and temples. In South India extensive medieval temples expressed obeisance to the ideal god or king, thus reinforcing the power of the god-king and subsequently the king's legitimacy. The southern king was venerated not in the transcendent office but in the man himself. This practice absorbed in turn the Hindu emphasis on the religious icon and personal veneration. Those Chola temples which are revealed by inscription to be funerary monuments support this view of the cult of the god-king. As in the north, the granting of land to temples and Brahmans consolidated the power of the priests. It reached its apogee during the reign of the Cholas. Gradually however, as the Chola dynasty fell into decline and with it the power of the monarchy, the king reverted to being a consecrated devotee, subservient to the Brahman and the temple.

The northern kings were slow to lay claim to temples. Until the eighth century in the south and the tenth century in the north, temples were not seen as the means to acquire power and legitimacy. Willis suggests that the imperial Pratiharas may not have sought identification with a fixed and therefore confining locus of power, but rather sought hegemony over wider dominions. Their aim was to control the nobility of North India who had a history of factionalism and competition.[77]

From the tenth century in North India, petty rivalries and political disintegration gave rise to an urgent need for legitimacy and this was reinforced by the patronage of temples and images. Temples reinforced the local authority of the king. Brahmans composed genealogies to help legitimize the position of any upwardly mobile social group and in return their temples were the recipients of generous royal land grants.

Prior to the reinforcing of royal power by investment in sacred architecture, the royal consecration ceremony was crucial to the acquiring of divine power. We have noted that in Vedic times this had been achieved through the sacrificial rajasuya ceremony. From the fifth century AD the number of kings engaging in the ancient ritual ceremonies of kingship declined. The rajasuya ceremony abandoned sacrifice to focus on ritual ablution as a means of the absorption of Sri or the divine feminine. The origin of these beliefs may well be sought in the Ikshvaku dynasty, where, as discussed above, there was strong archaeological evidence for the popularity of ritual bathing. Huntington also refers to the importance of water association and ritual bathing in South India. Linked to this ceremony with water was astronomical and astrological charting. The times of the full moon and positions of the planets in relation to one another were seen to be particularly important in arriving at an auspicious moment and festivals were planned to accord to astronomical configuration. There

was and still is believed to be a crucial link between the planets and the spiritual potency or degree of sanctity of the water.

Written evidence of the significance of this ceremony is given by Rastrakuta records. In a study of these documents Inden refers to several terms used to name the Rastrakuta king's initiation into kingship by the ritual bath or abhiseka, one being rajyabhiseka, 'affusion into kingship', which Inden suggests referred to the ceremonial bath in which water and other auspicious substances were poured over the king's head. Coronation ceremonies refer to sea water and water from no less than 500 rivers which was brought in jars and used during the abhiseka ritual.[78] Inden refers to holy water which was believed to infuse the divine substance of the king through ritual bathing. It also suggests the fertilizing of the king's marriage to the earth: 'The ceremonial bath was a rite that not only purified, it also imbued the king with the divine power or energy, or, as I prefer to put it, with divine will.'[79]

The rite was believed to put divine strength into the king's hair[80] and for the first year after his coronation he was not permitted to stand on the earth with bare feet to prevent his power from 'flowing away'.[81] It was also believed that the king would impair the sri conferred on him if he had his hair cut off. Hair is still believed to hold life today and the ceremonial offering of hair as an ascetic on renouncing the world, as a penance or to win merit and the first cutting of a child's hair are continuing examples of this. This form of offering can be seen in a carving at the Pallava Varaha cave (Figure 5.7) shrine at Mamallapuram.

Every day the king had a ceremonial bath, abhiseka, before holding court. This is

Figure 5.7 Carving of a figure holding his hair and about to offer his own head, Varaha cave, Mamallapuram. Late seventh century. Robert Elgood.

echoed in the daily puja of the idol which first receives lustration and feeding before dressing. Ritual bathing was the means by which people in association with the gods purified themselves, not only of the darknesses that impeded action, known as tamas, but also imbued themselves with the 'luminous energy' of Vishnu vaishnava-tejas, using as its medium the water into which the royal priests had invited it. The priests while sprinkling water are said to have invoked deities, to purify the king of previous sins and to fortify him for the next stage of his life, a ceremony much like Christian baptism, but repeated.

Indeed, virtually all of the rites having to do with the making or remaking of a Hindu kingdom during the period of the Hindu kingdom's glory, the eighth to twelfth century, consisted of a more or less elaborate bathing ceremony either of the king or of an image of a god.[82]

The daily ritual bath was supposed to be taken by every Hindu and also applied to a large variety of objects such as sacred images, animals, weapons and tools. The practice continues today. In the ritual consecration or reconsecration of images, the water in which the image was lustrated which now contains the spiritual essence of the god will be stored in jars wrapped in

Figure 5.8 Gajalakshmi, Varaha
cave, Mamallapuram. Late seventh
century. Robert Elgood

cotton to contain the precious force. This
sacred water will then be used to lustrate a
new image, transferring its potency from the
discarded icon.[83] An actual example of water
being inherently divine and containing the
essence of Vishnu is demonstrated by the
sixteenth-century Varadarajaswami temple
at Kanchipuram. Here a wooden Vaishnavite
image is ceremonially placed in the temple
water tank for twelve years. It is removed at
an auspicious time and placed in the temple
mandapa for 45 days before once again
being placed back in the tank.[84]

The Gajalakshmi image is a portrayal of
the lustration of the goddess by elephants

which was probably meant symbolically
to portray the act of royal consecration
(Figure 5.8). In this image the elephants
imbue Lakshmi with auspicious waters,
representing fertility which she herself
possesses, and she in turn infuses the
elephants with the same qualities. The
elephants, analogous with clouds and
therefore synonymous with rainfall, stand
on lotuses and demonstrate their relationship with the pre-eminent Lakshmi. The
earliest appearance of the female with
elephants is seen on the railings of the
Buddhist stupa of Bharhut (second century
BC). Other symbols associated with water

173

are found as part of the ornamentation of temples, for example, the protective river goddesses Jumna and Ganga, or the amalaka and water pot on the top of the temple.

The appearance of the river goddesses on the outside of shrines from as early as the sixth century AD suggest a new emphasis on the infusion of divinity.[85] An early historical reference to these images can be seen by an actual recorded event. The Chalukyan ruler Vijayaditya acquired Palidhvaja banners from a northern king on which these goddesses appear. It is interesting to note that following this event these images appear on southern architecture. The transference of sacred power, or the bringing of fertility and prosperity to the kingdom, may also be symbolized by bringing water from the sacred rivers. The river goddesses appear, for example, flanking Gupta temple doors in the second quarter of the fifth century and subsequently at Ajanta in the latter part of the fifth century. They also appear outside the Ramesvara cave at Ellora from the mid-sixth century, in the Gaudargudi temple at Aihole and in the temple at Pattadakal, where the linga is shown receiving lustration in the act of worship. Rajendra Chola successfully waged war in the north and brought back with him to his capital, Gangakondacholapuram, water taken from the sacred river Ganges. Despite the river's feminine character she also absorbs the essence of the male deities.

Spilling out of heaven from Vishnu's foot, containing Vishnu's liquified essence according to some myths, and falling onto Siva's head, where she meanders through his tangled locks, the mighty Ganges appears in this world after having been made more sacred by direct contact with Vishnu and Siva. The river then spreads the divine potency of these Gods into the world when she flows onto the earthly plane. She gives their sacred presences to the earth in liquid form.[86]

Identification with the deity, the infusion of divine power through the ritual bathing of both monarch and image enshrined in the temple and reference to lineage were all believed to confer power, legitimacy and fertility. The kings compared themselves with mythological archetypes and re-enacted noble deeds of the gods. Regional princes frequently used imperial titles and competed vigorously with one other in the arts of peace and war. In the absence of a recognized imperial centre there was no impetus to return to the detached role once played by the Pratihara monarchs. The king attempted to harness the power of the deity through identification with either Vishnu or Siva.

The seizure and worship of tribal aniconic images by Hindu rajas was also an accepted means of extending legitimate authority. The worship of these tribal images also served to mediate between vana and ksetra, Sanskrit terms for the wilderness and settled space. One effect of this was to maintain the acceptability of ancient tribal gods and religious practices alongside orthodox Brahmanical Hinduism. In classical Indian ideology, great import-ance is given to the conquest of the wilder-ness and also the giving up of the norms of society and the retreat to the forest during the final stage of life. A study of the acquisition of royal authority in Orissa prior to the British rule has recently been conducted, in which Schnepel argues that

One can find in south Orissa (and in Orissa generally) numerous instances where persons striving to become kings, or kings competing for dominance in a given area, fought for access to a sacred spot and for a prominent position in a local goddess's cult.[87]

Orthodox images of Durga were also brought in from outside the region and installed to give additional weight to royal legitimacy. The image of Sri Nathji at the temple of Nathdwara in Rajasthan is one such example. These images were often stolen and then installed in the disputed territory. The act of stealing an image demonstrated the king's courage and, far from its being considered an act of treachery and illegality, was seen to make him a worthy owner of the image. His offering of sacrifice to the deity cemented the alliance. References to such acts in the state of Orissa links the worship of the goddess with the ritual killing of a tribal leader and with human sacrifice in general which, according to Schnepel, was an important royal ritual practice in a number of south Orissan jungle kingdoms.[88]

Fertility and prosperity

One of the king's main responsibilities was to ensure rainfall. According to Gonda, Prthu, the first archetypal model of a ruler, was invested with dominion and compelled the earth to yield a sufficient supply of food.

> Indra seeing that all the ksatriya sovereigns ruled their kingdoms very virtuously, poured down vivifying showers of rain at the proper time and at the proper place, and thus protected all creatures.[89]

Liquor, which is forbidden to Brahmans (to prevent them from exposing the *Veda* to profanation by reciting it out of season), was said to help love, and the custom was to sprinkle it on brides to stimulate the generative powers.[90] Kings were associated

with the regulation of the meteorological process and other natural forces. Various forms of Vedic sacrificial offerings of sustenance to the gods were believed to contribute to the gods' task of world maintenance. These rites are recorded in ancient hymns and ritual prescription as well as in the Sanskrit *Epics*. One aspect of ritual was the gift (dakshina or dana) given by the patron of a sacrifice to the priests, to guarantee the success of the ritual. Soma, the god rather than the ritual drink, was seen as the king of the Brahmans and was also identified with fertility and fecundity.

In the Hindu context there is also a sense of the spiritual obligations incumbent on the monarch for the sake of auspiciousness, harmony and the subsequent fertility and prosperity of the community, which was a further factor in temple building. The contractual exchange of gifts for fertility and abundance is a further aim of temple building. The king's duty was to bring abundance and to protect his community, and this the temple was believed to do. For example, certain ornamentation of the temple was believed to be inspired by the desire to protect from drought, one of the crucial duties of the king.

Royal consecration's ritual bathing was, according to the scholar Marglin, intended to provide the king with female procreative powers. This is interpreted as vanquishing the drying powers of heat by the infusion of female procreative powers, believed to bring rain and prosperity to the king's subjects.[91] This may be likened to that of the courtesan or devadasi, who by her sexual activity is said by Shulman to vanquish the drying powers of ascetic heat. This interpretation is reinforced by the fact, as has been already mentioned, that the rivers are perceived as both female and divine and that the river waters bring about a fruitful marriage of the king and the earth. The king's marriage to the earth formed a part of the coronation ceremony in India until the sixteenth century. Even today when the priest wishes to sanctify water for ritual purposes he evokes the river goddesses into the water.

The king had a duty to protect his subjects, but also to cause them to increase and become more fertile and prosperous. There was a requirement that each level of society was in proper relationship with one another. An interesting parallel has been pointed out by Marglin, that of the king with his kingdom, and the wife with her domestic realm.

> The king is conceptualized as the increaser and the maintainer of his people. At his coronation he is symbolically infused with female procreative powers. On him depends the prosperity and well-being of his people who are also called his progeny (praja). Royal power is sakti power. The king is particularly responsible for the fertility of the land in the form of good and timely rains, a role parallel to that of the courtesan or the devadasi who by her sexual activity vanquishes the drying powers of ascetic heat.[92]

The king's responsibility for ensuring sufficient rainfall may well explain the fairly frequent occurrence of mithuna imagery on temples. These erotic images have direct links with ideas of fertility, the vanquishing power against heat, and were also thought to attract the rain/life-giving clouds. The Lakshmana temple at Khajuraho, wherein inscriptions were the result of royal patronage, is a good example of the use of erotic imagery intended to assist the king and reflect his duties. However, it is important to note that erotic imagery, like most Indian iconography, is multivalent. The king's association with the sun and

moon, and therefore with the round of seasons and time, reinforced his significance as the fertile provider of regeneration in all its forms. Even the menstrual cycle is given the Sanskrit name rtu, meaning season. The link between water and planetary positions and astronomy was understandably regarded as very significant.

Prestige

Another motive for kings to patronize grand architectural projects was self-aggrandizement and the potential for demonstrating his wealth. The exercise of royal power was as important as the fulfilment of expectations of his subjects in maintaining the reputation of his office. Successful kings fought military campaigns and acquired booty which had to be disposed of. Distributing wealth and booty was an expected part of a king's maintenance of the pillars of his state and consequently of his power. The Indian kings were understandably concerned to extend their territory. The temple in its sacred geometry symbolized the totality of the universe. Only if there is room can the blessings of heaven reach the earth. The kings sought to extend their boundaries and in their temples provided their philosophical expression of the universe. The elements of kingship, including his power as a universal king over the four quarters of the universe and all the planetary and other deities, were represented in the temple which reflected the king reflecting the temple reflecting the king.

The monarch achieved prestige by contributing to a temple that stood as a mark of his own personality, prowess and artistic imagination, as the inscriptions demonstrate. An example of this can be seen from the time of the Gurjara-Pratiharas at

Pehowa, where an inscription refers to a local Raja of the Tamara family who was eulogized by his successors for the construction of numerous temples in every region.[93] The inscription suggests that these temples with their lofty pinnacles look from afar like posts fixed at the horizon in order to establish the king's fame. The great Chola emperor Aditya, having built several elegant stone temples at the end of the ninth century, would have been pleased to read inscriptions describing him as the monarch

> by whom the row of large temples of Siva, as it were banners of his own victorious, lofty and unacquainted with defeat (collapse) were built of stone on the two banks of the Kaveri from the Sahya mountains – even to the ocean.[94]

In South India by the end of the Chola period there developed a rivalry between the patronage of the king and that of the temple. In this competitive climate kings sought to demonstrate their power and economic status through the grandeur of their temples. The small temples gave way to large and elaborate projects. An example of this, in the north, is the patronage of the mid-tenth century Chandella kings, who sought to elevate their former tribal origin to royal status. Their inscriptions stress their mythic genealogy, royal matrimonial alliances and make comparison with the heroes of epic literature. One inscription records that the temple celebrates the consolidation of the power of the king, who had captured a religious image crucial to the power politics of this region from his former overlord.

Wish fulfilment and gift giving

Under the Pallavas, ritual kingship involved royal beneficence which resulted in large land endowments and gifts to Brahmans, temples and lesser chieftains. This had been an extension from the earlier sacrificial ritual dues to Brahmans from Vedic times, combined with the tendency for the southern warrior king to demonstrate power by sharing wealth among his nobles.[95] The practice of gift giving to temples and Brahmans spread throughout North and South India.

A further reason for the building of temples was the commemoration of a victory or the promise of constructing a temple to the gods to ensure a victorious outcome of an impending war. Evidence of this is seen in an inscription which was added to the temple of Konarak where it was claimed that the king built the temple on the suggestion of his mother to fulfil a vow to the god following a great victory. On a village level the fulfilment of vows is common practice and demonstrates the interrelationship between the folk and monumental tradition to which reference has already been made.[96] According to Luschinsky, by AD 500 a new type of religious activity and thought based on the *Puranas* was well established in North India and largely under the control of women.[97]

Atonement

The Hindu concept of ahimsa or non-violence was sometimes a factor in encouraging monarchs to atone for a bloody victory by using booty for religious ends. Evidence of this is seen by the example of the eighth-century ruler Meruvarman who campaigned against his neighbours and then sought atonement by undertaking acts of piety with the booty brought home from his defeated adversaries.[98] Another example of this desire for atonement is demonstrated by the eighth-century Lalitaditya from Kashmir, who was apparently driven by the need for conquest and to placate the gods through continuous building and religious dedication.[99]

A clear example of the need to propitiate powerful deities and to beseech their aid in defending territory is shown by the erection of the Yogini temple of Beraghat (c. AD 1000).[100] It has been assigned to the Kalachuri ruler Yuvaraja II. He is said to have assigned one-third of his state revenue to maintain monasteries and temples and, when the neighbouring Chandellas threatened to invade, built the Yogini temple to gain the god's assistance.

Commemorative and funerary monuments

Temples were sometimes built as funerary monuments. This continues a practice that commenced in India with megalithic graves which were later followed by Buddhist stupas, eight of which were built to contain a part of the mortal remains of the Buddha himself. It has been noted that the stupas were often placed in close proximity to the earlier graves, a prominent example being Amaravati. Willis refers to two inscriptions from North India, one of which notes that the king Baladitya erected a temple of Vishnu to commemorate his deceased wife. The other inscription from Rajor records that prince Mathanadeva granted a village to a Siva temple to maintain rituals and named the temple after his mother.[101] The Chola king Parantaka (AD 907–55) was responsible for building the funerary temple Pallippadai over the remains of his father.[102] It has also been suggested that the Pallava Dharmaraja ratha may be a commemorative monument because a portrait of king

Mamalla I is placed on the south side of the ratha, which is the side associated with death. In the tenth century the Siva temple ascribed to Bhoja and the Matagesvara temple in Khajuraho appear to be examples of memorial or funerary monuments.

Literature also provides evidence for the existence of funerary temples.[103] A text exists which affirms that a memorial temple should avoid a regular sikara, and instead use a phamsana roof of receding tiers with decorations of bells at the corners.[104]

The naming of temples after a donor, esteemed person or demon is a long-established practice known from at least the fifth century, and which still continues today. In North and South India it can be observed in the villages in small shrines which commemorate heroes, ancestors and bhutas. In South India the Tamil classic *Jivaka Cintamani* tells the story of how a servant named Sutanjanan, a friend of Jivaka, died on the battlefield to secure victory for his master.[105] Jivaka built a commemorative temple to the memory of his friend and placed within it a consecrated gold portrait sculpture of Sutanjanan. Jivaka then arranged for daily worship in the temple, a great festival and composed a drama on the life of the dead hero and arranged for its performance in the temple. Nagaswamy cites this example to demonstrate the custom in South India of erecting a temple to a dead hero who is deified and worshipped and whose life is enacted through dance as a part of the festival. All over South India and Sri Lanka there are temples and shrines erected for the dead heroes Nadukal and Virakkal who as folk deities are worshipped under different names, where a ceremony is performed known as bhutam attam in which the bhutam is invoked in a living man and thereby brought to life. According to Nagaswamy the aim of the bhutam ceremony is to bring the hero to life and by so doing confer prosperity on the community. The invocation of the dead in a live person is also seen in the Brahman practice of performing the ritual sraddha to the dead parents, except that in the latter there is no colouring of the face or wearing of bright garments, ornaments, etc. Monuments which commemorate the dead and spirit possession serve a cathartic role, resolving the tensions and conflicts that arise from the dangerous thresholds of life.

Portrait sculpture

The earliest portrait sculptures take two forms, both relating to service to the community. There are statues of donors or donor couples from the Buddhist sites from the second to first century BC, such as Bharhut, Sanci and Karle, as well as hero stones. The headless portrait of Kanishka resembling the sun-god Surya is an early example of this practice. Inscriptions in the Kusan period refer to the king as the 'son of God'. The Gupta period also has portraits of Gupta emperors on coinage and images of the kings placed in temple shrines. Portrait sculptures of royal patrons are however comparatively rare in India after the sixth century AD until the Chola period.

The Pallava patron, however, Mamalla I, is believed to be represented with an analogy of himself as the boar and trivikrama referring to his victory over the Chalukyas. This visual allegory is supported by Kasakudi plates which state that the Pallavas resemble partial incarnations of Vishnu. The Dharmaratha also has a portrait sculpture of Mamalla I on the southern side (Figure 5.3) and, as has

already been mentioned, the king and son are portrayed in the Adivaraha temple in Mahabalipuram (Figure 5.1).

Several examples exist of portrait sculptures in the Chola period, when the god-king axis was at its height. King Rajendra, who erected a temple to Siva at his capital city Gangakondacholapuram to celebrate a march to the Ganges, is depicted in a niche beside one of the doorways of this temple. It has already been suggested that this may represent king Rajendra receiving a floral garland of victory from the god Siva (Figure 5.5).

On the entrance porch of the temple of Adinath of the tenth century AD, at Mount Abu in Rajasthan there is a rare portrait sculpture of the patron Vimala seated on a horse. Temple architecture in Nepal also sometimes incorporates commemorative stone columns, upon which an image of the ruler is placed facing the principal entrance to the temple.

Further portraiture is seen in the sun temple of Konarak assigned to King Nrsimhadeva in 1258. Below the image of Surya and his seven horses is a kneeling figure in anjali mudra next to the image's right foot which may well be Nrsimhadeva himself. It has been suggested that several other reliefs may represent king Nrsimhadeva and events in his life. Certain aspects of the iconographic programme seem to be personal to him rather than related to the deity. In the *Baya Chakda* manuscript it is noted that the king, on returning from war, ordered an image to be made showing him 'in the attitude of a triumphantly returning warrior'.[106] Although this image is not known, others relating to events in his life have been identified. One sculpture shows the king as an archer and is apparently the carving described in the *Baya Chakda*. Another shows the king worshipping a shrine with an image of Durga Mahisamardini. Several reliefs in the sun temple of Konarak portray the patron. One depicts Rama and Sita which may be interpreted as symbolically representing the king and Sitadevi, his wife. The identification of the king with the deity is a common occurrence in royal portraits.

In medieval Indian art the king is often portrayed in a more informal everyday manner. For example, in Khajuraho he is seen sitting with his courtiers. In the Belur temple he is sitting in his court giving dana; and in the Sun temple at Konarak he is shown practising archery and sitting on a swing amidst the women of his harem. However, scenes of royal coronations and personal triumphs form the subject of much temple art in which rulers attempted to link their lives with the world of the gods.

The later Vijayanagara Rayas and their successors the Nayaks were also keen on portraiture which took the form of full-length realistic portraits, usually found in gopuras and mandapas. The kings usually stand in anjali mudra, signifying that they are devotees of the god and often hold their swords under their arms; examples of these are the statue of Krishnadevaraya in the north gopuram at Chidambaram, and Tirumalainayaka on the south-west pillar of the Nardimandapa at Tanjavur.

A means of crossing

Temples are the destination of pilgrims but it is important to appreciate that arrival is not the end of the journey. Several inscriptions describe the temple as a 'great ship for crossing the ocean of existences'. The construction of a temple according to one inscription was considered a pious and noble work, 'an even path to beatitude, a great ship for crossing the ocean of existence, the seed of the tree of spiritual merit which bears endless fruits and the permanent abode of goddess of prosperity'.[107]

Inscriptions at the Chaturbhuj temple at Gwalior and another now in Udaipur both refer to temples, which were built as a means of crossing over from this temporal world to the spiritual.[108] The concept of crossing is likened to a ford and is therefore called a tirtha. The king, as patron, derived particular spiritual benefit from the temple. On entering the temple the monarch had access to the spiritual world and returned with his powers renewed through the powerhouse of energies which the temple represented. An object as well as a place can be considered a ford, but the principle remains the same, namely a means of passing from the temporal to the spiritual world.

The temple also gave the ordinary devotee the potential to become temporarily divine by identifying with the deity in his devotions and thereby making the crossing. An inscription at Pehowa states that three brothers built a temple because 'they were afraid of the dreadful ocean of mundane existence which is difficult to cross by men of little wisdom'.[109]

Religious obligation

In early Jaina inscriptions found on sculpture of the Kusan period at Mathura (first to third century AD), it was made clear that patronage of art was part of the code of religious duty (dana-dharma) which included the donation and preservation of images, sacred texts, buildings and monastic institutions. This giving is known as deya-dharma or deva-dharma. This philosophy also appears in Buddhism but in Hinduism cannot be substantiated at such an early date due to the lack of written evidence. However, it has been suggested that royal patronage in the Buddhist period was generally extended to more than one religious sect since at that time kingly patronage was not expected to be partisan.[110]

The medieval Hindu king's obligations were based on immemorial customs which were as sacred as written texts. Aside from the necessity to make gifts the medieval Hindu king's duty was to provide a stable environment for the worship of the gods and for the conducting of the key rituals which governed the life and death of his subjects. He had a duty to protect his subjects and the religious institutions, not just by statecraft but also as principal patron of worship. In different centuries in the various parts of the subcontinent the king was expected to build a temple or to be closely involved with the maintenance of an existing religious institution. By seeing to the well-being of the Brahmans the king ensured that rituals in his kingdom were properly conducted, for any deviation from the prescribed ritual threatened the prosperity of his state. The king's responsibilities were also to uphold artha and fulfil his dharma. In theory his right to kingship existed as long as he continued to fulfil his secular and religious obligations. The king's relation to his kingdom and the Brahman's to his idol have been compared to a woman and her home. There was an interlocking relationship in which the priests offered services to the gods, the gods preserved the king, the kingdom and his subjects, and the king protected the temples.

Protection

The temples provide a climate of devotion and service to God which was believed to secure God's pleasure, to propitiate him and to bring prosperity to the community and protection from malevolent forces. Ritual with its familiar continuity gave a sense of purpose and control to assuage the fears of men and women.

The title Raja or king was, according to Gonda, derived from the Sanskrit root raj, which expressed the idea of 'stretching out'. The king was seen as someone who stretched himself out and protected lesser men under his powerful arms. Long arms were considered a prescribed attribute of kingship and were believed to be essential to a king for the protection of his subjects. The seventh-century AD portrait of Mamalla I (Figure 5.2) shows such extended arms. According to Gonda, in the royal consecration the monarch received ritual lustration with raised arms while standing on the throne, and it is suggested that in this position he represented the axis mundi, the pivot of the universe.[111] Indra is associated with the pillar and it is clear that the king as chakravartin was seen as heir to the god Indra and to possess extraordinary superhuman power. The king's power, however, had to be renewed periodically and therefore the monarch came to the temple for regeneration and protection.

Conclusion

Hindu patronage of the religious arts from the first century AD shows certain key features. Before the sixth century BC in the north, the Vedic monarch depended on the priest for the acquisition of his powers. In the south he claimed warrior status by successful campaigns and the sharing of booty. The Vedic warrior king was believed to make an ascent to heaven through the smoke of the sacrificial fire and to seize power from the gods. Underlying this mythology was the concept that the acquisition of divine power required coercion not grace. During this period the open-air ritual did not require permanent housing, nor did the king or priest gain legitimacy from great monuments. According to the *Upanishads* the building of temples and images was meant for fools who were destined for the lower worlds,[112] while the practice of tapas produced merit.

A belief which had temporarily lapsed, that priestly intercession was essential in the ceremonies to divinely empower the ruler, was reinstated and gained momentum through North and South India from the first century AD. The popularity of Buddhism which had severely undermined Brahmanic influence gradually declined and there was a corresponding reaffirmation of priestly influence. The Kusanas, an immigrant dynasty, initiated a concept of the 'god-king', claimed to be the 'sons of God' (devaputra) and commissioned portrait sculpture of the monarchs. Ecumenical by choice, they also supported Jain and Buddhist shrines through donations.

The central Vedic cosmo-regal sacrifice was supplanted by the great gift mahadana, which was in turn inspired by the Buddhist tradition of gift giving for the acquisition of merit. This, together with formal consecration, abhiseka, and crowning (tying the fillet) were ways of acquiring divine powers and thus consolidating the king's secular authority and power. The domestic rituals were continued by Brahmans however, who began to codify prescriptive action and to ensure the king's and devotees' interest and investment in these activities. Until the medieval period kings were not interested in laying claim to temples, preferring to worship in small shrines and finding greater status from Brahmanical support.

From as early as the first century AD, women's patronage whether of Jain icons, Buddhist stupas or Hindu temples was also strong. Inscriptions testify to the fact that not only did queens invest in sacred architecture, but they encouraged their sons to atone for or build temples out of gratitude to the goddess, who they believe was responsible for military victory. As we will see in Chapter 6, women are also seen to have responsibility for the protection of home and family which involves them in propitiation and devotional offerings.

Investment in monuments for the acquisition of merit rapidly grew in popularity from the second century. Renouncing and gift giving were common in Buddhist and Jain devotion, and may have inspired popular Hinduism as it began to emerge in recognizable form. In the south under the Satavahana dynasty, communal patronage developed strongly and archaeology reveals that under the fourth-century Ikshvaku dynasty small permanent covered shrines began to be constructed. This patronage cannot be directly connected with the kings and, as in the Buddhist period, probably reflected the needs and preoccupations of society as a whole. The availability of the resources to finance such development reflects the rich trading economy of the time.

From the third century AD, kings were more interested in employing bards to eulogize their power and magnificence than in building temples. Sacred monuments were not at this time perceived as powerhouses for kings and it follows from this that identification with sacred sites was not an essential requirement of kingship. Gradually the Brahman priests re-established their claim as essential intermediaries in the major ceremonies of life, yet the need for temples to reinforce kingly power had not yet become established. In the Puranic literature, however, we find the claim that purtadharma was greater than the performance of Vedic sacrifices, a reversal from the earlier dismissive attitude.[113] Despite this literary reference kings seemed to be slow to make inscriptional claims to temples in the north. Evidence of Gupta and Chalukya patronage of Jain temples reinforces the idea of giving to acquire merit, as distinct from the payment to Hindu priests for their ritual services, which continued for some time in the puranic period.

It was not until the sixth to seventh centuries that we have evidence of kings laying inscriptional claim to temples. It was only when god and temple became synonymous and ritual sacrifice had been eclipsed that kings made themselves pre-eminent as temple builders. In the south the Pallava kings practised gift giving in the form of large tracts of land to Brahmans and temples, while in the north during the Pratihara period there was still a lack of inscriptional evidence linking kings with buildings. Princes, nobles and groups are more likely patrons of temples in North India during the Pratihara period, a continuation of an earlier tradition of patronage by a wide social group, as seen in the Buddhist period.

From the seventh century AD, royal consecration as in the north depended on priestly intercession but began to focus on a further important element, the purification from ritual bathing and the transmission of divine power by lustration or abhiseka. Water became a feature of royal initiation and this is given prominence in architectural design and temple iconography. Ritual lustration also reflects the fertilization of the symbolic marriage of king and earth. Tamil literature with its emphasis on the warrior hero whose immortality lived on through the worship of the hero stone may well have contributed to the growth of the concept of the individual who was both king and god. The ruler was strongly identified with the god, which reinforced legitimacy in times of political fragmentation and competition. This is seen particularly in the medieval period of the tenth century in North and South India. The apogee of the god-king identification was reached under the mid-Cholas, following which the king became a consecrated devotee of his deity.

By the tenth century there was a proliferation of royal inscriptions on temples and a clear use of temples to consolidate and extend power. The king increased his divine power by his identification with both the temple and the deity itself. The deity which was originally associated with figurative sculpture became increasingly identified with the temple building itself. The fragmentation of authority in medieval North India and the questionable lineage of some of the medieval kings was an added incentive for them to patronize grand temples where Brahmans created suitable genealogies. These were inscribed on the temples to emphasize the king's legitimate right to rule. This action had not been necessary in the days of heroic kingship when the kings depended on the Veda Srauta ceremony for their authority.

There was a huge change in the relationship between king and god that took place between the fourth and the seventh centuries AD. It can be seen in the *Bhagavad Gita*, where for the first time in an Indian context God acknowledged his love and concern for man. Society no longer only confronted and propitiated the gods but came to believe in a benevolent and caring god. The king became the god's divinely infused agent on earth. Water replaced fire as a bridge with the heavens. The sacrificial smoke rose up to heaven in contrast to the water which came down from heaven. In religious terms, the active warrior Vedic king hero was succeeded in typology by a passive devotional ruler. The first took and the second received divine power. Both however maintained responsibility for preserving the prosperity of their community, perceived as the power to bring rainfall and fertility.

A further dimension of this is given by Marglin, who suggests a link between kingship, female sexuality and time.[114] She suggests that the infusion of female procreative powers was necessary for the king to fulfil his obligation as provider of prosperity. As a corollary to the passive submission of the kings in relation to the deity, we find from the fifth to seventh century AD the rise of the martial goddess Durga as a manifestation of the goddess Sakti. The goddess became even more popular with the rise of medieval tantrism from the eighth to ninth century in North and South India. This period coincided with the rise of tantrism which had a profound influence on many levels of Indian society.

It is apparent from the above that spiritual merit, spiritual power, legitimacy, secular prestige, ancestor worship or commemoration, identification of king and god in temple and portrait sculpture, fertility and prosperity, religious obligation, atonement, protection, and the creation of a threshold or place whereby one may cross from one world to the next were all factors in encouraging the monarchs to invest in the expensive and time-consuming building of sacred architecture. The building of a temple became a further extension of the king's obligation of service to the deity and to his subjects and the temple became a vital element in the ordering of society. The temple was the pivot of the spiritual and social life of the community. It was not only the focus of worship but also an important employer, economic generator for the community and patron of craftsmen, including painters, sculptors, musicians and dancers. The belief that the deity can become temporarily manifest in a structure, which in turn became a powerhouse for kings, was integral to understanding the changing nature of patronage from ancient to medieval Hindu India. The consistent feature of medieval royal patronage in North and medieval South India was the dependence on Brahmans for intercession. This was believed to be essential to evoke the deity as a radiating presence from the inner sanctum of the temple, from whom authority and power devolved. The king's essential pragmatism in his adoption of the patronage of Brahman ritual underlies much of the art and a great deal of the political powers that survived into the later period.

Notes

1 Kennedy 1976, pp. 1–2.

2 I am grateful to Madhuvanti Ghose for her information on this aspect of the development of Hindu iconography.

3 Inden 1982, pp. 132–6.

4 Dirks 1987, pp. 28–9.

5 See Kinsley 1986, pp. 21–2.

6 Willis, in Mason, 1993, p. 50.

7 For further information on the organization of the temple of Madurai see Fuller 1991.

8 Luders 1961, p. 135.

9 See Anand 'In praise of Aihole, Badami...' in *Marg* p. 12.

10 See Sarkar and Misra 1966, p. 30.

11 See Anand 'In praise of Aihole, Badami...' in *Marg*, p. 12.

12 Ibid., pp. 12–13.

13 See Sarkar and Misra 1966, p. 26.

14 Michell 1989, pp. 192–3.

15 See Willis, in Mason 1993, p. 52.

16 See Huntington 1985, Chapter 20, fn. 3. Inscriptions left by Gurjara-Pratiharas provide extensive evidence of patronage and building by their rulers and subjects, but remains are not as plentiful as epigraphic evidence. See also Puri 1957.

17 See Inden 1985, p. 59.

18 *Agni Purana*, Chapter 38.

19 *Indian Antiquary* 1886, Vol. 15, pp. 105–13 and 138–41.

20 *Epigraphica Indica* Vol. VII (1) (1889–92), pp. 122–35. The inscription dated vikrama year 1011 AD 954-55 was found among the ruins at the base of the temple known as Lakshmanji at Khajuraho.

21 See Desai 1974, pp. 12 and 10–17; see also Desai 1985, Chapter VII.

22 See Desai 1986; Meister 1979, pp. 226–8.

23 See Desai 1988, p. 45.

24 The temple was originally known as the Marakateshvara (emerald lord) Pranathanatha (lord of goblins).

25 They had originally been feudatories of the Pratiharas.

26 Keilhorn 1892, verse 22.

27 Ibid., pp. 135–6.

28 See Desai 1988, p. 45.

29 This later inscription and evidence for the patrons' involvement with the temple does give rise to doubt the dependence on inscriptions for attribution to patrons; it confirms that just because the temple does not claim royal patronage it does not mean it did not receive it. It also demonstrates the importance of women

and their influence on patronage, and the many other elements involved in the selection of a site and an auspicious time for construction.

30 Boner 1972. Some scholars however doubt the authenticity of the manuscript.

31 See Huntington 1985, p. 435.

32 According to Huntington, religious dedications occur on auspicious dates. She suggests that 'right-handed' doctrine dedications are made during the bright half of the month and 'left-handed' tantric dedications are made in the dark half of the month.

33 For further discussion see Huntington 1985, Chapter 19, fn. 18.

34 An epigraph reveals that the temple was dedicated in the year Saka 556, equivalent to AD 634.

35 See Huntington 1985, Chapter 15, fn. 3.

36 Ibid., Chapter 16, fn. 2.

37 See Meister 1986, p. 111.

38 See Srinivasan 1975, pp. 197–8.

39 For discussion see Huntington 1985, p. 292.

40 Dirks 1987, pp. 28–9.

41 Suggested by Huntington 1985, p. 304.

42 For the inscriptions see E. Hultzch, 'The Pallava Inscriptions of the Seven Pagodas'. *Epigraphica Indica* Vol. 10 (1909–10), pp. 5–8.

43 See Nagaswamy 1962, pp. 37–8.

44 Dirks 1987.

45 See Balasubrahmanyam 1971.

46 See Balasubrahmanyam 1966, pp. 82–5.

47 Ibid., pp. 18–19.

48 Srinivasan, PhD thesis, 1996.

49 See Beteille 1996.

50 For illustration see Huntington 1985, Chapter 22, p. 541, Figure 22.1.

51 See Fuller 1991.

52 See Hardy 1983, p. 225; Shulman 1985, Chapter VII; Dirks 1976.

53 I am grateful for Michael Willis' suggestion that the Pratihara rulers, particularly under the rule of Harsa, did not want to be usurped by a deity, who was seen as a royal personality, or to limit their power by identifying themselves with a specific region.

54 See Inden 1985, pp. 53–73.

55 Anand p. 12.

56 Sarkar and Misra 1966 [1987], p. 26.

57 The most holy river Ganga which flows through Siva's hair is shown in Hindu iconography as a goddess.

58 Anand p. 12.

59 A.V. Nai, 'Inscriptions of the Deccan: An epigraphic survey (*c.* 300 BC–AD 1300)' *Deccan college Postgraduate and Research Inst Bulletin* 9 (Poona 1948), insc. 63. The queen and her sister were both married to Vikramaditya II.

60 See Willis, in Mason 1993, p. 54, n. 27.

61 Ibid., p. 53.

62 I am grateful to Profulla Mohanti for this information.

63 See Willis, in Mason 1993, p. 54.

64 Ibid., p. 52.

65 *Epigraphica Indica*, Vol. 1 (1889-92), pp. 154–62.

66 See Willis, in Mason 1993, p. 55.

67 See R. Salomon and M. Willis (1990), 'A nineteenth-century Umamahesvara Image', *Artibus Asiae*, Vol. 50, pp. 148–55.

68 *Epigraphica Indica*, Vol. 4 (1895–7), pp. 29–32.

69 Cited by Willis, in Mason 1993, p. 42.

70 See Michell 1977.

71 Two donative inscriptions on wooden beams spanning the vault of Bhaja chaitya. These inscriptions were intended to proclaim the names of the donors and yet were not visible from the ground. The recording of the gift was perhaps all that was necessary for the donor to feel secure about receiving his religious merit.

72 From the text the *Brhat Samhita*.

73 See Kennedy 1976, p. 3.

74 I am grateful to John Marr for this information.

75 Kennedy 1976, p. 2. See also Hart 1975, p. 38.

76 See Kennedy 1976, p. 15, and Desai 1974, p. 12.

77 See Willis, in Mason 1993, p. 59.

78 See Gonda 1966, p. 93.

79 Inden 1990, p. 236.

80 The concept of strength being in a man's hair reminds one of the Hebrew tradition and Samson.

81 This mirrors one of the distinguishing features of gods from mortals which was that the gods did not actually *stand* on the ground. Nala is thus picked out from celestials by Damayanti in her svayamvara by the fact that he, unlike they, had his feet on the ground, cast a shadow, and sweated.

82 Inden 1990, p. 234.

83 I am grateful to John Marr for this information.

84 I am grateful to S.R. Balasubrahmanyam for this information.

85 It is, however, suggested that the river goddesses appeared on the banners captured from the north and were seen for the first time on Chalukyan shrines.

86 Kinsley 1986, p. 189.

87 See Schnepel 1995, p. 150.

88 See Schnepel 1992 and 1995.

89 See Gonda 1966, p. 7.

90 Ibid., p. 9. This is also found in tree worship where alcohol is sometimes spat on the tree by the worshipper.

91 See Marglin 1985, p. 301.

92 Ibid.

93 See Krishna 1989, p. 35.

94 The Rajarajesvara in Tanjore built by Rajaraja Chola.

95 Dirks 1987, p. 29.

96 I am grateful to Stephen Huyler for information on the terracotta tradition in India.

97 For more information see Chapter 6; see also Luschinsky 1962, p. 377.

98 See P. Pal, in Dehejia 1988, pp. 9–10.

99 See R. Fisher, in Dehejia 1988, p. 36.

100 For discussion of this temple see Dehejia 1988, p. 44.

101 See Willis, in Mason, 1993, p. 53.

102 See p. 158.

103 Dehejia 1993, p. 72.

104 Ibid., fn. 8.

105 Paper entitled 'The dead and the living in dance' given by Professor Nagaswamy at a conference at SOAS on the performing arts in June 1996.

106 See Boner 1972, p. 118.

107 Cited by Willis, in Mason 1993, p. 55.

108 Ibid.

109 Krishna 1989, p. 36.

110 Stoler Miller, 1992, p. 28.

111 See Gonda 1966, p. 109.

112 *Mundaka Upanishad*, Vol. 1, Chapter 2, pp. 10-1.

113 *Agni Purana*, Chapter 38.

114 See Marglin 1985, p. 301.

CHAPTER 6 Village and Tribal Patrons and Their Religious Arts

India has been described as a land of villages. Even today, even if they no longer live there, a large percentage (82 per cent) of the population continue to identify with a rural community or area. In the villages a strong sense of local identity, tradition and caste status remains. The Indian home, be it mud hut or palace, is a sanctuary, a place which must preserve ritual purity. The home is also seen as the source of life and regeneration. Women make use of specific rituals to fulfil their responsibility for the care of the family and spiritual protection of the home. These traditional practices acknowledge an inherent understanding of impermanence and the need for constant renewal and vigilance and are conducted on a regular basis. Numerous local deities are worshipped in rural India, with an inherent hierarchy. The form of popular worship is dependent on the specific requirements of the individual deity.

The size of the tribal population[1] in India is immeasurable, with estimates ranging from 30 to 60 million people, a large proportion of whom do not declare themselves Hindu. These tribal groups are mainly concentrated in the hilly and forested areas of central India where they still live primarily by hunting, fishing and gathering. The largest tribal groups of India are the Bhils (Rajasthan, Gujarat,

Maharastra and Madya Pradesh); the Gonds (Madhya Pradesh, Maharashtra, Andhra Pradesh and southern Uttar Pradesh); the Mundas, Santhals and Hos (eastern Madhya Pradesh, Bihar and west Bengal), and the Nagas (Nagaland and Manipur). Others mentioned in this chapter are the Todas (Tamil Nadu) and the Saoras (Orissa). Small pockets are also found in the Nilgiri hills in Tamil Nadu and in the western ghats in Kerala.

Despite the fact that there are differences between rural and puranic Hinduism, the importance of rural legends and crafts for understanding the complex development of Hinduism is now appreciated. Recent field studies have demonstrated that tribal and agrarian culture contain elements which show us the evolution of early Hindu art and ritual practice. Jain argues strongly that regional myths, previously considered as Sanskrit derivatives, have in fact coexisted alongside the puranic versions for centuries.[2] With the acknowledgement of the important contribution of Tamil tradition and mythology to the development of Hinduism, it is now possible to see these diverse strands as an important part of the syncretic whole.

Village or tribal communities have relatively simple practical and spiritual requirements. Patronage, commission and exchange of goods is largely achieved through barter (known in Hindi as jajmani) rather than cash.[3] Agricultural tools, wood-carvings, basket-making, textiles, jewellery and pottery are produced locally and these combine an aesthetic sense of rhythm and colour with functional efficacy. Their decoration often provides the wearer or user with spiritual power, protection or wish fulfilment. One such motif is the parrot, the vehicle of Kamdeva, the god of love, which decorates the trousseau and walls of the marriage chamber. The lotus is another motif frequently employed by women on textiles, jewellery and in the ritual decoration of their homes. Decorative detail can also provide caste and occupational identity. An example of this may be seen in the individual and distinctive designs on hathwara cloth produced in the Rajasthani village of Pipar near Jodhpur.

Rural India's religious art includes terracotta votive figurines, wall and floor painting and the illustration and recounting of legend and stories. Like Brahmanic ritual arts, folk art is dependent for its efficacy on ritual preparation, performance and sound. It does not aim at representational accuracy or realism but comes from a common cultural pool of symbol and metaphor. These symbols parallel myth and legend, occupying the middle ground of human consciousness between the visible world and that of the imagination and the unconscious. Some religious art is commissioned from craftsmen, who belong to exclusive endogamous guilds, while more simple images are made by non-professional

individuals or tribal priests for ritual use. Rural religious art is linked to wish fulfilment, communion with the spirits, gods or goddesses and protection. The crucial requirement was the propitiation of the unpredictable deities by gifts. Gift giving still provides one of the chief vehicles for the interaction of man and god in rural and urban areas of Hindu India. Historically it took several forms, the most powerful being the sacrificial offering of live victims to be devoured by the deity. Linked to a belief in the transformation of the victim through sacrifice is the offering of terracotta votive figurines which are made in vast numbers and are commissioned from the potter in the fulfilment of vows to the deity.

Tribal religious art is largely ephemeral, made to endure the time of the ceremony and only efficacious if combined with ritual performance and a religious chant. The simplification and abstraction of the depiction of animal or humans may enhance their magical properties. In tribal society the impulse to adorn, to fulfil protective requirements and to provide status is satisfied by appropriate jewellery, body decoration in the form of painting and tattooing and highly coloured and patterned textiles. For similar reasons tribal houses, like village houses, are also decorated with ritual patterns.

This chapter will comprise three sections. First, it will examine village Hinduism; second, it will focus on the historical and contemporary production of terracottas, wall painting, and illustrated story-telling; third, it will look at the patronage of these arts.

Village Hinduism

Village Hinduism shows local variety and a greater emphasis on the worship of the goddess than does orthodox Hinduism. The religious life of the villagers involves respect for the orthodox Brahman priest alongside the worship of the local deities. The division between village and orthodox Hinduism is not clear-cut, with much overlap and coexistence. Many villages possess a temple dedicated to a Hindu puranic deity, tended by a Brahmanic priest as well as shrines dedicated to local gods and goddesses, who often receive a more intense loyalty. According to the scholar Sekine, 80 per cent of the faithful of South India are said to be devotees of 'village gods' and cults centred on the great gods of Hinduism outside the village are relatively limited.[4] The local deities have an acknowledged hierarchy, a multitude of different names, and yet exhibit certain similarities. Gramadevatas or local deities are predominantly female. In many cases it is a local goddess who has pre-eminence and is believed to be united in marriage with the village.[5] Unlike puranic deities the local goddesses are unmarried, although the male village gods do sometimes have their own consorts. The goddesses, and the lesser male village deities such as Aiyanar in Tamil Nadu, are worshipped in separate shrines within the boundaries but often in different parts of the village.

One major difference between orthodox puranic and rural Hinduism may be seen in the ease of individual access to the deity in the latter. The villagers do not require priestly intercession for access to or for their devotions to these gods and goddesses. All castes, with the exception of people from outside the village boundaries, who are excluded, have access to the local deity. Another characteristic feature of rural Hinduism in North and South India is the lack of a clear-cut division between man and spirit seen in a belief in a hierarchy of gods, spirits, animals and man.

Studies by Luschinsky and other anthropologists have revealed a hierarchical attitude to deities which is characteristic of rural beliefs in North and South India. For example, in one area:

> While most men and women place Bhagauti Mai, representing the seven disease sisters, in second place. Then come other Gods and goddesses of the Hindu pantheon, godlings of the Senapur area, and finally the host of evil spirits which wander the earth [6]

Conversations with informed villagers reveal belief in a pantheon of gods where the supreme deity is more an overseer than an active participant in the phenomenal world, while his qualities are represented by other gods and goddesses. The range of deities can be extremely complex, with as many as five different types such as a village, caste, lineage, family and personal gods. Religious concerns of devotees in rural India reveal both dependence on and apprehension of local deities whose power may bring prosperity, protection or calamity. Preternatural beings from the lower echelons of the spirit world are also seen to haunt the village, forest and collective mind of the community.

Goddesses

As mentioned above, examples of regional goddesses are Mariyamman in South India

Figure 6.1 'Seven sisters' at a village shrine in Tamil Nadu. Robert Elgood.

and Manasa in North India. All across North and South India we also find the recurrence of the theme of the seven sisters (Figure 6.1). Other goddesses are known only to a small local area and sometimes the deity will share the names or epithets of deities from the Sanskrit pantheon. These village and tribal goddesses are without consorts and demand blood sacrifices, usually but not exclusively a male animal. Different godlings and goddesses are approached for different requests. For example, in South India Mariyamman of Aruppukkottai would be sought for the relief of smallpox (Plate 6), Mariyamman of Madurai for fertility and the male deities Aiyanar and Kuruppan in Madurai would be worshipped for protection. Different gods and goddesses also make varied demands on their devotees. Many goddesses expect severe penances such as fasting and abstinence, fire walking, and the goddess Mariyamman insists on blood sacrifices. On the other hand, godlings do not require such severity of ritual but often accept live offerings. In South India it is customary to offer liquor to Maturaiviran, and Murukan[7] is pleased for his devotees to offer hair, Karuppu the protector appreciates weapons or meat, while Aiyanar prefers clay offerings.[8]

Goddesses and Sacrifice

During periods of disease or disaster the goddess is honoured and propitiated by the celebration of festivals. These involve the participation of the whole village community and commonly include spirit possession rites. One component of village festivals in honour of the goddess is her ceremonial marriage to the village headman. The buffalo in some parts of South India is also called the husband or devotee of the goddess.[9] Before 1947 (when it was banned), buffalo sacrifice was widespread and is still practised in some rural areas and in regions such as Andhra Pradesh. Today, however, the animals most frequently immolated are male goats, pigs and fowls.[10] The sacrifice of the buffalo used to be the climax of village ceremonial in many festivals in North and South India,[11] and is still widespread in Nepal.

Interpretation of sacrifice

The purpose of the male animal sacrifice has various interpretations; for example, it has been suggested that it may be the assuaging of the unleashed power of the female, while Shulman describes it 'as a means by which the blood sacrifice of a male victim transforms him into a devotee of the goddess and effects his union with her'.[12]

Beck, on the other hand, does not perceive this sacrifice as creative but as appeasing the goddess's anger.[13] The sacrifice has many functions and can most accurately be interpreted as the climax and the focal point of the entire festival and the means of the creation and activation of sacred power. The victim may be seen as an intermediary or substitute for the self-immolation of the offerer.[14] The villagers appreciate the inherent danger in the presence of the ambivalent and unpredictable goddess and, after a period of intense creativity, negotiate her departure to reinstate the normal order of daily life. The goddess's power remains in the village until its dissolution at the end of the festival,

when the image is immersed in water. Harman also intimates that sacrifices are sources of power, beset by unpredictable dangers involved in their accumulation.[15]

Sekine refers to the South Indian devotee's liberal contact with the sacrificial blood, regarded as a pollutant in North India. He argues that the goddesses, in their affirmation of blood sacrifice, symbolize the dynamism of death and the regeneration of life. This idea is also reinforced by the scholar Yamashita, who makes the distinction between the northern concept of the link between sacred power and purity;[16] and evidence from Tamil literature of the southern belief in the generative qualities and the inherent mystical power in the 'impure', seen most specifically during the practice of sacrifice.

This release of an inherent sacred power through sacrifice may be echoed by the ancient Tamil concept referred to by Zvelebil as the release of 'ananku'. This, argues Zvelebil, is 'The most fundamental 'prime' of all ancient Tamil, possibly Dravidian, religious concepts, but it is also the most abstract'.[17]

Ananku is described as the sacred force inherent in certain places, objects and powerful animals and beings, most particularly in Murukan, which is both creative and destructive. In some humans, according to Zvelebil, release of this force may lead to possession and a kind of sickness. He suggests that shamanistic possession attempts to harness this force and render it creative.

> In these goddess rites there was sought through the creative paradigm of the 'demon devotee', that is to say, through the sacrificial self-transformation of what appeared to be a demon – in other words, through the 'pollution'

of his destructive death symbolized by the blood sacrifice – the acquisition of the powerful sakti (sacred force) that is nurtured in the very midst of this process.[18]

Here, Sekine may perhaps also be referring to the power of ananku which Zvelebil himself suggests is contained by powerful animals such as the buffalo, and, according to Hart, by woman during menstruation and widowhood.[19]

Blood is one of the hallmarks of ritual offering associated with fertility and regeneration in rural Hinduism, a widespread form of early ritual devotion which survives even in the Christian tradition of communion. This liberal blood-letting which involves the deliberate splashing on stones, the shrine or the devotee may also be interpreted as an attempt for closer communion with the goddess. It may express the absorption of the released power of the buffalo victim through blood, or contact with the union of the goddess with the transformed victim. Associated with this may be ananku which, according to Zvelebil, assumed the meaning of a personalized demonic–divine force.

Whitehead also argued that the buffalo sacrifice may be an intimation of an older practice where the aim was communion with the spirit of the buffalo. He went on to suggest that this would explain the customary practices, such as wearing the entrails of the victim or the voluntary splashing of blood which went beyond appeasement and propitiation.[20] The buffalo was a beast of valour and a most valued offering. In the tribal community of the Todas it was and still remains a sacred animal.[21] This and the reference to the puranic myth of the buffalo demon points to an ancient reverence for the buffalo.[22] It

is one of many examples of the reinterpretation and demonization of non-Vedic deities, which were supplanted by the Brahmanic order.[23] The buffalo demon and its relationship with Durga in her manifestation of Mahisamardini is strong throughout India but is distinguished in the south by Durga standing on the decapitated buffalo's head, rather than the body as in northern iconography.[24]

The ritual violence required to invoke and appease the village goddesses can be seen as forcing the villagers to confront a deeper level of psychological experience. Through fear of the goddess and the confrontation with death itself, the sacrifice reaches to the root of regeneration of spiritual power and the heart of personal experience. The loss of personal control through spirit possession leads to personal chaos and trance, where the goddesses and devotees meet in terrifying spiritual union. This transformation leads to a commonality of experience and a temporary liberation from caste discrimination. The intensity of the power released by the worship of the goddesses cannot be sustained on an everyday basis; nor is it safe for the community to prolong the great and unpredictable power of the goddesses within their environment.[25] The male gods temper this sacred power while maintaining social order.

Male Deities

A variety of male deities is worshipped in the rural areas. Well known in the south are Murukan, in some senses associated with Karuppu;[26] and Aiyanar, the popular village god of Tamil Nadu. Murukan is a particular favourite in South India, where he is worshipped with a greater intensity

Figure 6.2 A village shrine with tridents and spears, sacred to Murukan, Tamil Nadu. Robert Elgood.

than the puranic gods. The most noticeable feature of the Aiyanar shrines are the huge clay horses which are left in groves near the shrines at the edges of villages for him to ride at night to protect the village. Aiyanar is a peaceful god who does not require violent sacrifice and is therefore presumed to have subsumed Brahmanic prohibitions. Aiyanar is seen as more detached and responsible for the community as a whole rather than the concerns of the individual,

and for this reason perhaps receives less intense devotion than other personal gods and goddesses. The temple to Aiyanar is always on the outskirts of the village where it tends to be neglected except on special ceremonial occasions.[27] In contrast, the temple to the goddess Mariyamman is normally sited within the village.

The subordinate gods who sometimes appear with Aiyanar are known as Karuppu, Maturaiviran and Muniyan (Plate 7), and are sometimes represented by stone images scored with rough carvings or by bricks or tridents (Figure 6.2). This lack of consistency in the appearance of these village gods suggests that iconography is of minor importance to the villagers. Yet these gods are also represented figuratively in the form of colossal, free-standing, highly coloured statues with a wrathful appearance. They are sometimes referred to as 'evil gods' and believed to act maliciously. Aiyanar's dependence on these evil or impure beings for his own power rests on the Tamil concept of the power of the impure.[28] The subordinate godlings are worshipped from fear and villagers offer vows to them. Sekine states that this apparent contradiction may indeed

> be understood as constituting a dynamic continuum, with the former (the villagers' need for blood sacrifices) representing the need for the creation of sacred power by means of sacrificial death and the latter (the need for a pure god) the need for the stabilization and preservation of that power.[29]

Rural India worships a range of gods, godlings, ghosts or spirits, tree spirits or snake shrines, for reassurance and protection. In rural India, coexisting with the worship of local deities is the worship of trees and associated male and female tree spirits, yaksha and yakshini, and the worship of snake shrines which are associated with anthills. Subramaniam argued that the notion of the immanence of sacred places may have been inspired by the Tamil concept of the fixed localization of the sacred.[30] Unlike Vedic sacrifice, which was mobile, the Tamil spiritual force was bound to a specific place. Mackay, writing in 1931,[31] stated that offerings and occcasionally animal sacrifices were still

made to certain trees to placate the spirits who dwelt within them. Crooke[32] also referred to the existence of a forest tribe known as the Pavras in Khandesh, who sacrificed goats and chickens to local deities called Bara and Rani Kajhal who occupied adjoining sacred trees at harvest time.

Ghosts

Another pervasive preoccupation in village and tribal communities is respect for ancestors and the related fear of ghosts. According to Fuller, the ghost is enshrined and worshipped as a deity so that its malevolent power may be controlled.[33] Minor deities such as ghosts may be merged with other deities to become forms of them, such as a deified hero, who might be identified as a form of Bhairava or a deified heroine as a form of the village goddess. In Karnataka large sculptures are carved from jackfruit tree wood representing the spirits of deified heroes, fierce and evil beings, Hindu deities, the mother goddess, animals and the serpent spirit. These figures are for use in the bhuta (literally ghost or spirit) cult and are propitiated in shrines located near a pipal or banyan tree. Naga stones are also commonly found nearby. These bhutas are ambivalently perceived as both demons and benefactors as long as they are pacified by worship and offerings. Bhuta worship involves the usual offerings of water, flowers, lighted oil lamps and incense, a periodic propitiation in the form of possession rituals amidst the chanting of paddanas or Tulu folk narratives describing individual biographies of the bhutas. During the invocation the spirit is believed to enter the bhuta spirit medium or impersonator rather than the sculpture.[34]

The derivation of the word 'yaksha' is to become visible and also implies a ghost or spirit. This association of spirit and tree and by extension wood sculpture reminds us of the beginnings of Hindu iconography.

As already mentioned, according to Majumdar, village and tribal religion is inspired by a belief in a universal power, bonga, which is reflected in ritual. Bonga is believed to be the power contained in the natural elements such as the sun, moon, trees and serpents. This is close to Zvelebil's description of the Tamil belief in a sacred force called ananku which is immanent in certain places, objects and persons and not as the property of well-defined transcendental gods. Ananku was held to be a force which was capricious and dangerous, neither solely auspicious nor malevolent.[35]

Shrines

The localization of sacred power, called 'topographical localization'[36] by Zvelebil, began very early in Tamil Nadu. This concept may have given rise to sacred shrines in Tamil Nadu and their later proliferation throughout South and North India. Sacred sites existed *ab initio* or acquired recognition. Some shrines may have arisen from marker stones. These may have acquired sanctity by their demarcation of a place where a spirit once appeared, subsequently becoming in anticipation the regular site for sacrifices to that spirit. These shrines link the everyday world and the supernatural and are still the focus of individual devotion.

The shrine to the deity is often placed on the edge of the village, thereby protecting the village from the dangerous outside world while keeping order within the village boundaries. Village deities are

Figure 6.3 Sacred termite mound, Tamil Nadu. Robert Elgood.

predominantly female and are not usually represented by anthropomorphic images.

Each Hindu community, whether large, urban or rural, has its own local shrines. The shrines may be a pile of stones placed in the open fields (Figure 3.9), or on the bank of a river or stream in an area of natural beauty, or more usually at the boundary of the village. In West and South India shrines may also be associated with snake shrines which are placed beside termite or anthills and covered with yellow turmeric (Figure 6.3). The shrines are often uncovered, with a mud, stone or cement platform and a low wall on three sides, sometimes with a bamboo and palm leaf cover.[37]

The images of the deities in shrines sometimes appear as roughly carved stones only recognizable by their ornamentation. Decoration is often as simple as a blackened surface daubed with red, the result of offerings, ablutions and a smearing of vermilion, while other images may be adorned with ornamental clothes and garlanded with flowers. Sometimes the sacred image is merely a pile of stones marked by a flag or pole or a large earthenware vessel. Some shrines in Tamil Nadu possess a large trident (symbol of Siva), or a spear (symbol of Murukan), often topped with limes which act as propitiatory offerings to the evil spirits.

As already mentioned in Chapter 3, these shrines are maintained and served by a local priest, male or female, often from a family and any caste traditionally associated with the shrine, but rarely from the Brahmana caste (Figure 6.4). Unlike the Brahman priest these local priests do not mediate between devotee and god or goddess but they do observe rituals on a daily, seasonal or annual basis depending on the local tradition and individual inclination. The upkeep of the shrine is shared by the community either in the form of a tax levied by the local council or by regular patrons, who vow to provide incense, food and flowers on a regular basis. Terracotta votive figurines are given as offerings to the shrines, many of which use terracotta accessories such as ghatas, kalasas and dipas as offertory vessels.

In most villages several shrines exist that are dedicated to different deities. In some examples in Tamil Nadu, northern shrines hold a predominance of female deities who require blood sacrifices strongly linked to Tamil traditions, while shrines in the south of the village have a pre-eminence of male deities who do not require live offerings.

The tribal peoples also have simple shrines tended by temple keepers. These tribal sanctuaries are situated in remote areas, in mountain regions or in dense groves, near rivers or waterfalls. All tribal groups have a priest or sacred specialist. The ceremonies of the tribal deities show a remarkable similarity throughout India. The tribes have priests with no special status such as the Badava in the case of the Bhils and the Baiga Kanikkars in the case of the Gonds. A tribal image can be as simple as a large vermilion marked stone or a few wooden poles. Tribes do not however believe that their gods, represented by these wooden posts or clay pots, are embodiments of the deities and merely act as a focus for prayer. Some terracotta pots placed on an earthen altar plastered with cow dung may also represent the deity. In Santal villages the shrine is a raised mud platform over which there is a well-kept thatched roof supported by four corner posts. The roof is covered with grass during ceremonial occasions. In sacred groves, under trees or in these simple free-standing constructions many clay figures of elephants and horses are left behind after being ritually offered to the deity. In some tribal areas small dolmens, standing stones and capstones serve as memorials to the dead. The Gonds, Khasi, Mund, Oraon, Bhil or Kurumba still construct these memorials and they are common throughout tribal India.

Forms of Worship

In the study of ritual practised in village worship, it is difficult to distinguish between orthodox Hindu village ritual, remnants of non-Vedic ancient practice, and tribal custom. These are often combined in today's religious devotions and the principles of bhakti are found in all three. As we shall see in the conclusion to this

Figure 6.4 A priest of
Aiyanar shrine, Tamil
Nadu. Robert Elgood.

chapter there are varied objectives in the patronage and practice of the religious arts and customs. Central to these practices is the belief in the power of a hierarchical spirit world which can be evoked but is inherently unpredictable. The community feels propelled to propitiate the gods or goddesses in the ways known to please them in order to protect themselves from divine malevolence and to secure divine benevolence. As we shall see, this involves among other ritual practices the offering of diverse gifts to the gods and goddesses.

Terracottas are offered to the more Brahmanized deities such as Aiyanar, while blood offerings are given to the non-Vedic godlings such as Karuppu or the goddesses such as Manasa or Mariyamman.

The actual practice of worship is most commonly an individual affair which takes place at the orthodox Brahmanic temple, at a variety of local shrines or in the home. At a local shrine or temple it involves the individual bringing offerings to the deity in the form of food, money, terracotta votive figurines or live sacrifical offerings. Each

197

house has its own sacred area, a room, niche or a special space given to the worship of the gods. Sacred domestic space contains images in stone, metal, wood or terracotta, while posters or paintings of the gods or goddesses, often purchased from local temples or places of pilgrimage, decorate the walls. Domestic worship is without priestly mediation involving incense, an oil lamp, prayers and an offering of food or money to the deity. Personal reverence is given and specific guidance or help is sought in the everyday relationship with the deity.

The principal practitioners of these local rituals are women. Women take responsibility for the well-being of their homes and families and use various methods such as vrats to win the protection and assistance of the goddess Lakshmi or the local deities. Vrat stands for votive observance and votive rite and was originally derived from the verbal root *vr*, 'choose or will', or simply vow, in Sanskrit, literally 'what is willed' or 'will'.[38] These are domestic rituals practised mainly by women. The vows are made individually to a variety of popular village deities who offer protection against disease and disaster, or fulfilment of wishes. The contractual nature of vrats involves customary practices such as fasting, ritual wall painting or the offering of gifts when the deity has delivered the required result. Vrats are generally cyclical and some are performed on certain days of the week as a regular pattern of reminders to the gods of the devotees' commitments, such as a fast on a certain day each week. Sometimes this is more complex and arduous. There are over 2000 vrats, some of which are integral to the great festivals and are common to the whole country, while others are particular to local areas and are receptacles of ancient autocthonous rites.

Pupul Jayakar suggests that the vrats were an ancient ritual practice, acquired from non-Vedic priest magicians called Vratyas.[39] These she suggests travelled from village to village in a cart, accompanied by a woman who served as a prostitute and a musician who sang and danced in ritual performances. She indicates that these vratya priests were mentioned in the *Atharva Veda* and that they transmitted an oral tradition which permeated the culture of village India. According to Huyler, vrats originated in the early Aryan ceremony of vrata stoma which was intended to cleanse and purify non-Aryans so that they could join the Aryan rites of sacrifice and be accepted into the new society.

References to vrata rites are made in puranic literature as well as being linked in origin to the spells and hymns of the *Atharva Veda* and to the *Stri Karmani* rituals described in the ancient text the *Kausika Sutra*. Vrats found in the *Kausika Sutra* contained spells and included magic, for example, for acquiring a husband, a child, to destroy a rival, to protect pregnancy or to capture a truant woman. The *Grhya Sutras* and the *Manu Smrti* manuals dealing with samskara rites and vrata observances, obligatory for any Hindu householder, enjoined the drawing of mandalas by women in rituals connected with the worship and adornment of the earth and home at the time of celebrations of pregnancy and birth, initiation to adulthood, and marriage. Vrats include charms which range from those used to increase sexual vigour, rites for procuring rain, to the making of a picture or an effigy for benevolent or malevolent purposes.

The basic aim of vrat or vow is the attainment of divine help which involves the devotee in prescribed penance, such as fasting. The essence of rural Hinduism is expressed in this direct relationship between the individual and the deity. Vrats do not require the intercession of a priest and are largely conducted by women. They allow the individual to approach the god directly through methods which involve commitment by the devotee with, on the other hand, gentle coercion of the deity. They are passed down from mother to daughter and provide society with a more direct access to the deity than the hierarchical caste restrictions of Brahmanism. They stand in direct contrast to the male-dominated Brahmanism, and have been the principal means by which women achieved their objectives in the maintenance and well-being of their husband and family. Vrats may be silent or expressed where he, or more usually she, makes a contractual promise to the deity in return for the fulfilment of a request. The root of vrata ritual lies in the belief that desire, when visualized and made concrete through image and activated through spell and ritual gesture, generates an energy that ensures its own fulfilment. Some vrats are extremely severe and involve fasting and the promise of gifts to the goddess once the wish is fulfilled.

Aside from fasting most vrats include the drawing of a magical diagram, the repetition of specific mantras and the recitation of a katha (story or legend) associated with the particular deity to whom the prayer is directed. They sometimes involve the painting of elaborate patterns on the walls and floors of houses, often during festival times and in some areas on a regular daily basis. They are centred within the house although the devotee may be required to perform some ceremonies outside the home. Today vrats still exist in innumerable variations in urban and rural communities involving specific domestic concerns such

as curing illness in the family, the desire for children by the childless, need for financial luck for the poor, or rainfall for a good crop.

Festivals

In times of disaster the villagers gather for a festival during which a live sacrifice will be made to a deity, usually the village goddess. The vital presence of the deity is often demonstrated by shamanistic spirit possession and the whole community interacts in this catharsis. Some festivals are annual, while others are solely celebrated at the outbreak of disease or disaster. These latter festivals are believed to arise when the goddess loses power due to insufficient propitiation and withdraws her protection. The belief in a malevolent as well as a benevolent power inherent in the nature of the goddess is fundamental in rural India and is particularly strong in those villages where the goddess has pre-eminence, especially in Tamil Nadu. What, then, is the significance of the sacrifice of a buffalo? As usual the interpretation is multivalent. It may be interpreted as a propitiatory gift of blood to please the goddess; or as the subduing and destroying of the troublesome demon seen as the buffalo; or, as is suggested by Zvelebil, the taming of the power of the goddess Ananku by her marriage to the buffalo demon. In all these cases there is a transfer of power marked by the spilling of blood caused by this conjunction, a spiritual recharging. A frenzy of devotion takes place during these festivals when severe penances and vows are fulfilled. Fire walking, carrying hot coals in pots on the head and hook swinging are practices associated with these occasions.

The Rural Arts

In rural India there can be no sharp division in the vital relationship between ritual action, customs and art. As early as 4.30 a.m., married women clean and adorn their homes to honour the goddess, which they believe brings prosperity and protection. Art and associated ritual is used to revere the deity with a belief in the dynamic relation between spiritual forces and the creative potential of the craftsman. This is seen in the belief in the village potter's ability to bring life to clay in the form of terracotta figurines. It is also apparent in the belief that drawn lines may contain and control the potentially destructive forces that threaten the home, while coincidentally attracting the entry of Lakshmi. Reverence for objects is believed to bring auspicious returns; for example, rough stones splashed with blood become markers for the divine and the subject of ritual performance. Despite the fact that they are not the result of specific aesthetic rules, there is a belief that they have, together with terracottas and sacred wall decoration, the potential to become spiritually charged.

The origin and historical development of the rural arts is difficult to document due to its intentional impermanence and the lack of inscriptions regarding patron or artist. Much of what is produced is destined for eventual destruction, and the usefulness of such objects expires once they have served their ritual and religious purpose. The artist or craftsman expects to renew his art and the community believes that the numinous spirit or deity is transient. The continued presence of the goddess or the spirit is also believed to be undesirable, in that it may sometimes provoke unforeseen consequences. This belief is demonstrated by the example of the offering of terracottas where after the ceremonial the figurine is thought to be empty of spirit and is allowed to dissolve back into the earth. This also happens in the case of ritual wall paintings which dissolve in the rain and floor patterns which are distorted by the scuffing of feet. The materials used for these arts contribute to this transience.

Despite the difficulty of tracing any development of these rural arts, some information is obtainable from literary sources and archaeological finds, particularly in relation to terracottas.

Historical Development of Terracottas

In India, pottery and terracottas have a magico-religious function and the potters, despite their low caste, are believed to have the power to bring life into their creations.

Literary references to terracottas can be seen as early as the seventh century AD, when the poet Bana wrote that the emperor Harsa employed artists to make terracotta figures of auspicious fruit, trees and aquatic creatures for decorative purposes on the occasion of the marriage of his sister.[40]

The earliest terracottas so far discovered are those from the north-west regions of the subcontinent, products of the communities of the Zhob and Kulli cultures. Hand-moulded clay images of the earth mothers (Matala), with archaic, mask-like faces and schematized bodies have existed in a 6000-year unbroken tradition.[41] Art historians have referred to them as 'mother goddess' figurines. There are numerous references to earthenware, especially painted pottery and terracotta figures, in the archaeological findings of the pre-Harappan, Harappan and post-Harappan periods. The pre-Harappan pottery found at the Kalibangan site in north Rajasthan is characterized by black decoration on a red background.[42] Numerous terracottas including female figurines, bulls and other animals have been excavated from the Indus valley culture of 2500 BC (Figure 3.11). Many of the numerous animal figures found in Harappa may have been votive offerings but it has been suggested that some may have been toys, recognizable by their moveable heads and wheel mountings. With the disappearance of the Indus valley culture the use of moulds appears to have ceased and did not reappear until the third century BC.

Terracotta female images survive from the earliest times. A female torso modelled in clay with applied breasts dating from the third millennium BC was excavated in Baluchistan. Some 500 years later the creators of the Indus valley female figurines are at pains to emphasize elaborate head-dresses, pinched eyes and elongated breasts, again modelled to the waist and ending in a pedestal base.[43] Later forms have thin legs which subsequently grow rounded and bulky, with a heavy girdle emphasizing the pubic triangle. A further version of the earth mother from the second century AD shows her with heavy thighs and rounded breasts. Sometimes these images have animal faces or beaks instead of noses. The feet may also point backwards, suggesting that these images are of spirits.[44]

The purpose of these ancient figurines remains obscure, although the discovery of terracotta female figures holding two infants reinforces the suggestion that they were linked to fertility. A bulging abdomen also strongly infers pregnancy. Huntington casts doubt on the divine aspect of these figures, suggesting

> that the popularity of the female as a subject in terracotta art from pre-Harappa and Harappa times is associated with the ideas of motherhood and hence fertility, procreation, and the continuity of life, although the presence of any divine status is unknown.[45]

Evidence from tribal terracottas of recent centuries may throw light on the original purpose of the innumerable Indus valley figurines which hitherto had been identified as mother goddess images.[46] The scholar Jayakar suggests that tribal groups such as the Rani Paraj of Surat describe terracottas as possessing the essence of 'woman' while not being inherently goddess images.[47] Village women of the local potter community make these figurines (Figure 6.6). During the rituals of the Rani Paraj, figures of terracotta votive offerings of animals and humans are offered to the spirits which the tribe believes inhabit certain trees.[48] These images are perceived as 'man' and 'woman' and not as any form of deity. A selection of trees[49] is worshipped by the Rani Paraj, together with a stone cave where no image of a god is ever placed. Clay horses are offered by the Rani Paraj to the samar tree in the belief that the 'bhut' or spirit (inhabiting the tree) will ride it at night to protect the village community. This rite is believed to be linked with fertility rites at harvest time when images of a horse, man, woman and coconuts are offered to the samar tree.[50]

Despite finds of early terracottas in South India in the Nilgiri hills the majority of images are found in the North. These terracottas comprise only animal figures, among which the most predominant are bulls. The early farmers of this period (1900–1300 BC) also made some female figurines and these were applied sometimes to storage jars. This association would underline their connection to ideas of fertility.[51] Excavations at Inamgaon revealed unbaked clay figurines of the late Jorwe people, c. 1200–800 BC. Similar figurines made of wheat flour are still today made by the villagers in the surrounding area today and which are invoked for success.[52]

The Mauryan period (300 BC) initiated a new era of royal terracotta patronage. The primitive types of the preceding ages largely ceased to be made and an entirely new type of human figurine appears, outstanding because of their size and stylistic traits of physiognomy and expression. Several have come from the city of Pataliputra and its environs and others from urban centres in the Ganga valley. In some Mauryan sculptures the figures were pressed from moulds, with finer modelling done by hand.[53]

In the Sunga period terracottas were made throughout North and East India, the style and ornamentation being identical to Sunga stone sculpture. In addition to modelled figures, plaques became popular and these were sometimes displayed on walls. The plaques usually depict secular subjects such as young women at their toilet, making music or dancing. Their nudity and overt display of the generative organs may link them with fertility cults, this probability being reinforced by the survival of several Mithuna terracottas. The Sunga period reveals terracottas as a popular art and several can definitely be identified as specific gods and goddesses. By contrast, production of terracottas in the Deccan and South India was apparently not prolific. The only early terracottas seem to be those of the neolithic settlements and megalithic burials. The Satavahana terracottas reveal, however, the skill of professional craftsmen. A new class of plaque depicts a nude female figure, usually headless, known as Lajja Gauri. This image may well be connected with fertility, and is supposed to be Graeco-Roman in inspiration.[54] A further advance in technological processes can also be seen in this period in that the craftsmen were able to produce hollow terracotta figures in the round.[55]

The Kusan period marks the further proliferation and development of terracottas which are found all over the empire but with two main centres, Mathura in the north and Taxila in the north-west. Secular and religious terracottas are numerous. Stone sculpture however seems to have found greater favour than terracottas as major religious icons, but this may merely reflect stone's greater chance of survival. Interesting images of Brahmanical and Buddhist deities in terracotta do exist, inspired perhaps by the bhakti cult or the cult of the personal god of the time. The probable inference to be drawn from this is that terracottas served an indigenous folk tradition and held less appeal for the immigrant royal patrons. One of the finest terracottas is a plaque showing Kamadeva within a flowery border. Around the first century AD Gandhara was another important centre of Kusan terracottas. These show strong Hellenistic influence with many of the terracotta figurines appearing to portray Greeks or Graeco-Romans.

From the fourth century AD the rise of the Gupta empire and the rapid spread of its culture throughout India led to a widespread production of terracottas. Brick and stone replaced wood as the predominant building material used in the construction of religious structures. The increased use of brick was paralleled by the manufacture of terracotta panels not for village use but as an integral part of the royal temple serving an orthodox religious function. Some fine examples of this work are found at Brahmanabad (Sindh), Nagari and Bikaner (Rajasthan), Ahicchattra, Bhitargaon (UP) and Majasthan and Paharpur (Bengal). In contrast to these temple plaques there are also secular plaques depicting the daily life of the higher castes of Gupta society.

One can only speculate on the expectations and aims of the early terracottas and who was responsible for their production, though the quality of the Kusana and Gupta terracottas suggests royal patronage. After the political decline of the Guptas, royal patronage of terracottas also declined though it remained strongest in the lesser courts of Bengal and Bihar in East India, with some production also in Kashmir. The art of terracottas has continued up to the present day, but from the ninth to tenth centuries it became solely a rural art.

Despite the archaeological evidence the history of terracottas can in no way be considered comprehensive. Permanence was neither an expected nor desirable phenomena in much of it, since clay was believed to absorb negative energy and pollutants. Pots were purified by contact with the water they carried and had a longer life, but terracotta images served their brief ritual purpose and were then disposed of by immersion and dissolution in water.

Present-day Terracottas

The potter, as well as producing conventional cooking and drinking utensils, performs a magico-religious action in creating clay spirit vessels as votive offerings for the deity; and in making pots which have a symbolic significance in their own right. The villagers believe that clay figurines come alive when transported to the spirit world. The ritual use of terracottas was based on the belief that clay and human and animal flesh was interchangeable, and that clay was permeable to malevolent forces. As well as the substitution of terracottas for live offerings, clay can also replicate afflicted parts of the body in an enactment of sympathetic magic, where the image is offered to ward off the sickness and to bring health and wholeness to the devotee.

Jayakar affirms the magico-ritual aspect of these images:

> Fired or left unbaked, depending on the rituals for which they were intended, these icons of the Mothers, the holders of the secrets of the earth, epitomised magical rites of agriculture, fertility, life and death. At the time of the sowing of seed and harvesting and in rituals to the dead, icons of the virgin mothers were made of clay, installed, worshipped and then cast into the waters, or offered to ancient sites of the goddess – to caves, clearings in forests, or to trees – or were abandoned at village boundaries. By their very nature impermanent, the earth Mothers could not be kept under a householder's roof except for short ritual purposes.[56]

Terracottas for ritual purposes fall into two categories. First, votive offerings commissioned from the potter, which are mostly auspicious animals of varied sizes such as bulls, elephants or horses (Figure 3.13); second, unfired images, crudely made by the devotees themselves, usually women, such as elephants, horses or female figurines. Accompanied by prescribed vrats, the unfired female images may be worshipped as the goddess until their dissolution.

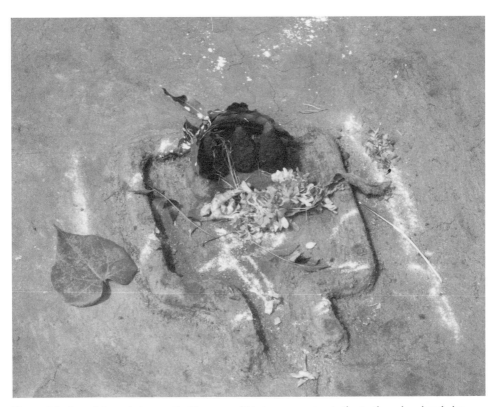

Figure 6.5 A crudely made terracotta Aiyanar and his two consorts, similar to those handmade by women, rural shrine, Tamil Nadu. Robert Elgood.

These terracotta figurines, made on commission throughout India, have in common the provision of transport to the spirits, and a belief in their magico-ritual quickening with the spirit of the animal simultaneously and instantaneously at the moment of offering. The style of these figures does have local variation; some mix wheel and hand techniques of production, some are undecorated, while others are painted white after firing to reinforce their ghostly qualities. Terracottas are particularly prevalent in Tamil Nadu, culminating in the giant spirit horses and the huge multicoloured tableaux associated with the worship of Aiyanar, while Kerala is the only state in India where clay figures are rare.

The crude unfired images are common and usually linked with magic and ritual made privately by women. Jayakar refers to unfired crude terracotta figurines made by women (Figure 6.5) which are offered during the Yama Pukura Vrata, a ritual which is connected with the primordial mysteries of the rains and the waters and the quickened energy of life. This invokes Yama, the lord of death, and is celebrated by virgins. The Yamabudi figurines, though not regarded as the goddess, are, according to Jayakar, potent with magic. While not conclusive, the continued use of these Bengal figurines today may explain the ritual purpose of the similar early terracotta figurines from Baluchistan (Zhob and Kulli).

Votive terracotta figurines used in devotional Hinduism and in village worship also became customary in tribal society. The tribes do not produce pottery objects but commission Hindu craftsmen to produce offerings for votive or funerary purposes. Bhil tribesmen, for example, travel several hundred kilometres to the Rajasthan village of Molela near Nathdwara to purchase terracottas from their favourite potters, the Maru. The village potters make various items according to the needs of the tribes such as male and female figurines, horses, elephants, tigers, bulls, calves and buffaloes to offer in adversity; and animal and human parts such as hands, feet, navels, eyes, ears, knees, stomachs, breasts, lungs, testicles, limbs and insects such as worms to offer if there is sickness.

Producers

Pottery today is produced chiefly by professional potters of the caste of Kumhars. Each of the nearly one million potters working in India today believes that he is descended directly from Prajapati, the first potter created by the gods. With local variations the legend is the same throughout India. The potter's livelihood and his tools are perceived as gifts from the gods. The majority of potters are Hindu and belong to a distinct class or jati, a subgroup of a larger varna of the caste system. The potters usually marry from within their own community, a bride from the same or similar background. They work for varied patrons and fulfil different requirements. The demand for the potter's wares is seasonal, the greatest number of commissions being during the planting and harvesting of crops and before festivals. Not only do potters produce bowls, pots and cups used in daily life but also special vessels used in weddings and other ritual images. The potter receives commissions to make toys, ordinary drinking and storage vessels, and to sculpt terracottas. The most common votive terracottas are horses, which are given to the various gods and goddesses to protect the donor from inauspicious omens, to cure illness or to guard the village.

The community's attitude to potters is curiously ambiguous, regarding them as dirty because they work with the unclean clay, but powerful. They are believed to possess a kind of magic, are honoured and are allowed to perform special ritual duties within society. Pupul Jayakar refers to one such example where the potter, having created the terracotta image and ritually evoked Sakti to enter into it, put a nail through the figurine to render the goddess harmless and buried it.[57] In South Indian rural communities the potter occasionally acts as a priest or shaman, where he becomes the medium for the messages of the god or goddess to the community.

Once the potter has been asked to make a specific votive offering he assumes the ritual responsibility, imbuing the sculpture with both the form and potency it requires. The patron pays the potter when he collects the image, sometimes with food, new clothes, money or even a cow or goat. Payment severs the potter from the sculpture and transfers the merit to the patron. According to Huyler, 'the deity breathes life into the image transubstantiating its essence into reality in the spirit world: A sculpture of mud placed in a shrine becomes a living gift to the gods.'[58]

The training of the potter begins from childhood, when children play with the tools and clay of their fathers. According to Huyler, boys begin to use the wheel from

Figure 6.6 Women decorating pots, Jhun Jhunu district, Rajasthan. Stephen Huyler.

temperature kilns and fuel which glazing required.

Only men work on the wheel, with the exception of the region of Manipur, where women work on the wheel while the men prepare the clay and the kilns. In most areas of India the women, deprived of the wheel, make pots by building lengths of clay in a manner similar to coiling. Terracotta figurine production is predominantly a male occupation although women do make clay images in some communities. Despite the fact that the man has pre-eminence in the crafting of the pot on the wheel it is the woman who is responsible for the decoration of the pot or painting details such as the eyes on the figurines. Women of each family have their own distinct designs, which are adhered to and passed on to the next generation (Figure 6.6).

Huyler, in his study of a working potter, describes the extent to which the potter gives time to preparatory rituals and engages in meditation while working on the clay:

> Touching his forehead with the fingers of his right hand before he begins his daily work, a potter acknowledges the power of his gods and their gift to him of creativity. The clay he employs is the embodiment of earth, usually viewed as a goddess. By honouring his deities, he ensures his right to change soil into sacred form and he maintains his link to his earliest ancestor: Prajapati, Lord of Creativity.[60]

At least once a year the family worships its tools during a special celebration, usually Dasara.

Painting

Parallel to the belief that a tree, shrine or terracotta may house a spirit is the concept that ritual drawing or diagrams may contain

the age of 8. The girls are trained to clean and prepare the clay, to slip and paint the terracottas and to help with the firing.[59] In South and East India pots are not usually painted before firing. This creates an ephemeral design which gradually wears off. All terracottas except those from Gujarat are painted after firing. The potter uses sticks, roots, bark, straw, animal dung and anything else that will burn to heat kilns which are often temporary, made in flat open spaces or in small pits near the potters' homes. Several factors gave rise to the unpopularity of glazing: the taboo on the reuse of drinking vessels; the fact that the local red clay did not readily hold a glaze, and the lack of china clay. Finally, most potters could not afford the high spiritual power. The ritual act of wall painting is a common and significant practice in many parts of India, where women employ it to protect the home from disruptive and maleficent spirits. The apertures of the home such as the windows and doors are thought to need particular protection. Women make the household decisions and undertake the religious tasks to protect the family. These include regular wall and floor decoration, consisting of a variety of patterns and designs which are believed to be auspicious, having special appeal to the goddess: 'The designs applied to the surfaces of a house are not only prophylactic, as protection against evil, they are also reverential, celebrations of the beneficence of the deities which protect the home.'[61]

An essential preparation for any religious action involves personal purification and cleanliness, where there is a direct relationship between purity and the sacred. Purification of the individual involves ritual washing and the recital of prayers, while purification of the village home is achieved by the regular renewal of the manure coating of the walls. The porous qualities of cow dung give rise to a belief in its capacity to absorb malignant energies, and since these forces are ever present the walls require periodic renewal. The uric acid in the freshly applied manure is believed to have purifying properties. The replastering of walls is often followed by wall painting which is also believed to spiritually recharge and protect the home.

The ephemeral nature of painting requires the re-enactment of these rituals on a regular basis. The walls and floors are resurfaced and ornamented with new designs on many different occasions during the year. In South India the earth which lies at the threshold of the house is washed and cleaned early each morning before sunrise and applied with a new pattern of coloured powder which will almost disappear by mid-morning. Some households use a different pattern for each day of the year.

History of Wall Painting

The earliest evidence for the practice of painting can be seen from mesolithic and neolithic times in pictographs scratched in red and yellow ochre on cave walls. These have been discovered in Mirzapur in Uttar Pradesh and Bhimbetka in Madhya Pradesh. According to Heinz Mode and Subodh Chandra, the most important evidence of continuity are the contemporary tribal pictographs of the Saoras and the Warlis; and the wall and floor paintings of the Gond and Kol tribes. These contemporary tribal pictographs can be compared with images which appear in the early rock paintings and Hrrappan picture writing on early coins from 2500 BC. Very little has survived, however.

The earliest extant post-Harappan wall painting in India is that found in the Buddhist caves of Ajanta. This seems to have a permanent narrative and inspirational intention and was a sophisticated, highly skilled art, perhaps executed by monks on behalf of a patron. In South India the wall paintings in the Pallava temple at Kanchipuram, or on the Brhadisvara temple in Thanjavur of 1000 AD, are a continuation of the narrative tradition.

The *Vishnudharmottara Purana*, the ancient Sanskrit treatise on painting, mentions the making of dhuli chitras, paintings drawn with powdered colour on the earth, and rasa chitras, outlined in liquid colour. According to Pepul Jayakar, the liquid colour is known as pithar or pithali and is made by mixing rice or corn starch with water. The treatise prescribes the worship of the sun-god through an eight-petalled lotus flower drawn on the ground.[62] Several other puranas speak of the art of drawing the sun on the ground and suggest that the sun was worshipped in the form of a circle in earlier times.[63]

Wall Painting

Wall and floor decoration is widespread throughout India and has different names in different parts of India, though sometimes the same word serves for both wall and floor painting. It is called alepan (wall) or aripan (floor) in Bihar, alpona in Bengal, chowka purna and sona rakhna in Uttar Pradesh, mehndi mandana in Rajasthan, sathiya in Gujerat, and rangoli in Maharashtra, kolam (and muggu) in South India, and chita in Orissa. Only in Orissa does the term used to describe this art indicate painting rather than writing, and indeed, the diagrams are intended to serve as a form of script for communicating with the deities. In West and South India the patterns are strictly geometrical while richer symbolic shapes are used in Bengal, Bihar and elsewhere in North India[64] (Plate 8). Paintings illustrating stories from the *Bhagavata Purana* are frequent. These themes are passed down from mother to daughter and the whole community shares in the moods expressed in the well-known stories. Wall and floor paintings vary across India from the painting of elephants and riders in Uttar Pradesh before the Divali festival to a white chalk painting on a red mud background, found in Rajasthan. Each festival and every occasion has its own repertoire of specific designs and symbols, with the most common motifs in Rajasthan being geometric and abstract symbols, such as six-pointed stars, hexagons, lotuses and swastikas.

Kramrisch suggests that the purpose of these ancient diagrams was to propitiate the earth as a source of fertility, to awaken sakti and to seek protection. She describes wall painting as acting in conjunction with other ritual actions to form a concentration of willpower, describing these symbols as the 'shape of conceptions...intuited and functional diagrams transmitted by women'.[65]

> It is believed that within the confines, within the more or less intricate geometrical lines of the diagram an invoked presence finds its allotted place. Its power is confined and thereby held in its place and for the purpose for which the diagram was drawn. The magic diagram makes it possible for power to be present, and it brings this presence into the power of the person who has made the diagram.[66]

This expresses the belief in the power of the lines to hold or contain power, which in turn becomes controllable by the executor of the diagram. Huyler describes it in the following way.

> Into it the power of the god is invoked. It is assigned to its enclosure, it is spellbound. It cannot escape; it is controlled. It is held in its confinement, bound in a plane by the outline of the enclosure so that it cannot escape into the ground where, like lightning, it would be rendered impotent.[67]

This description clearly expresses the belief in the potency of the circle and the relationship of this power with the person who performs the ritual act.

Mulk Raj Anand describes it as:

> a woman's art, born of unconscious and ancient knowledge potent with power and energy, to be

used by women as the mark of the auspicious for the worship and adornment and protection of the earth and home. The making of Aripan is referred to as writing, a medium of communication and never as painting.[68]

One of the most well-known styles of wall painting is from the area of Mithila surrounding the Madhubani district in north Bihar. Mithila women of Brahman families and upper caste Kayastha women paint the walls of their homes to celebrate the major events of life following the pictorial tradition of the family and caste to which the painter belongs. The nuptial chamber and the verandah outside it as well as the room of the family deity are painted with particular care. Many of these paintings narrate myths and legends, especially scenes from the *Ramayana*. The paintings on the bridal room floor are intended to break down inhibitions and to awaken desire between the bride and bridegroom who may be totally unknown to each other. The same symbols appear on both walls and floors. The spell that accompanies the rites is from the *Artharva Veda*.[69]

Producers

The art of wall painting is largely the prerogative of women. Its traditions are handed down from mother to daughter, and girls from the ages of 5 and 6 begin to learn the skills of the craft and become competent by their twelfth year. In most parts of India the women replaster their homes during periods of seasonal transition, such as the beginning of winter, planting, harvest time and before summer. Often these seasonal changes coincide with festivals like Holi, Sivatri, Dasara and Divali. Wall paintings are also produced during rites of passage which include birth, puberty, betrothal, marriage and death.

For the production of wall painting women use their fingers, the sides of their hands or their palms dipped in the liquid colour. Alternatively, a cotton rag held in the palm is used, soaked in paint which is allowed to drip down a finger and on to the wall. Paint is also sometimes thrown at the wall or brushed on using hair, coconut fibre or the chewed ends of sticks. Domestic utensils may also be used to apply block patterns.[70] A modern development is the use of stencils that are either cut at home or purchased locally. These wall paintings are sometimes made as part of the performance of a vrat. Exterior lines are applied to create a sacred and contained space and then the symbols are drawn to the accompaniment of spells to invoke the spirit or deity to inhabit the diagram.

Floor Painting

Floor paintings are made with white rice paste but also with coloured powders, or with white local chalk. Most of the pigments used in wall and floor painting are natural organic substances, although chemical powdered dyes and paints are now becoming more popular. White is the most popular colour for outlines and motifs and in many homes white and red are the only two colours used.

Floor designs are usually drawn freehand by women trickling rice paste or powder down their middle fingers on to the ground or they may be daubed or sprayed (Figure 6.7). Some of these are drawn freehand but most are created by connecting or drawing around a series of dots laid out in rows according to the required pattern. These patterns are achieved by a delineation from

Figure 6.7 Kolam, Tamil Nadu. Stephen Huyler.

the centre outwards. In most cases dots or dashes are aligned in the various sacred directions to form auspicious configurations such as the circle, star and the square or mandala. Other symbols used are the naga or snake symbol, the crescent moon, swastika, conch shell, lotus flower, sword, disc or pot. Some are geometric, some flora or fauna compositions, while others are portraits of deities. Designs range from geometrical diagrams to symbols such as footprints, believed to be those of the great goddess.

In South India floor painting is more common than wall painting and is known as rangavelli, rangoli, kolam or muggu. In Tamil the word kolam means beauty, form and play. In Tamil Nadu every morning for a month before the Festival of Pongal the women rise early and decorate the ground

in front of their homes with designs to honour the goddess. Each day the scuffing of human and animal feet gently blur the designs until their renewal the following day. Most of these designs are made with rice powder, and women say that in using rice powder they feed the insects and ants, a duty prescribed in the ancient texts the *Dharmasastras*. 'The making of the kolam involved pouring rice through the fingers with an even flow, almost as if you were pouring "dry water" from the hand.'[71]

According to Vijaya Nagarajan, the kolam is painted on the 'front threshold' of the house where the private domestic world encounters the outside world. Nagarajan describes the kolam as a net which can catch the ill feelings people have when feeling covetous and jealous of one another. With the correct performance this sacred

Figure 6.8 Brahman celebrating Pongal, making puja inside an elaborate Kolam. Nepattur village, Tamil Nadu. John Marr.

drawing is believed to have the potential to hold force and protect the threshold from the inner and outer world and to encourage the auspicious entry of Lakshmi. The symbols that stand for Lakshmi include the lotus flower, the conch shell and the chariot. The kolam is usually associated with the fulfilment of vrats or vows to the deity or with the fertility or samskara ceremonial. Some of these designs are drawn in the morning or evening; others are made to coincide with an important life sacrament (samskara) such as the birth of a child, a boy's investiture with the sacred thread, or at the time of marriage. Others are drawn as acts of devotion when taking a vow (vrata) to achieve a desired result (Figure 6.8). The latter are drawn on certain significant days of the year in the course of the sun.

Before the Mandala is drawn, the earth or the floor of the house is freshly plastered with cowdung and the Mandala drawing executed by women on the prepared space. The thumb and the first finger of the right hand is used to draw the alepan diagrams except in the Dvadasa aripan...one finger of the left hand is used to draw a complete circle in white on the ochre colour of the earth.[72]

Tribal Wall and Floor Decoration

Tribal communities also paint their houses. In Orissa their homes are adorned with broad bands of earth colours: yellow ochre, reddish brown and white. In Madhya Pradesh the designs are executed in low relief and parts accentuated with colour. In Gujarat entire walls are covered with designs painted in white, with wide vertical

211

panels within which are horizontal bands of geometrical shapes interspersed with floral and vegetal designs. The Warli tribe of Maharashtra produce distinctive and well-known paintings for family marriages, known as the chowk, the essential element being a square painted on the mud-plastered inner wall of the room where the wedding is to take place. The tribal goddess Palaghut with the sun and moon is contained within the square. This boundary is drawn in red ochre with four ritual lines which represent the clan deities. Once the goddess has been represented the area outside the diagram is embellished with scenes of everyday life. When this has been ritually installed the painting is covered with a large cloth and unveiled during marriage ceremonies so that the deity may bestow her blessing on the union. This marriage diagram may only be drawn by married women, but men and women decorate the walls of their homes with scenes from the forest and daily life. In the last few years these paintings have become popular with Western collectors and tribesmen are now commissioned to produce these paintings commercially.

The tribal Saoras of Orissa paint pictographs within their homes to serve as shrines called ittal which portray the spirit world. The present-day Saoras give no anthropomorphic forms to their gods, merely outlining an area within a square or rectangle for the habitation of the deity. These icons are generally commissioned by a family which feels itself to be suffering from the evil influence of a particular spirit and the male artist is regarded as a magician priest. The paintings are also made in times of crisis to propitiate deities and ancestors as well as for fertility.

In the Kumaon region of Uttar Pradesh, no important samskara ceremony or religious festival propitiating a deity is complete without the jyonti or painting of three female deities along with Ganesa, and the pattas depicting a particular deity.[73] The Rathva and Bhilala tribes of Chhota Udaipur in Gujarat and the area of Alirajpur in Madhya Pradesh use wall painting to demarcate special sanctified areas in their homes for the installation of deities.

While in most tribal areas it is women who paint the walls of the houses, magico-religious wall painting is also produced by male priests. This has been noted in tribal groups such as the Gondhs of Mandla and the Warlis of Maharashtra. In areas where the tribe has come into close contact with a settled village community, however, both men and women paint. In north Gujarat among the Bhil tribes painting is done by men known as buas, who paint the sacred pithoras, images in red, yellow and black of horses and riders, on the internal mud walls of the Bhil huts. Like the Warli paintings, a headless figure is invariably represented with five sheaves of sprouting corn emerging from his neck. As part of ancestor worship the Bhil buas make a liquid paste of grain and spray it by mouth on to the walls of their huts to make shadow outlines of the palm of the hand or a sickle. These symbols are believed to protect the huts from malevolent forces.

With growing urbanization there has been a decline in the performance of ritual painting. The most persistent forms are vrata diagrams and those floor designs (kolam and rangoli) used on wedding daises and altars which are integral to these rituals.

Story-telling and the Transmission of Culture and Education

Story-tellers

For centuries in India it has been customary for male story-tellers who belong to a specific caste to travel from village to village, telling stories illustrated by colourful paintings on scrolls, large pieces of cloth or wooden temple boards.[74] The paintings used a visual language familiar to the local community. These performances did not have an expressly didactic purpose but were expected to propitiate the gods thereby bringing rain, fertility and prosperity. This tradition, which continues today in many parts of urban and rural India, is very ancient. As early as the second century BC Patanjali refers to Saubhikas who disseminated moral and religious doctrines among the people with the aid of pictures.[75] Early Buddhist literary sources refer to charan-chitra or 'mobile paintings' and Buddhist stupa panels of the first to fourth centuries AD may be compared with contemporary scroll paintings.

> There are Brahman heretics who, having prepared a canvas booth (pata kotthaka), and painting (lekhapitva) therein representations of all kinds of happiness and misery connected with existence in heaven or hell, take this picture and travel about (vicaranthi) pointing out; If you do this you will get this.[76]

Coomaraswamy suggests that charan-chitra was the Buddhist equivalent of the better known term Yama-pata. Jain cites the Vishakhadatta's *Mudrarakshasa* where there is a reference to a spy who described himself as a Yama-pattika (a picture show-man of the panel of Yama, the god of death) and carried with him painted scrolls of hell's punishments. 'He habitually entered the house of his patrons, where he displayed his Yama cloth, and sang songs, presumably of a religious type.'[77]

Bana's *Harsacharita* also mentions the Yama-pattikas and explains that they showed pictures and gave sermons on vice and virtue, reward and punishment. According to Jain, the Garoda caste of story-tellers in Gujarat using the vertical painted paper scrolls are the direct descendants of the Yama-pattika tradition.[78]

The emergence of the vernacular languages – Maithili, Braj Bhasa, Avadhi, Oriya – led to a revival in story-telling, while the introduction of paper in the fifteenth century in India also encouraged the production of these illustrated tales. The practice of painting vertical scrolls has survived mainly in west Bengal and Bihar, whereas the large horizontal scroll paintings are chiefly found in Rajasthan. In Bengal the story-tellers are known as patuas and in Bihar as jadupatuas. From the late nineteenth century, the patuas of Bengal produced paintings for sale to pilgrims at the Kali temple in Calcutta. The jadu-patuas (literally magic-painters) in contrast are itinerant aboriginal mendicants, 'Hindu' magicians, brass-workers and painters who paint for the Santal tribe from Singhbhum and Bihar as well as for the inhabitants of settled villages. The Santals believe that the jadu-patuas possess magical powers that protect their followers. According to Jain, the Chakshudana-pat or the 'eye bestowal painting' is one carried by the Jadu-patuas to the family of a recently deceased individual with all but the eyes painted, which signifies the wandering spirit of the dead. It is to free the spirit from this odyssey that the family commissions the eye bestowal ceremony to the picture. The ceremony is particularly interesting because it links a tribal practice to orthodox Hindu concepts of darsan and the eyes being the seat of the soul and the inauguration of statues.

In Rajasthan stories are told by itinerant magician bards from the Bhil tribe called bhopas about a hero called Pabuji, a Rathor chief. His adventures are painted on large horizontal scrolls (phad) of up to 30 feet in length, originally painted on cloth though modern versions are on paper backed by cloth. The central figures of Pabuji and his black horse are larger than the other figures in the story and the illustrations use flat washes of red, black, olive and yellow ochre. Story-telling involves singing or 'reading' the painted phad to the accompaniment of music and dance while a ritual oil lamp is held over the relevant area of the painting in a manner resembling the ritual illumination of orthodox Hindu icons. It is widely believed that the deity inhabits the painting and therefore these paintings should never be sold and may only be discarded by ritual immersion in Lake Pushkar, the abode of Lord Brahman.

In the Warangal, Khammam, Adilabad, Karimnagar, Hyderabad and Medak districts of Andhra Pradesh the Nakkash caste of painters use both horizontal and vertical scrolls of starched cloth nine metres in length for painting stories on a characteristic orange-red ground. These paintings depict Puranic legends and are carried by story-tellers to different patrons, such as the weavers who patronize the Konnapalli group, and who narrate the *Markandeya Purana*.[79] In Mysore the principal figures are ornamented with gold in the manner of temple images.

Nineteenth-century paintings from Paithan, Maharashtra and Central India depict local variations of the *Ramayana*, the *Mahabharata* and the legends of the *Puranas*. These themes are produced on both sides of thick ivory-coloured handmade paper and serve as visual counterparts to the stories told and sung by two narrators who create a dialogue and reverse the pages during their recital. It is suggested by Jayakar that the style of these paintings may be derived from the court art of Vijayanagara.[80] The oldest paintings seem to be from 1830–40. According to Jayakar and Dallapicchola, there are stylistic similarities between these paintings and Karnataka puppets. A functional parallel is also noted in the didactic role of the puppets and the Paithan paintings.

Production and performance

Illustrating and telling stories is a male occupation. The professional story-tellers recite passages from the *Mahabharata*, *Ramayana* or legends of the Puranic gods. These sometimes combine folklore and stories of local warriors in performances which are rarely one-dimensional and often integrate dance, dialogue, recitation and epic theatre. The essential role of the bards is to interpret the pictures to village audiences, while many also practise magic, astrology and palmistry. Other caste members are accomplished painters and musicians.

In Rajasthan the scroll painting is hung on a bamboo frame revealing the part of the story currently being told to the audience while the rest of the scroll is rolled up. The bard recites the piece while his wife illuminates the relevant scenes with an oil lamp. Performances of the Pabuji ka phad are held at night, with the bhopa and his wife singing and dancing. The story is accompanied by mime, song, drumbeat and occasional acrobatic feats. A parallel tradition of painted narrative in Rajasthan is the custom of adorning the temples with painted cloths. A well-known example of this is the Sri Nathji temple at Nathdvara, where sacred hangings are regularly renewed which portray the idol surrounded by devotees.

In South India cloths known as vasamalai are painted in Kalahasti, Nagapattam and Pallakolu in Andhra. These cloths are used for hanging on temple walls and as screens on wooden carts (rathas) that carry the icons in procession around the town.

In Gujarat a cloth which recounts the exploits of the seven mother goddesses, known as the mother Mata ni Pachedi, is printed by the artisans of the lower castes for use during the Navaratra festival. The cloths of the mothers are hung around the shrine and form its roof. On the last of the nine nights the bua or magician-priest drinks fermented rice wine and is possessed by the goddess.

He dances and sings wildly and wrapping the pachedi cloth of the goddess around his shoulder, he leads a procession to the river side. Virgin girls follow him carrying on their heads the earthen pot containing the sprouting corn. At the river bank they worship the departing mothers and the sacral pot is consigned to the waters.[81]

In sum, despite the fact that story-telling was primarily performed to induce rainfall and fertility and thus orchestrated to coincide with calendar events and festivals, a consequence was that itinerant story-tellers kept alive the local legends and folklore among the urban and rural communities. The paintings were also believed to be sacred and, together with ritual song and dance, capable of evoking the deity within the audience. The low caste status of story-tellers and the lack of Brahmanic prescriptions for the painting or literary content reinforce the non-Vedic roots of this bardic practice.

Section III

Who Were the Patrons in Village and Tribal India?

Female patrons

As we have seen, apart from male story-tellers, rural women in India have always been largely responsible for creating magico-religious 'art'. They commission and offer terracottas to the goddess and approach a range of local godlings or tree spirits for protection, fertility and the well-being of their families. Women also create elaborate wall paintings to beautify and protect the home. The pre-eminence of women as religious patrons in rural India was well established from the earliest recorded times. Recent studies show a decline in the religious and social status of women in relation to orthodox Hinduism over 4000 years though their status in village India has remained constant.

From about 2500 B.C. to about 500 B.C., girls of higher class families were well educated and could provide intellectual companionship for their husband. They participated with their husbands in all religious rites and in the making of family decisions. The high status of Brahman, Kshattriya, and Vaishya girls relative to boys of the same castes could be explained in part by the fact that they, like boys, were ceremonially initiated and wore the sacred thread.[82]

Luschinsky suggests that women enjoyed a high standing in ancient India from 1500 to 800 BC, but during the Classical Period, from 800 BC to 500 AD they experienced a gradual decline in status, demonstrated by the fact that women were no longer permitted to wear the sacred thread or to participate in Brahmanic rites.[83] Women were no longer able to participate in sacrificial ceremonies, to study the *Vedas* or to become wandering ascetics and their religious role was confined to the domestic rituals which accompanied the marriage ceremony.[84] Despite losing ground to the Brahmans in mainstream ritual activity, from AD 500 a new attitude developed which perpetuated the importance of women in domestic religious rituals.[85] It is interesting to note that women's diminishing status in orthodox rites seems to coincide with an increasing fear of women's ritual power and the growth in the cult of sakti. The male takeover of the women's role was not without trepidation. This is most obviously perceptible in the male attitude to, and apprehension of, the ambivalent goddess who required propitiation with blood and sacrificial offerings; and visually in the changes in sculpted female imagery which became more sensual from the first century BC to the third century AD. No longer seen solely as the earth goddess with a critical role in creation, women were regarded as possessing potentially dangerous sexual power if untamed by marriage, exemplified by the power of the goddess in all her manifestations.

Despite Aryan patriarchy, remnants of a matriarchy can be observed, particularly in the south where the use of the mother's

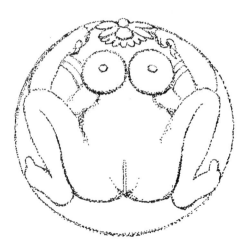

Figure 6.9 An image of Lajja Gauri. Drawing by Christopher Glanville RWA.

name persists in secret rites and fertility rituals.[86] Goddess images such as the fourth-century Lajja Gauri fertility image found at Nagarjunakonda (Figure 6.9) are further evidence of the patronage, social and religious responsibility of women and the worship of the goddess. The inscription on the image reveals that it was installed by the Ikshavaku queen, Mahadevi Khanduvula, described as A-vidhara (whose husband is alive) and Jivat (all of whose children are alive).[87] The inscription by implication refers to her auspicious status, proven by the fact that her husband and offspring were living; their deaths would be taken as evidence of her failure to undertake the necessary ritual protection or of an inherent malevolence.[88]

Within the Indian village women have never appeared to suffer any inferiority with regard to religious status and to have retained their ancient ritual responsibilities.

Hindu women have not been quite as subjugated as some texts would have us believe. Women continue to be versatile experts in ritual matters in a variety of ways. We may conclude therefore, that the brahmanical attempts to oust women from ritual involvement have more or less failed. Their failure is probably due to the fact that local practices have a tendency to reassert themselves over scriptural models and to rework them in their own way.[89]

In the village women have the responsibility for most of the calendrical and life cycle rites as well as the votive offerings. Luchinsky observed that village women felt that they contribute to the welfare of their family and village by their religious and magical activities.[90]

Most of the magical and religious activities of Senapur women are based on their desires to attain certain ends: to protect themselves and their families from harm, to cure illness and overcome adversity, to ensure procreation, to maintain spiritual cleanliness, and to ensure good crops, among others.[91]

A series of interviews of village women by Mary Mcgee reveals that few women performed votive rights (vrat) for their own health and prosperity. Most were motivated by a desire for children, marital happiness or for the well-being of their children and husbands together with a concern for this world rather than an afterlife. In this way they are seen to fulfil their dharma, social responsibility and to find liberation.[92] In contrast, it has been found that the men of Senapur make vows when they are ill or involved in a court case or when they have some personal or family problem.

The making of vows is not an elaborate procedure. Villagers do not go to the shrine of the god whose help they seek when they make a vow. They simply make a silent promise to a god when the idea occurs to them. They may or may not tell others what they have done. If their requests are fulfilled, however, they usually tell friends and neighbours of their good fortune and hurry to fulfill their promise.[93]

These religious activities appear to satisfy many of the needs felt by women. These might include a change from the daily routine; emotional catharsis through spirit possession; a sense of sisterhood; and a sense of importance and power. Above all, women's ritual provides them with the satisfaction of making a crucial contribution to the protection of the family unit which gives them their purpose and identity in life. Women who are distressed or anxious may also turn to shamans and spirit possession to obtain relief. The manifestation of the spirit in the medium reinforces the villager's belief in the omnipresence of the spirit world.[94]

Despite the importance of women as patrons and non-professional producers, the professional craftsmen forming the ancient guilds such as potters, goldsmiths, carpenters and wood carvers are without women members. These craftsmen were the link between the monumental forms of the orthodox tradition, the rural gods and the tribal deities of forest and mountain.

Tribal patrons

Potters from village communities are sometimes commissioned by tribal groups. Terracotta offerings are made either individually or collectively at large sanctuaries in special places away from the village to fulfil specific vows, but each village has its own small abode of the god of the area which is a miniature form of the larger sanctuary. 'With these terracottas tribals climb mountains or cross rivers or go into thick forests. They walk miles to reach the gods' sanctuary which is always at a remote place, with a mystical atmosphere.'[95]

The concept underlying clay offerings is the link between clay and flesh. The tribals believe in the offering of a whole clay figure to make oneself whole, a clay cow for a cow, etc. The offering of the greatest merit is that of the horse, which has become an animal of great significance and value. Elephants are also highly valued and sometimes offered in clay. They may be made at different stages in the growth of crops; for the well-being of an individual or village; to protect against ill health or to avert evil for men and animals; during the disease curing ritual, or when installing the spirits of the dead in domestic shrines; for offerings to ancestors; to wish for children or for fertility in animals; when cows or buffaloes do not give milk; to recover a property if there is a theft or if the village wishes to offer a new 'Pedhi'.[96] For small offerings, the tribals take their chosen terracotta to the sanctuary together with chickens, incense, flags, rice, coins, wine and coconuts.

> For more important occasions, it starts with the sending of invitations to friends, relatives and others. People then get together at one place and musical instruments are always played. They sing and dance all the way even while approaching the god. At the sanctuary, they offer their different gifts first marking them with dots of orange. Flags are offered and the lamp is lit. The Bhuva, Priest, goes into a trance and offers the rice, wine and chicken, and calls all the gods there while chanting and singing. Towards the end, a man climbs a tree or on to a higher platform and throws rice over the assembled people which each member of the group tries to catch. They take that rice home with them. Finally, a feast and dancing complete the ritual.[97]

Motivations for Patronage

To understand the motivations for rural patronage and the practical rationale of the rural arts, one cannot turn to ancient sastric texts or inscriptions or cite the reasons that apply to royal patronage. Instead one has to rely on the contemporary investigations of anthropologists, ethnologists and village art historians. The acquisition of prestige, legitimacy and spiritual power underlying the patronage of the grand sacred monuments are not factors in the rural arts. Rural art does however share with the decoration of temples, the conceptual link between pollution, and regeneration. Concepts of power such as titular legitimacy are not village preoccupations, but prosperity, protection, health and purification and fertility are. The rural arts are not bound by Brahmanic prescription nor are they subject to priestly intercession in their approach to the spirit world or the deity.

The desire to acquire spiritual merit which gave rise to so much imperial patronage is less prevalent in the patronage of the rural arts. The average village woman does not show much concern for the next life but believes that the supreme deity is always watching and will punish her if she does wrong. However, her principal concern is the resolution of everyday problems. To achieve this, in most cases the individuals turned to a variety of gods, who ranged from the detached supreme Ishvar also known as Bhagvan, to caste deities, village gods and, for the most intimate spiritual relationship, personal gods or goddesses. The more aloof Brahman village gods do not require literal sacrifice but the fickle village gods or goddesses require bloody propitiation.

Figure 6.10 Terracotta horses offered to Aiyanar. Stephen Huyler.

As has already been noted, most of the rural ritual practices include vrats to the gods or goddesses together with devotional offerings or gift giving. These are the chief means for fulfilling objectives such as fertility, prosperity, protection, purification, healing and installing a deity.

Gift giving and vow fulfilment

In the *Mahabharata* Bhishma told Yudhisthira:

> Indeed I shall tell you, O Bharata! how gifts should be made to all orders of men. From desire of merit, from desire of profits, from fear, from free choice, and from pity gifts are made. O Bharata! Gifts therefore, should be known to be of five kinds[98]

Gift giving is a common feature of life at all social levels in India. Vratas, as we have already observed, usually involves the giving of an offering alongside some personal penance, such as fasting and the accompaniment of magical verses. The commission of a terracotta is a ritual that begins with the devotee promising his deity on the fulfilment of a request to honour this by a gift or vrata. Another aspect of this gift giving is the belief that removal of bad luck may be achieved by its absorbence into a clay vessel which is then given away or placed outside the community. As has been noted, the offering of terracottas has become a symbolic alternative which accompanies many acts of worship to Puranic deities, certain village deities such as Aiyanar and certain tree and snake shrines.

Gifts can be in the form of live animals which is required by some local deities such as Karuppu in South India and many goddesses, but it is expensive and is discouraged by many orthodox Hindus. Horses and elephants are the most common forms of votive terracottas, although cattle, camels, tigers, many other animals and figures of gods and humans may also be found. Both horses and elephants have been associated with power and prestige. In South India the large terracotta horses offered to the god Aiyanar have a longer life span than most votive terracottas.

219

Devotees believe they continue to serve the God as spirit horses and that they cross into the spirit world for the god's personal use. The large terracotta horses are renewed but often the old horses are preserved (Figure 6.10) and still receive devotion unless they get broken or damaged.

Most Hindus participate in annual festivals which require as part of the ritual the offering of terracotta sculptures which represent the gods. These sculptures are usually made by professional potters on commission and purchased by devotees. They are not included in jajmani transactions and are specially commissioned as required and paid for in cash or bartered with other trade goods. Clay objects are also involved in the custom associated with the dead and ancestor worship which is linked to the worship of the sacred banyan tree. The Rani Paraj tribals from Surat place a clay temple under the tree and put a stone within it in the name of anyone who dies. From that day they believe the dead person dwells there. On festival days several clay images of horses, cows and buffaloes are taken to this sanctuary. Jayakar refers to similarities between these images and those figurines found at Harappa (2500 BC), Sunga terracottas, and also to those made for the Toda cattle cults of the Nilgiris of South India.

Terracotta offerings are believed to be capable of holding the spirit which is the essential offering to the deity. This potential is perhaps linked to the belief in the permeability of the earth or clay. The small votive figurines are believed to absorb the essence of the animal they represent, which is released once the image is offered to the deity. Haku Shah suggests that the terracotta is quickened by sacrificial offering, the chanting and the trances. The sculptures, perceived as actual live sacrifices, provide the devotee with the equivalent merit of a live offering. The terracotta image immediately after the ceremonial offering is like an empty husk, and is therefore meaningless, unusable and insignificant and is left to disintegrate.

As has been noted, many of the tribal peoples in the western part of India give votive terracottas to their gods. The western tribes, particularly the Bhils, have adopted some devotional Hindu customs including the making of vows and offerings. While a few tribesmen make unfired clay figures, most commission Hindu potters to make the required votive images. The favoured terracotta image is the horse. These are used to placate the malevolent spirits of tribal ancestors who have their own sanctuaries.

A need for healing is one reason for the propitiation of the god or goddess who is brought into the community through spirit possession and the ceremonial of festivals. An example of this is the initiation of festivals to the goddess of smallpox during epidemics. Associated with the ritual of gift giving and vow fulfilment is the idea of the transference of disease into offered animals or substitute images. Stutley gives the example of Siberian shamans transferring disease from a sick man to the body of a sacrificed reindeer. Among west African Ewe people, for example, sickness is swept away with small brooms after its ritual transference; and in the Nias Islands dolls are substituted for the patients and the diseases transferred to them. In Wales as late as the nineteenth century cocks or hens were taken by sick people to the parish church of Llandegla and the well of St Tecla which was circumambulated three times in the belief of a cure.

Figure 6.11 Women at a tree shrine. Stephen Huyler.

Fertility and prosperity

We have noted research showing rural women's desire for children, prosperity, a good harvest and for the general protection and purification of the home and household. This gives rise to some of the performance of vratas. Women desired a happy, fruitful marriage and more often performed votive rites for their family than for their own health and prosperity. A perception of themselves as an integral part of the collective family is thought to inspire women rather than a sense of their independent personal self-interest. In contrast, men are seen to make vows when they are ill or involved in a court case.

Women who desire children often resort to devotional offering of terracottas to certain goddesses and at certain shrines (Figures 6.11 and 6.3). The snake shrines or naga kals, often located at the base of sacred trees or beside anthills, are also associated with the fertility offerings. Miniature cradles are hung on sacred trees to act in a sympathetic manner and to ensure the health and protection of an existing child (Figure 2.5). Wall paintings are specially made for wedding ceremonies of the Mithila tribe in the Madhubani district which are believed to arouse the young bride and to bring about a fertile union.

Ritual story-telling and its illustrated performance which is still believed to bring prosperity, rainfall and fertility probably derives from ancient agricultural rites.

Penance, propitiation and protection

These are all fulfilled by the offering of terracottas to the deity. Penance is also undergone through physical hardship such as fasting, walking on nails or hook hanging, often performed during festivals as part of a vow to the goddess. As has been observed, the deity is propitiated partly by the offering of terracottas, food, money or other gifts, and by the painting of ritual diagrams on the walls and floors of the village houses. The kolam on the threshold protects the inner world of the household from the outside world.

Protection was also believed to be acquired by offerings to the deity or by ritual wall painting. Connected to the idea of protection is the fear of the evil eye. Mothers put a preventive dot of lamp black on the forehead of each child and a black cord around the child's neck or arm. Black pots painted with demon faces are also placed outside houses and in the fields and are believed to be protective.

In Senapur according to Luschinsky,[99] the villagers worship three gods: their house god, the village protector and the god who protects the area of the village, while some villagers worship the village goddess. She suggests that villagers seldom trust one god to fulfil their requests and therefore enter into obligations with more than one god.[100] If their demands are satisfied they worship all the gods to whom they made vows.

Conclusion

Rural religious art provides the means for individuals to attempt to control an unpredictable environment. All those social groups which are excluded from direct access to orthodox Hindu deities by the Brahman monopoly of ritual such as women, non-Brahmans, sudra castes and tribal groups have found an alternative means of communicating with the divine in the rural arts. This expression was free of the prescriptive discipline of the Brahmanical canons, though these groups have absorbed the traditions of bhakti

which Brahmanical Hinduism has woven into its own ritual fabric.

The patronage of folk art, restricted by limited resources, is predominantly inspired by women in the community, who take ritual responsibility for the well-being of their family. Devotional offerings are believed to provide protection from and to propitiate the spirit world. Women offer figurines, which they believe act as vessels or vehicles for a transient spirit, eventually transformed in its contact with the deity. Wall painting is a further means used by women to contain malevolent forces and evoke the protective goddess. Inherent in this art is a belief in the power of the line to demarcate and contain force, and the concept that a deity may be evoked and temporarily confined within the home or in an area of two-dimensional space. Stella Kramrisch suggests that the making of these images invokes and contacts a superhuman presence, which is communicated with by the drawing of certain shapes.[101] Folk art is ephemeral and is aimed to concentrate power on a temporary basis. Yet historical evidence for magical rural customs can be seen in such texts as the *Atharva Veda*, which records spells and formulae from this non-Vedic tradition. This reinforces the universality of arts, which often pre-dates Brahmanic principles and points to a pool of ancient rites.

Brahmanic and village Hinduism coexist in rural communities and yet are distinct. One difference is revealed by the freedom in the latter for the individual devotee to directly approach the local deities without the need of priestly intercession. Although local priests preside over shrines, women through their domestic rituals have direct access to the deity. Also special to the village is the hierarchical array of non-

Brahmanic godlings, which coexist with Brahmanic deities and a range of powerful, potentially dangerous goddesses who require blood offerings.

Connected also to the woman are the underlying concepts which are intuitively understood and lived in the rural context. One of these is the belief in purity, the need for purification in preparation for the arrival of the deity and the need for regularly re-purifying the home. Diverse practices relating to domestic purification include ritual bathing, particularly popular with women, and the re-plastering of houses with cow dung which is said to remove the malignant forces absorbed by mud-encased walls. The women are themselves perceived as pure, partly due to the high percentage of time they spend in the home. The woman's involvement in the preparation of food and ritual practices also requires a lack of contamination and her assumed state is an expression of her domestic respons-ibilities. The woman's potential power is also manifest in her ritual wall painting. Here she is believed to be instrumental in concentrating protective forces in the ornamentation of the house and floor. This is regularly renewed either daily or for ceremonial occasions.

The goddess of disease is known as polluting and dangerous and yet this does not prevent her from being sacred. The hierarchy of purity and impurity extends to a range of deities, with at a lower level ghosts and malingering spirits from which the rural community seeks protection. Another aspect of this hierarchy is the lack of distinction between the spirit and the human world in the rural imagination. Perhaps the mystery of the ambivalent goddess, who represents a reality where tragedy and joy are ever present, is more

real than the single-minded optimism, or pessimism, of Western culture. This cannot be understood rationally, though the rural communities were sufficiently resilient that they were able to confront the powers of chaos and destruction evoked through the goddess and trust in the darkness from which grew the seeds of regeneration. The community anticipated the whim of the goddess and recognized the extent to which she could determine life and death. Manasa, the North Indian goddess, typifies this unpredictability of life, associated as she is with the snake who suddenly strikes. The goddess warns her devotees of the fragility and uncertainty of their hold on life and by so doing helps them digest and prepare themselves for the fears that haunt them.[102]

Notes

1 Although there is little agreement on the definition of the word 'tribe', one can say that the tribe is non-industrialized, speaking a common language with a common ancestry and living in a homogenous territory.

2 Jain 1993, pp. 58–64.

3 Jajmani is an ancient system dating from the laws of Manu, whereby services or objects of equivalent value are exchanged or bartered. The term jajmani is derived from the name jajman, which literally forms the nucleus of the exchange.

4 Harman 1989, p. 98, and Sekine 1993, p. 134.

5 Brubaker 1978, p. 298.

6 Luschinsky 1962, p. 719.

7 The original Murukan was, according to Zvelebil, the son of Korravai, the goddess of war and victory (see Zvelebil n.d.). It has been suggested that Murukan was originally a tribal god, a proto-hunter who underwent a transformation into the god of the social elite in such later works as *Tirumurukarruppatai* and *Paripatal*. Two forms of Murukan exist: one is worshipped by kings, nobles and Brahmanic priests with six heads and twelve arms; one is worshipped by villagers symbolized by a spear adorned by a red cloth and red blossoms carried by the folk priest, the shaman and offered a

sacrifice. According to legend, Murukan originally had no father. This concept may perhaps express an ancient idea that women bore children without men. Siva was later included, as his father and he becomes identified with Karttikeya in the Brahmanic cult.

8 Harman 1989, p. 145.

9 See Whitehead 1921, p. 62, 'Devaru Potu' devoted to the Goddess.

10 See Fuller 1992, p. 84. Smaller animals are offered to male and female deities but buffaloes are reserved for goddesses, although this is now rare in India, and only in East India are animals regularly killed at major temples served by Brahman priests. Elsewhere, animal sacrifices are confined to smaller temples and shrines of local deities, which are officiated by non-Brahmans.

11 See Biardeau 1984, p. 5, fn. 3. Biardeau argues that buffalo sacrifice has been banned officially since 1947, so that it is almost non-existent in towns, but still persists in some regions, and is vivid in the memory of old people. In the north there is a close association with the festival of Navaratri and the Devimahatmya myth whereas in the south the connection is less strong and the buffalo sacrifice or Vijayadasami may take place on a different occasion. Biardeau explains that this difference is due to the absence of Brahmans from the sacrificial ritual in the south. In Tamil Nadu the ceremony is not linked to the great feast of the goddess. The ritual Vijayadasami is simple and has one name, Vanniyasurasamhara, 'the murder – or reabsorption – of the asura Vanni'. At Maduvettimangalam which was one of the great centres of buffalo sacrifice in Tamil Nadu (meaning 'blessed site of buffalo sacrifice'), the ceremony of the great feast of the temple is performed. In front of the temple is an enormous pipal tree alongside a half-dead sami tree. Underneath it are seven stakes to which are attached seven buffaloes which are sacrificed for the seven villages. It is the sami tree which is essential to the ceremony, and the possessed untouchable man must remain beside it during the ceremony. Both the pipal symbol of the wood of the vertical arani of vedic sacrifice and the sami tree are essential for the ritual.

12 Shulman 1980, p. 317.

13 Beck 1991, pp. 113–15.

14 Fuller 1992, p. 84.

15 See Harman 1989.

16 I am grateful to John Marr for pointing out the links between blood sacrifices in Rajasthan and Nepal in the context of Ksatriya rather than Brahmanical rituals.

17 Zvelebil, undated, pp. 10–11.

18 Sekine 1993, p. 173.

19 See Hart 1973, pp. 233–51.

20 Whitehead 1921, p. 146. This blood bond is a universal phenomenon seen among North American Indians, in Africa and in the Christian communion.

21 See Emeneau 1971.

22 Erumai maram or 'Buffalo valour' is one of the poetic themes in the Sangam work *Purananuru*.

23 An example of this is seen by the range of attitudes in the Vedas to the yakshas, from red-eyed demons and ghosts to benevolent spirits sought for prosperity. Biardeau (1984) also refers to the custom whereby the low caste god can become a demon who is transformed or married into the orthodox range of deities (p. 108).

24 See Whitehead 1921, pp. 143–58. It has also been argued by Biardeau (1984, pp. 11–13) that in the south, particularly in Tamil Nadu, the buffalo sacrifice is strongly linked to the sami tree, and may be less concerned with the Brahmanical mythology of Durga. According to Biardeau, the sami tree is the fire tree and is also seen as the feminine – the womb of fire, in which fire dwells in a state of calm once extinguished. The word 'sami' is from the root sam, to calm or extinguish, or put to death in the causative form.

25 The puranic expression of this concept is provided by the story of Narasimha. After slaying Hiranyakasipu, Narasimha is garlanded in his entrails. Narasimha is then so bloody and powerful that Siva is forced to quell him, which he does in the form of Sarabha.

26 Shulman (1980, pp. 313 and 421) sees Aiyanar as an 'allotrope' of Murukan, which is a parallelism also referred to by L'Hernault (1978, pp. 121–2).

27 Karuppu sometimes shares the shrine with Aiyanar, in which case sacrificial posts are placed there for blood sacrifices to Karuppu.

28 See Hart 1979, pp. 15–17.

29 Sekine 1993, p. 153.

30 See Zvelebil n.d., p. 4.

31 Mackay 1931, p. 393.

32 Crooke 1912, p. 5.

33 Fuller 1992, p. 49.

34 Jain and Aggarwala 1989, pp. 73–6.

35 Zvelebil n.d., p. 23.

36 See Bolle 1969, p. 129.

37 See Stutley 1980, p. 6. Anthills are seen as living entities and ants (upajihvika) are regarded as beneficent insects, with the power to reveal the presence of healing water. Monier-Williams states in his Sanskrit–English dictionary that one of the three forms of the term for ant, namely upajika, may have been the name of a water deity. I am grateful to John Marr for informing me that Siva at Tiruvarur is, in one of its mulasthanas, worshipped as Valmikanatha, 'lord of ants' and his shrine is subterranean.

38 Mary McGee, in Leslie 1991, p. 71.

39 Jayakar 1971, p. 290. Vratyas, according to the *Atharva Veda*, were non-sacrificers and worshippers of Eka Vratya (single principle). Later texts describe them as wandering magicians dressed in black, holding a rod and bow and wearing a magical amulet around their necks. During the solstitial festival they were said to draw mandalas on their carts which served as an altar and to perform sacred rites. See Jayakar 1980, p. 40.

40 Agrawala 1953, p. 71.

41 Jayakar 1980, p. 250.

42 Jain and Aggarwala 1989, p. 174.

43 Jayakar 1980, p. 252.

44 Ibid., p. 254. In Gujarat there is a superstitious belief that ghosts have feet which point backwards.

45 Huntington 1985, p. 17.

46 For further reference to terracotta images of the mother goddess see Dasgupta 1961, p. 16. See also Dasgupta 1936.

47 Jayakar 1980, p. 254.

48 These terracottas may well represent a reference to an earlier custom of sacrifice of animals to propitiate the tree spirit. Mackay (1931, p. 393) refers to the existence of a clay tablet found from the Indus valley which shows a row of naked figures under which is a kneeling figure on the left holding a broad-bladed object in one hand. In front of this figure is a goat; before which is a defaced object resembling a tree, while in the centre of this tree is a human figure. Mackay suggests that

a priest is about to sacrifice a goat to a tree spirit. In most parts of India at the present day, offerings and occasionally animal sacrifices are made to certain trees to placate the spirits that dwell within them. The cult of the tree was also commom to most ancient religions throughout the world. For example we have the Dryad and the Hamadrayad of Greek mythology, and Hathor who dwelt in the Sycamore fig-tree of ancient Egypt.

Crooke refers to the existence of a forest tribe in Khandesh, the Pavras, who sacrifice goats and fowls before harvest, and make an offering of corn to a pair called Bara and Rani Kajhal who occupy adjoining sacred trees (Crooke 1912, p. 5).

49 See Jayakar, 1954. Trees worshipped by the Rani Paraj are the samar, samadi, vad (banyan), the pipal and the mango.

50 A further ritual is that if there is a theft in the village the aggrieved party takes a vow that if the stolen articles are recovered he will offer a horse to the samar tree. These horses are hung on the branches of the tree.

51 For further reference see *Marg*, 'The Terracotta Art of India', 1954, Vol. VII, p. 33, Figure 5.

52 They are known as Ganesa (a name given in imitation of the later Ganesa as mangalamurti). Similar unbaked clay male figurines have been recently found in Shahr-i-Sokhta, a chalcolithic settlement in Iranian Sistan. See *Marg*, 'The Terracotta Art of India', Vol. VII, p. 38.

53 Figures recovered from excavations at Bulandi Bagh show costumes and poses which suggest dancing girls. A comparison of these with the present-day Manipuri and Naga dance poses shows great affinity. For illustration of figures see *Marg*, 'The Terracotta Art of India', Vol. VII.

54 See Sankalia 1960.

55 This is suggested to be the result of a double mould adopted as a result of contacts with the Roman world.

56 Jayakar 1980, p. 250.

57 Iron or steel nails were believed to possess magical powers and were commonly used to defeat spirits. In Kerala, for example, it was usual to nail a malevolent spirit to particular trees.

58 Huyler 1996, p. 78.

59 Ibid., p. 31.

60 Ibid., p. 57.

61 Huyler 1994, p. 174.

62 *Vishnudharmottara Purana*, Part 2, Chapter 169. The text is of the sixth century AD but is of earlier sources.

63 Puranas are encyclopaedias of ancient knowledge.

64 See Huyler 1994.

65 Kramrisch 1983, p. 106.

66 Ibid.

67 Kramrisch 1968, pp. 65–6. Also note the association of the circle with the Yezidi tribe, some of whom still live in Iran, who are unable to move outside a circle drawn in the dust or in chalk around any one of them.

68 Anand 1969.

69 Jayakar 1980, p. 139, Figure 126.

70 See Huyler 1994.

71 Nagarajan 1993, p. 194.

72 Jayakar 1980, p. 145.

73 Jain and Aggarwala 1989, p. 103.

74 Kramrisch 1946, Vol. 1, p. 9.

75 Coomaraswamy 1929, pp. 182–4.

76 Jain 1980, p. 105, fn. 21, citing the Samyutta Nikaya 111.15.5.

77 Quoted in ibid., fn. 23.

78 Jain 1980.

79 Ibid., p. 105.

80 Jayakar 1980, p. 158.

81 Ibid., p. 169.

82 Luschinsky 1962, p. 376. See also Majumdar and Pusalker 1951, 1954 and 1955; Altekar 1938; Upadhya 1941.

83 Menski, in Leslie 1991, p. 49.

84 See Leslie 1991, pp. 18 and 43.

85 See Luschinsky 1962, p. 377.

86 I am grateful to John Marr for informing me of the matrilinear marumakkattayam among the Nayars in Kerala, and a similar structure among the Bants of coastal Karnataka (around Mangalore and Udipi).

87 See Sonawana 1988, p. 33, and Narasimhaswami 1951-2, pp. 137-9.

88 Hart 1973, pp. 233–51.

89 Menski, in Leslie 1991, p. 50.

90 Luschinsky 1962, p. 645.

91 Ibid., p. 646.

92 McGee, in Leslie 1991.

93 Luschinsky 1962, p. 692.

94 For a description of spirit posession see Luschinsky 1962, pp. 702-3.

95 Shah 1985, p. 17.

96 Ibid., p. 16.

97 Ibid., p. 18.

98 Cited by Huyler 1996, Chapter 3, fn. 3.

99 Luschinsky 1962, p. 650.

100 Ibid., p. 652.

101 Kramrisch, in Stoler Miller 1983.

102 The death of Diana Princess of Wales and the devotion shown by the world to her image as a goddess, with offerings of flowers and candles in reverence, in some senses expresses the archetype of devotion on the one hand and the consciousness of the unpredictability of life on the other. Diana represented and represents the paradox of a person who was in life seen for her compassion on the one hand and her suffering and inadequacies on the other. Her death evoked in England an unprecedented spontaneous public adulation and reverence.

■ CHAPTER 7 Conclusion

This study has shown the extent to which an understanding of the relationship between images and ritual is essential in the exposition of the development of the devotional cults of Vishnu, Siva and the goddess, popularly known as Hinduism.

> Historians of religions have too long looked only at words. Religion can exist as much inside a durbar hall as in a temple. Clues to the presence of a religious culture can be as much embedded in a decorated elephant as in an ancient myth....The word of bureaucratic documents, the paraphernalia of the court, the style of dress, the colors of a painting – all these 'things' must be added to the words of theologial and mythic discourse we have learned to read so well.[1]

As Waghorne powerfully argues, the clues to understanding the voices of the past lie as much in the coalescence and impurity of current orthodox ritual as in the lifeless texts of the past. She also argues that popular religion escaped the deadly disinfectant of the textual tradition,[2] suggesting that the actual remnants of Vedic culture exist now within the Vedic texts only as 'the scattered and fossilized remnants of a lost and discredited world'.[3] This book has proposed an alternative route to the lost worlds of Hinduism by tracing the evolution of Hindu sacred imagery. Images, intentionally multivalent, continue to play a central role in ritual and are therefore made with faithfulness to prescription and exacting reverence. This book has a debt to the vital contribution of ethnography seen in the inspired works by Fuller, and has also drawn on the profound insights of scholars such as Biardeau, O'Flaherty and Shulman in their work with textual sources.

From as early as 1500 BC, all the available evidence suggests that Vedic ritual did not require icons, despite the survival of large numbers of terracotta figurines, generally believed by scholars to point to a coexistent non-Vedic tradition. From the fourth century BC, there is more substantial evidence of the use of cult images in India. These cult images and their shrines were adopted by a developing orthodox Puranic Hinduism. Icons of deities grew from a folk belief in the potentiality of divine spirits to arise from and inhabit trees and by extension wood, which transferred to a belief in the capacity for stone to become vivified with the correct procedures. They came to form a vital focus for prayer in Brahmanic Hinduism and in the village traditions. Shrines from the first century AD grew to localize and root the sacred in areas of sanctity. From this followed the need for protection of the sanctuary and for formal rules about the optimum housing of the image. As a result of the Buddhist and Jain opposition to live offerings to the deity, *yajna*, the central cosmo-regal sacrifice, was supplanted by domestic rituals, which transmuted and transformed the mundane to the spiritual, the impure to the pure. In the Puranic period purtadharma (gift giving) received more acclaim than the performance of the central cosmo-regal sacrifice. Vegetal offerings were transmuted by the sacred fire; prayer, gifts, gesture and feeling were all transformed metaphorically by prescriptive action. The ultimate symbolic offering of the self was believed to enable the worshipper to become one with God through death's transmutation.

Many scholars have convincingly demonstrated that sacrificial rituals, both actual and symbolic, provide the strongest common feature and link between popular and orthodox Hinduism. Yet as pointed out by Biardeau, the ritual prescribed in the texts governing ritual in the temples of Vishnu and Siva is never described by Hindus as 'sacrifice', for linguistically and conceptually, puja is differentiated from bali (blood sacrifice) for inferior deities.[4] Despite this distinction every ritual may be seen as an expression of devotion, and self-sacrifice was the ultimate offering in the cult of bhakti. Madeleine Biardeau argues that popular religion reflects the devotional practice of bhakti which arose during the Epic and Puranic periods and explains how low caste village practice became absorbed into the Brahmanic tradition.[5] She speaks not of covering up the popular tradition but of 'englobing', which is a process of ideological development. Shulman however, while admitting to the continuity of sacrifice and self-sacrifice in Tamil myths, argues that much of Tamil tradition was given an orthodox slant engineered by Brahmanic

intervention rather than natural progression. An example of this practice is found in the Tamil story of the god offered in sacrifice to the goddess, a matriarchal myth which the patriarchal Brahmans altered so that the god was supplanted by a more acceptable surrogate such as a bull, his devotee or a demon.[6] It is the Brahmans (Figure 7.1) to whom much of the credit must be given for engineering an extraordinary tapestry of adaptation and reworking, of absorbing the challenge of Buddhism and through reformulation and adaption, sanitizing the Vedic ritual while preserving their own essential role. Even the popular bhakti movement with its emphasis on individual worship and emotional intensity came in time to provide an essential arm of the Brahmans' customary performance while preserving in the orthodox temples their intercessionary function.

The alchemy of sacrifice and ritual as agents of transformation are central to understanding the southern Tamil tradition and also the northern Brahmanic tradition. In order to gain a true understanding of Hinduism it is important to study religious practice as well as words and images. Customary practice is bound up with images, icons, ornamentation and prayers. The result of man's actions is karma but by extension he was also subject to change through action. Ritual may be seen as a process of alchemical transformation of the participant. An example of this is the transformation of the body, regarded as an unsanctified temple, which becomes sanctified through yogic practice. A further example of this transformation is seen in the potent symbol of the camphor flame. Fuller expresses the quintessentially Hindu idea of a blending of divinity and humanity. This, Fuller observes, can be seen in the

Figure 7.1 Brahmans at Srirangam. Robert Elgood.

transcendence of the icon which, dissolved in the flame, touches the disembodied self of the devotee. It is also observed through the icon's and devotee's mutual vision of the flame and therefore each other. The intensity of the flame can also persist in the vision of the worshipper once the eyes close and therefore reinforces the persistent presence of the deity within the mind of the devotee.

The transformation of the victim in the sacrifice, or of the terracottas offered in folk cults, lies in a change of substance from the material to the spiritual. The ancient urge for union with divine power lives on in the worship of the village goddess, achieved through connection with the blood of the sacrificial buffalo. These principles are reflected in bloodless Brahmanic puja which urges union, through symbolic self-sacrifice and the offering of gifts to be consumed by the deity. What links the village and temple worship is the transformation of the offering.

The gap between agamic theory (many of the agamas prepared in South India) and practice further reinforces the transmission of action rather than theory, despite a love of classification. Belief has always been centred on the pre-eminence of sound and words interrelated with ritual action, rather than the importance of ideas and concepts. Rural and urban Hindus do what they believe should be done, which in turn becomes common practice and this, faithfully repeated, is what becomes orthodox.

The Hindu view makes no clear separation between God and the world. The sacred is polished, worked and transmitted through the prescribed ritual acts which make the normal supranormal. In this sense Hinduism is concerned not merely with a faithfulness to ideas but the transformation of material substances through action and the vibrations of sound. Sound linked to breath was believed to empower the word. Thus the unit of sound, or mantra, was more important than the meaning of the whole; this led to the oral tradition taking precedence over written texts.

Religious language does not express itself in words but in a kind of ritualized practice. Linked to this sacred action is art, which does not obscure or refuse the challenge of the depiction of the sacred. Hindu art attempts to bridge matter and the immaterial; existence and non-existence; subject and object, expressing these through a subtle use of metaphors and paradigms. Hindu sacred art reveals not merely the abstract essence or framework of things but also the fullness of manifestation (prakriti), of abundance (purna) and an encompassing vision of reality. Religious objects are spiritual because they are artificial products of ritual.[7] Ornamentation, far from artifice and pretension, is seen to convey vitality and power. The figure of the king also receives this adornment for the same reasons.

Hindu kings had certain obligations; first, to secure ritual power by generous endowments to Brahmans, and second, by the patronage of temples to strengthen the deity's presence in his empire to ensure rainfall, fertility and prosperity. Insofar as he became God's representative, the divine monarch received sacred power through lustration with the sacred waters and was dressed like a religious icon with extravagant clothing and jewellery. Ornamentation, far from merely appealing to his vanity, is believed to strengthen and empower him. Individual jewels are believed to hold special power while pearls like the moon reflect the sun. His subjects offer the king the obeisance shown to their cult deity. Although from the third to the eighth centuries kings preferred to promote their munificence through courtly bards

rather than temples, by the eighth century temples became powerhouses for kings. The apogee of the identification of the god-king was in the Chola period. The king also appeared among his subjects in much the same way as an icon is carried in a chariot around a town.

The deities reveal a hierarchical pantheon with no sharp separation between the human and spirit world where humans require protection from maleficent forces. Icons and images serve as effective channels for the radiation of divine forces. The Hindu image, unlike the still and inwardly focused meditative and enlightened image of the Buddha or the Jain tirthankara, provides a range of moods and physical states. Siva can be immobile as the teacher or yogi or can embody the state of bliss and energy in action in his tandava dance. In Buddhism the aspiration to the non-worldly spiritual was embodied in stone and grew to be revered. Unlike the simplicity of the outer manifestations of the images of the Buddha or the Jina, Hindu gods and goddesses require ornamentation and a complex array of attributes, arms and jewellery to enhance their power and auspicious qualities. The figures of Buddhism and Jainism are concerned with experience and the relationship and nature of man, while the Hindu images concern themselves with the evoking of the gods among men. In Hinduism the radiation of spiritual essence evoked in the icon as a consequence of appropriate ritual commands reverence.

The Buddhist icon represents the enlightened human state which was intended to inspire and evoke in the disciple a corresponding detachment and enlightenment. By contrast, Hindu icons depict gods and goddesses who play here on earth and beyond and are intended to assist in bringing their powers to act in this world. The aim of the Hindu devotee was, through inner transformation, to become qualitatively similar to and therefore capable of becoming one with the deity. The objective of each facet of worship is the purification and making sacred of the transforming action of the total ritual. Essential components are meaning and order in thoughts; sincerity of feeling is expressed in a corresponding intonation and correct physical action in gesture. The experience of the sacred is not merely through the eyes but through all the senses: taste, sound, and the purification of smell through the use of incense. These are parts of the body of action which encourage the god's manifestation on earth and make possible the communion of god and devotee. Finally the divine presence (sri) is assured by the lustration of sacred water, the purifying and transforming power of the flame, and the vibration of sounds. All elements and senses are involved in this amalgam of space, wind, water, earth and sacred fire.

This book in its structure and emphasis has attempted to show the extent to which the Hindus' use of and attitude to images

and temples in the orthodox tradition or in lines in sacred wall painting, drawing or terracottas presupposes a belief in the interrelationship between the divine and inorganic matter. It suggests a hierarchy of material of varying density or divinity matter which is, under certain conditions, permeable to higher forces and can become qualitatively transformed with the application of certain elements of sound, light or fire.

Hindu arts are however in the final analysis part of maya, reflections or milestones on the journey to the individual's direct experience of their micro- and macrocosmic identity. They are spiritually endowed aids to liberation from this world of the non-real.

Notes

1 Waghorne 1994.
2 Ibid., p. 120.
3 Heesterman 1985, p. 99.
4 See Fuller 1992, p. 99.
5 Biardeau 1981, p. 238.
6 Shulman 1980, p. 132.
7 See Clothey 1983.

Glossary

abhayamudra – Be not afraid.

Abhisheka – the sprinkling of consecrated water over a sacred image or the head of a king at his coronation.

Agamas – set of revealed texts referred to by tantric sources and most temple rituals.

Agni – Vedic god of fire.

Agnihotra – the Vedic burnt offering.

Ahimsa – non-violence, a central concept of the *Jains*.

Akasa – the most subtle of the five elements; refers to the material support for sound known as ether.

Alankara – ornamentation, auspicious embellishment.

alepan – geometric drawings on the floor or wall. These are drawn on festival and auspicious occasions.

Amalaka – the flat circular, ribbed form which is placed as a crown on North Indian temple towers. The word derives from 'mal' meaning to hold or gather. Perhaps its circular ribbed form is suggestive of a ring.

Amrta – nectar of immortality.

Ananku – this concept is found in Tamil. It is described as the sacred force inherent in certain places, objects and powerful animals, particularly noted in *Murukan*, which can be creative or destructive.

Anjalimudra – the hand position of prayer and respect, with the two hands joined.

Annapurna – goddess of plenty, her symbols are the overflowing pot of rice and vessel of milk.

Apsaras – beautiful courtesans of the gods.

Arati – a temple ritual where the lamp is moved in a clockwise circular direction in front of the deity.

aripan – see *alepan*

Arjuna – the son of Indra, friend of Krishna.

Artha – wealth, one of the four goals of ancient Hindu life.

Asram – a retreat or the dwelling place of a mendicant in the forest.

Asura – inhabitants of lower regions. They become evil when they try to usurp the place of the gods in heaven or to come to earth to oppress the *Brahmans*.

Asvamedha – the Vedic horse sacrifice.

atharvaveda – fourth vedic text (see *veda*)

Atman – the name given to the eternal principle which imagines the empirical individual.

Avatara – literally 'descent', usually applied to Vishnu's ten incarnations.

Bali – an offering, often a blood sacrifice.

Bhagavad Gita – 'Song of the Lord'; a section of the *Mahabharata*, in which Krishna propounds a philosophy which forms the basis for much that is central to the later development of Hinduism.

Bhagavata Purana – a popular text which tells of the life of *Krishna*; refers to his childhood, the gopis and the rasalila but not to the person *Radha*.

Bhairava – Siva in the form of an ascetic with wild hair, a staff and erect penis. He is often accompanied by a dog. In North

India and Nepal he is known as Bhairon.

Bhajan – popular hymns sung by pilgrims or devotees at a shrine.

Bhakta – a devotee.

Bhakti – intense devotion to a personal god. Implies a relationship of exchange between the god and devotee, the worshipper receiving grace from the deity in return for gifts and devotion.

Bhopas – story-tellers, who tell stories of the hero *Pabuji* in Rajasthan.

Bhuta – ghost or spirit.

Brahma – deity; first of the Trimurti.

Brahman – soul or universal spirit.

Brahmana – the priest, the highest of the four Hindu castes.

Brahmanas – prescriptive texts which refer to sacrificial ritual.

Chaitya – a sacred place.

Chakra – wheel or discus weapon of Vishnu.

Chakravartin – title used by Hindu rulers to indicate a 'universal king'.

Chamunda – goddess created by *Durga* to destroy evil.

Chandra – moon god.

Caste system – the division of Aryan society into four classes: *Brahmans* or priests, *Ksatriyas* or warriors, *vaisyas* or traders, *sudras* or labourers.

Chitra – wall painting in Orissa.

Damaru – hourglass-shaped drum, carried by Siva.

Dana – the act of giving.

Darsan – the act of seeing the enshrined deity and being seen; this can take place in the temple or in front of any sacred image.

Deva – god.

Devadasi – temple dancers, also known as temple courtesans.

Devimahatmya – 'Glorification of the Goddess'. Part of the *Markandeya purana*.

Dharma – one of the four goals of Hindu life, the act of living appropriately, fulfilling ones appropriate role and place.

Dikpalas – door guardian.

Dravida – southern type of temple style.

Durga – destroyer of the buffalo demon.

dvapura – third of the four yugas.

Gada – the club weapon.

Gana – mischievous dwarfs who form part of Siva's retinue.

Gandharva – a celestial musician.

Ganesa – the son of *Siva* and *Parvati* who has an elephant head. He is invoked to remove obstacles at any new beginning.

Ganga – the river goddess, personification of the river Ganga. The goddess is associated with Siva in the iconographical detail in which she flows into Siva's matted hair.

Garbhagrha – 'womb chamber', the innermost sanctum of the Hindu temple.

Garuda – the vehicle of Vishnu, associated with the movement of the sun through the sky, based on the bird the kite.

Gavaksha – horseshoe-shaped arch, literally means 'cow-eye'.

Ghee – clarified butter, used for oil lamps and anointing images.

Gita Govinda – Sanskrit poem, which relates the love of the god *Krishna* with the cowherdess *Radha*. This was written in the twelfth century by *Jayadeva* and can be read on a literal or metaphorical level, expressing the human soul's longing for divine union.

Gopi – female cowherds in love with *Krishna*.

Gopura – pyrimidal entrance gateway of South Indian temple complexes.

Gramadevata – village deity, frequently a goddess.

Guna – term for the three components of the phenomenal world, i.e. *sattva*, *rajas* and *tamas*.

Guru – spiritual teacher.

Hamsa – goose, the vehicle of Brahma.

Hanuman – monkey god, referred to in the *Ramayana* as an ally of *Rama*.

Harihara – the conjoint figure of Siva and Vishnu.

Indra – Vedic god of war and god of storms.

Isvara – or Bhagvan, supreme lord, the unmanifest, the immeasurable and indescribable form of the ultimate divinity. More remote and impersonal than the puranic deities, such as Siva, Vishnu or the Goddess.

Jainism – this teaching emphasizes ascetic practices alongside a concern with *ahimsa* (non-injury to all living souls, human and animal). Twenty-four teachers are reknowned, of which the last, Mahavira, a contemporary of Buddha, promulgated the faith.

Jajmani – a village system of barter or exchange of service for produce.

Jatakas – stories of the previous lives of the Buddha.

Jati – the caste into which an individual is born (literally birth).

Jayadeva – twelfth-century author of the *Gita Govinda*, q.v.

Jnana – 'knowledge', with special reference to ultimate truth or reality.

Kailasa – the mountain home of Siva.

Kalasa – a water pot, which also acts as a finial on Indian temple towers otherwise known as *Sikhara*.

kali – fourth of the four yugas.

Kali – literally 'the black female'. One of the terrifying names and manifestations of Siva's consort; also known as *Chamunda*.

kali-yuga – the current period of time, the cycle described as the most degenerate in the series of four yugas: *krta*, *treta*, *dvapara*, *kali*.

Kali – the last of the avataras of Vishnu. He is depicted as a horseheaded human figure.

Kama – 'Desire', especially sensual, amorous desire. It is described as one of the goals of man.

Kama Sutra – 'treatise on love' attributed to the Brahman Vatsyayana. Date unknown.

Karma – the law of cause and effect. The effects of individual karma in this life are believed to have a bearing on the next.

Karna – corner of shrines in temples.

Karuppu – also Karuppan, popular local deity in Madurai, and other regions of Tamil Nadu, he is worshipped with sacrificial live offerings and weapons. He is a subordinate god to Aiyanar and can be malevolent; needs to be propitiated.

Karttikeya – warrior god, referred to as the other son of Siva, also known as Skanda.

Ketu – ninth planetary deity, god of the eclipse of the moon.

Kinnaras – heavenly creatures, with human heads and horses' bodies.

Kirttimukha – a lion-mask, which often appears at the top of an arch or as a frieze on Indian temples.

Kolam – threshold floor design made from rice flour, found in South India.

Korravai – warrior goddess, some identify her with *Kali* or *Chamunda*.

Krishna – the most popular avatar of Vishnu. In the *Mahabharata* he appears as a Ksatriya and advises the Pandavas, particularly Arjuna. In later periods he is worshipped with devotion, and numerous stories tell of his adventures in the forest and his love for Radha.

krta – first of the four yugas (time periods). These yugas show a progressively descending decline.

Kshatriya – the warrior caste, has its origin in the Vedic division of society into four castes.

Kubera – renowned as a guardian of treasures.

Kurma – turtle, the second incarnation of Vishnu.

Lakshanas – divine marks.

Lakshmana – younger half-brother of Rama.

Lakshmi – consort of Vishnu, worshipped for good fortune and

233

Glossary

prosperity, associated with the lotus, also known as *Sri*.

Lila – literally 'play'.

Linga – the aniconic form of Siva, appears in the form of a phallus, but is also known as a sign or mark of Siva and a symbol of Siva's cosmic energy.

Lingodbhava – the image of Siva emerging from the cosmic linga.

Mahabharata – Indian epic that tells of the war between the five Pandava brothers and the members of the Kaurava clan. The story was transmitted orally, established by the first century AD, until it was written down sometime around the fourth century AD.

Maithuna – couple depicted in sexual intercourse.

Makara – water beast resembling the crocodile in appearance, associated with the river Ganga.

Manasa – protective goddess of snakes.

Mandala – a circular cosmic diagram, representing the cosmos. It formed the ground plan for many sacred and secular buildings, according to the ancient treatises on architecture. This diagram also forms a dynamic part of prayer and meditation, where it may be referred to as a *yantra*. In the centre is depicted the deity or sacred syllable.

Mantra – prayer or sacred utterance. Different mantras invoke different deities. Mantras can be one syllable or a combination of sounds; the intonation is crucial to its efficacy.

Markandeya purana – One of the puranas, date unknown, see *Devimahatmya*.

Matrka – mother goddess; usually seven in number, the *saptamatrkas*.

Matsya – fish, first *avatara* of Vishnu.

Maya – the power of illusion, it is identified with nature, *prakriti*.

Mayon – a South Indian black deity. Krishna subsumes some elements of Mayon.

Mithuna – male and female couple, commonly depicted for magico-protective purposes and to engender fertility. *Maithuna* – stands for the couple engaged in sexual intercourse.

Moksha – liberation from rebirth. Last of the four goals of a Hindu.

Mudras – hand gestures; for example, suggest reassurance (abhayamudra) or adoration (anjalimudra); gesture in dance.

Murti – form, or image of a deity.

Murukan – the son of the war goddess *Korravai*, very popular in *Tamil Nadu*. He has been absorbed into the figure *Skanda* or *Karttikeya* and thereby linked to the Puranic deity Siva.

Naga – serpent or snake spirit, sometimes seen with a partly human form. The cult of snake worship is of great antiquity in India and Nagaraja is king of the naga and naginis.

Nagara – northern style of temple.

Nagi/nagini – femla *naga*.

Nandi – bull, the vehicle of Siva.

Narasimha – man-lion, the fourth incarnation of Vishnu.

Narayana – one of the names of Vishnu.

Nataraja – 'lord of the dance', refers to the god Siva in his form of the cosmic dance of bliss, especially at Chidambaram in Tamil Nadu.

Natysastra – 'Treatise of dramatic art and dance' attributed to the mythical sage Bharata. Refers to the theory of aesthetics of emotion, known as rasa.

Navagraha – nine planetary deities including the sun and the moon.

Padma – lotus.

Parvati – one of the names of the benevolent consort of Siva. She is the daughter of the Himalaya mountains.

Pasu – 'sacrificial victim'. In South India *Saivism* the term is also applied to individual souls, distinct from God who is their master.

Patuas – story-tellers in Bengal also known as jadu-patuas.

Pitha – the 'seat' or shrine of a deity (often a goddess) particularly those which commemorate the dismemberment of *Sati*, it can also act as a pedestal of an image.

Prabodhacandrodaya – play written by Krishna Misra for the Chandella court in the tenth century AD.

Pradakshina – the clockwise ritual circumambulation of the sacred monument or image.

Prakriti – primeval matter identified with the female principle, seen as nature, inclusive of energy, vitality, diversity.

Prana – breath, the control of which is the aim of yogic practices.

Prasad – literally 'grace', a gift of food given to the worshipper by the priests after its sanctification by the deity.

Prasada – the platform of God.

Pratirathas – intermediary offsets around the temple.

Prithvi – earth.

Puja – ritual Hindu worship, which can be practised either at home or in the temple.

Puranas – religious texts assembled during the first eight centuries AD, which formed the basis for modern Hinduism. They present the substance of treatises of ritual, codes of laws, the description of holy places, etc., all that a Hindu needs to know in order to act correctly.

Purnaghata – motif of pot overflowing with plants.

Purtadharma – involves the patronage of buildings.

Purusa – man, one of the names of the perfect man or absolute.

Radha – despite being married, she was Krishna's favoured cowherdess.

Raga – musical mode, melodic formula arranged within an octave.

Ragamala – series of paintings based on ragas, identified with the different times of the day and seasons of the year. They represent a variety of emotions, especially love and devotion.

Rahu – eighth planetary deity; god of the eclipse of the sun.

Rajas – the second of the three *gunas* associated with passion and energy.

Rajasuya – the king-making ceremony, involves anointing the king with holy water, which is believed to transfuse divinity to the royal person.

Rama – hero of the *Ramayana*, one of the *avataras* of *Vishnu*.

Ramayana – a great epic, the story of the ideal king, *Rama*, attributed to Valmiki, probably composed over many years.

Rasa – 'essence, relish, flavour, taste' received by the audience. The nine rasas are the erotic (sringara), comic (hasya), compassionate (karuna), fearsome (raudra), heroic (vira), frightening (bhayanaka), odious (bibhatsa), marvellous (adbhuta) and peaceful (santa). The person who so responds is called a rasika.

Ratha – a processional chariot, made of wood, bamboo and cloth, used during festivals to carry the image of the deity through the streets of a village or town.

Ravana – ten-headed demon king from Lanka who captured Sita in the *Ramayana*.

Rg Veda – early collection of hymns used at Vedic sacrifices.

Rshi – sage, seer. Mythic seers who, according to some, transmitted the revelation. In the epics and *Puranas*, they are exemplary individuals who were half-renouncers, half-householders, and acted as teachers or heroes.

Rudra – 'the terrible' the most common name for Siva in Vedic literature.

Rudraksha – dried berries which are made into rosaries worn by Saivite devotees.

Sadasiva – Siva with five heads.

Sadhu – holy man who is unfettered by the norms of society and pursues a religious path.

Saivism – followers of Siva.

Sakti – the power and energy of the goddess.

Salabhanjika – girl performing a ritual associated with tree worship, where she breaks the branch of the sal tree and kicks the trunk with the heel of her foot.

Salagrama – ammonite fossil sacred to Vishnu or Siva.

samarveda – third of the vedic texts (see *veda*).

Samhitas – collections of Vedic hymns. The most ancient texts of the Vedic corpus.

Samsara – transmigration, bound in the circle of rebirth.

Sandhyabhasha – intentional language of *tantricas* often hidden in symbolism.

Sankha – conch shell sacred to Vishnu.

Sannyasin – a renouncer, a religious holy man, who abandons his family and community.

Saptamatrka – the seven mothers.

Sarasvati – river goddess identified with knowledge, music and the arts. Consort of Brahma.

Sastra – ancient texts which prescribe various aspects of human behaviour. *Silpasastras* cover the production of sculpture, *Vastusastras* deal with architecture.

Sati – the perfect wife, faithful to her husband. The name given to the wife who burns alive with her husband on his funeral pyre.

sattva – literally 'white', state of purity.

Sikhara – 'mountain peak'. Tower or spire of a Hindu, Buddhist or Jain temple.

Silpa – the Sanskrit word for art.

Silpasastras – prescriptive texts which refer to art.

Siva – one of the chief gods who receive widespread devotion. He is known as the god of destruction, associated with the Vedic god *Rudra*, he is also associated with the unorthodox forms of renunciation; third of the *Trimurti*.

Skanda – son of *Siva* and *Parvati*; however, myths describe his birth as arising from the seed of Siva but from a woman's womb.

Smrti – literally 'memory'. The tradition as distinct from the revelation. It includes literature such as the great epics the *Ramayana*, the *Mahabharata* and the *Puranas*.

Soma – an intoxicant drunk during the Vedic ritual sacrifice.

Somaskanda – sculpture which depicts Siva sitting with Parvati and Skanda; very common in South India.

Sraddha – the offering to the ancestors.

sri – honourific, meaning splendour, glory.

Sruti – literally 'heard'. This refers to Vedic texts which are believed to be revealed.

Stambha – the cosmic pillar, linked to the idea of a world axis.

Stupa – a solid earthen burial mound. The early stupas contained reliquaries of the remains of the Buddha.

Sudra – the lowest of the four castes.

Surya – sun-god; first planetary deity.

Svarga – heavenly realms.

Svayambhu – 'self-manifest', i.e. a naturally occurring form which resembles and is believed to be the *linga*.

Svastika – an ancient symbol found in the Indus valley civilization from 2500 BC, linked to the sun, symbol of luck and auspiciousness; used particularly by *Jains* and Hindus.

Tamas – the third of the three gunas, associated with darkness, dullness, ignorance.

Tamil Nadu – state in south India.

Tantra – literally to 'expand or extend', an esoteric teaching involving secret rituals, used by Hindu and Buddhist devotees. The teaching centres on the worship of the goddess, and involves devices such as *yantras* and *mantras* to support prayer.

Tantras – texts based on the *Agamas* and the *Samhitas*, in the extreme form the *Tantras* place *Sakti* above the male God.

tantricas – Those who undertake tantric practices.

Tapas – literally 'heat'; austerities and penance.

Tejas – radiance, splendour.

Tilak – a mark ritually applied to a person's forehead on an auspicious occasion.

Tirthankara – 'ford makers', the 24 saints of *Jainism*.

treta – second of the four yugas.

Trimurti – the manifestation of the deity in three aspects to preside over different states of the cosmos.

Tulapurushadana ceremony – the ceremony where the king weighs himself against gold, which is subsequently distributed.

Tulasi – household tree (basil), sacred to *Vishnu*, tended by women.

Uma – one of the auspicious names of the goddess, wife of *Siva*.

Upanishads – philosophical and mystical texts which refer to the concept of rebirth and suggest the path to liberation.

Vahana – vehicle of the deity.

Vaikuntha – *Vishnu* manifest as a combination of the boar and the man-lion incarnations.

vaisyas – the third group in the fourfold division of Hindu society. It includes such occupational groups as merchants and farmers.

Vajra – double-headed thunderbolt of the god Indra.

Vamana – dwarf incarnation of *Vishnu*: his fifth incarnation.

Varaha – boar; third incarnation of *Vishnu*.

Varuna – Vedic god of the waters.

Vastusastras – see *sastra*.

Vasudeva – name of *Krishna*.

Vayu – Vedic god of the air.

Veda – literally 'knowledge', through revelation. The sacred texts of the Aryans. These were compilations of hymns and ritual prescriptions which were transmitted orally. The four Vedas are the *Rg Veda, Yajurveda, Samaveda* and the *Atharvaveda*. The first three relate purely to priestly ritual activity, while the Atharvaveda includes magic spells and incantations.

Vedi – Vedic altar.

Vesya – a courtesan.

Vimana – the pyrimidal tower which crowns the shrine of a South Indian temple.

Vina – South Indian musical instrument, similar to a long-necked lute.

Vishnu – one of the chief puranic gods, associated with creation and preservation. His ten incarnations restore cosmic balance in the universe: second of the *Trimurti*.

Visvarupa – the cosmic manifestation of *Vishnu*.

Vrata – literally 'choose or will', these are domestic rituals, performed mainly by women, involving penance and sometimes the saying of prayers and the making of sacred diagrams.

Vyala – imaginary lion-like beast, symbolizing animal and natural compulsions.

Yajna – the Vedic sacrificial ritual.

yajurveda – second of the vedic texts (see *veda*).

Yaksha (m), *Yakshini* (f) – literally 'to become visible', the ancient tree spirits, worshipped from the earliest periods to the present day.

Yama – ruler of the dead.

Yamuna – personification of the Jumna river: her *vahana* is the turtle.

Yantra – mystical diagram associated with the worship of the goddess. It is used to focus concentration and act as a path guide during meditation.

Yoga – physical and spiritual exercises, whose goal is to achieve experience of liberation in this life. This involves physical exercises to control the body and mental exercises to empty the mind of associative thought and reach silence and stillness.

Yoni – the aniconic form of the goddess, based on the shape of the female vulva.

Yuga – name for the cosmic ages which come in four consecutive periods: *krta, treta, dvapuna, kali*. The periods show a gradual decline of standards and quality of life until the cycle is destroyed and reborn.

Yupa – sacrificial post.

Index

Index

bull, images and worship of 55, 85, 86, 113, 202
business affairs 76

Calcutta 73
Cambaita 128
Camunda Raya 159
Candragupta II 26
caste system 4, 61, 121-2, 128, 166, 205; see also Brahmans
Caturvedimangalam 159
cave temples and shrines 25-6, 88, 94, 98, 153, 156, 162
Chakravartin 64
Chalukya Pulakesin 153
Chalukyan dynasty 150-4, 164-6, 169
Chamunda 54, 73, 75
Chandella dynasty 105, 146-8, 177
Chandra, Subodh 207
Chandradevi 149
Chandragupta 144
Chantamula 142
Charana citras 90
charity 168-9
Chaturbhuj temple 167, 180
Chhichha 147
Chidambaram temple 49, 159, 180
Chinnamasta 70
chitra, art of 89-91
Chitralakshana 89
Chitrasutra 30
Chittorgarh 107
Chola dynasty 81, 157-61, 165-6, 158-9, 170, 177, 183, 230
Cholisvara temple 157
circumambulation 9, 37, 129-30, 220
class discrimination 6; see also caste system
climate 125
cobras 84
coins, images on 57, 76, 80, 141, 143, 179, 207
colours associated with particular gods 31
conch shells, symbolism of 64, 87, 120
consecration
of images 14-15, 27, 32
of kings 138-9, 159, 168-9, 171, 173, 181
of temples 120, 124, 149
Coomaraswamy, A. 17, 19, 23, 97, 101-2, 114, 128, 213
coronation ceremonies 176; see also consecration of kings
courtesans 78, 87, 110, 112, 118, 175-6; see also vesyas
cow dung, use of 76, 83, 96, 207, 211, 223
craftsmen, work of 28-9, 39, 120, 122
Crooke, W. 194
crossing from the temporal to the spiritual world 180, 184

cult images and deities 2, 10, 136-7, 227
cult practices 9, 11
cultural activities of temples 168
Cutus 142

Daksha 52
Dakshinamurti Siva 49, 51
dana 10, 135, 145, 169, 175, 180; see also mahadana; purtadharma
dana-dharma 180
dance in temples 33
Danielou, A. 52
Dantidurga 138, 151-2
darsan 28, 36, 39, 101, 113, 129, 131, 214
Dasara festival 72, 88, 120
dawn goddesses 81
demigods 113
Deogarh temple 26, 124, 144
Desai, D. 107-10, 121, 147
devadasis 113, 132, 140-1
Devaki 61
Devangana Desai 87
Devapala, king 146
Devasena 142; see also Karttikeya
Devi 19, 54, 114
Devi Mahatmya 71, 73
Devidasis 33
devotional cults 29
deya-dharma and deva-dharma 180-1
Dhanga 147-8
Dhangadeva 147-8
dharma 3, 6-7, 11, 75, 81, 94, 136, 180-1, 217
Dharmaratha 179
Dharmasastras 7, 210
Dhiman 150
Dhyana mantra 32
Didarganj Yakshi 68
Dirks, N. 138, 152
discus, the, symbolism of 64
disease 69, 79, 199, 220, 223
Divali festival 76, 88
dolmens 96, 99, 196
domestic worship 198
doors of temples 102-3, 112
Dravida-style temples 124, 127
Dubois, Abbé 84
Durga 8, 26, 54, 71-3, 84-5, 97, 144, 153, 162, 175, 184, 192
Durga-puja festival 72-3, 88
Dyaus 19

earth goddess 68, 216; see also mother goddess
Eck, D. 37
elephant, symbolism and worship 26, 55, 76, 113, 115, 173, 219
Elephanta temple 150
Eliade, Mircea 108
Ellora 72, 151, 174
Ellura temple 98, 106
emblems associated with deities 87-8; see also Siva; Vishnu

emeralds, use of 147-8
Epics 7, 17, 117, 175
Eran 59, 96, 144
eroticism 33, 35, 45, 56, 62, 78, 85, 106-13 *passim*, 120, 132, 147, 176
ethnography 10
Ewe people 220
excluded groups 222

fertility symbols and rites 14, 20, 62, 67, 76, 78, 99, 105, 112, 139, 174-6, 190, 201-2, 211, 215-16
festivals 72-3, 76, 83, 88-9, 120, 131-2, 141, 190-1, 199, 209-10, 215, 220-1
fish deities 59, 64, 81
floor painting 209-12
flute-playing 62
folk art 188, 200, 222
folk beliefs and traditions 4, 106, 132, 139; see also village custom
forest books see Aranyakas
friezes 115
Fuller, C. 10, 32, 79, 194, 227-8
funerary monuments 158, 170, 178-9
funerary temples 148, 158, 178

Gail, Adalbert 30
Gaja Lakshmi 143, 153, 173
Gandhara 57, 112-13, 141, 202
Ganesa 7, 54-5, 71-2, 84-5, 113-14, 142, 212
Ganga (dynasty) 149, 159
Ganga (goddess) 54, 84, 115, 144, 174
Gangaikondacholapuram 157-8, 160, 161, 174, 179
Ganges, river 45, 49, 76, 144, 158, 174
garbhagrha (sanctum) 3, 93-4, 99, 101, 103, 106-7, 119, 121, 130, 152
gargoyles 104
Garoda caste 213
garuda bird 57, 84-5, 88
Garuda Purana 73
Gauri 54
Gautamiputra 98
gavakshas 102-3, 120
Gayatri mantra 81
genitals
female see yoni
male see phallic symbols
geometric diagrams 208; see also yantras
ghats 4, 25, 73, 142
ghosts 194-5
Ghosundi 98
gift giving 135, 182-3, 188, 218-19, 222; see also dana; mahadana; purtadharma
Girnar 148

242

Index